COLLEGE OF ALAMEI LIBRARY
WITHDRAWN

D0759081

E
91
C45

Chamberlin, J.E.

The harrowing of Eden

Date Due

MAR 25 '81			
JUN 16 82			
DEC 8 '82			
JUN 15 '83			
NOV 13 '86			
2/21/43			

JAN 24 '81

FEB 76 '91

LENDING POLICY
IF YOU DAMAGE OR LOSE LIBRARY
MATERIALS, THEN YOU WILL BE
CHARGED FOR REPLACEMENT. FAIL-
URE TO PAY AFFECTS LIBRARY
PRIVILEGES, GRADES, TRANSCRIPTS,
DIPLOMAS, AND REGISTRATION
PRIVILEGES OR ANY COMBINATION
THEREOF.

BRO
DART   PRINTED IN U.S.A.   23-364-001

WITHDRAWN

THE
HARROWING
OF
EDEN

THE
HARROWING
OF
EDEN

White Attitudes
Toward
Native Americans

J. E. Chamberlin

A Continuum Book

The Seabury Press - New York

The Seabury Press
815 Second Avenue
New York, N.Y. 10017

Copyright © 1975 by J. E. Chamberlin

All rights reserved. No part of this book may be reproduced in any form, except for brief reviews, without the written permission of the publisher.

Acknowledgment is made for permission to reprint two lines from "The Dance" by Hart Crane. From *The Collected Poems and Selected Letters and Prose of Hart Crane* by Hart Crane. Copyright © 1933, 1958, 1966 by Liveright Publishing Corporation. Reprinted by permission of Liveright Publishing, New York.

Designed by Publishing Synthesis

Printed in the United States of America

LIBRARY OF CONGRESS CATALOGING IN PUBLICATION DATA
Chamberlin, J   E   1943–
  The harrowing of Eden: white attitudes toward native Americans

  (A Continuum book)
  Index
1. Indians, Treatment of—North America.
2. Indians of North America—Government relations.
3. Indians of North America—Land tenure. I. Title.
E91.C45   323.1'19'7073   75-9941
ISBN 0-8164-9251-4

CONTENTS

To Jane

THE
HARROWING
OF
EDEN

CHAPTER ONE

Our Dance
Is Turned
Into Mourning

"There can be no injury," remarked John Locke, "when there is no property."[1] Neither can there be much profit, at least according to the standards which were accepted by Locke's seventeenth-century contemporaries and eighteenth-century readers. In particular, the generations of Europeans who followed Columbus to the shores of the New World were faced with a curiously ambivalent situation. They were anxious to profit by their bold venture and to gather a rich spiritual and material harvest; and yet they discovered conditions which contradicted the likelihood of either. Their first task, therefore, was to change the conditions and cultivate the fallow ground so that the civilization and Christianity upon which everything they valued depended might flourish; and so that those rewards on earth and in heaven which they eagerly desired might be harvested in abundance.

The initial inventory was unsettling. For one thing, the natives did not realize—at least not in the proper way—that they possessed souls, and land. For another, they were not suitably anxious to give up both into the care of the newcomers. It was an annoying impediment, but just the sort of challenge to which the energy and ambition of the white

3

population might wholeheartedly address itself. The metaphors and the machinery were ready at hand. All that was needed was enthusiasm, precisely what had been stifled in the Europe from which so many of the new settlers had escaped, and precisely what they now had in excess. For almost five hundred years this enthusiasm has been exercised, though in so long a time it is little wonder that there have been periods of fortunate exhaustion.

From the very beginning the focus was on one issue, which provided a context for the most important, and eventually the most urgent, question in the history of relations between natives and non-natives in the northern part of the northern continent. The question appeared to be simple: who owned the land? The answers that were given tell a perplexing story. Native conceptions of land and property involved a fusion of civil and religious beliefs; and non-native presumptions about individual property, including the individual soul, transformed their own basically European civil and religious ambitions sufficiently that the question of land, and the uses to which it was put, became predominant. The answers were complicated by native innocence, indigenous distrust and primitive intransigence on the one hand; and by European naïveté, Christian philanthropy and civilized greed on the other. And the answers were conditioned not by a wise discretion but by a fool's catalogue of excesses—religious, political, cultural and economic as well as individual, tribal and national; by visions of the future and memories of the past; and, usually most of all, by the demands of an ever-changing present. But all were the answers to that baffling enigma, the Indian Question.

As the years passed, the terms changed: the pieties of civilization and Christianity became the imperatives of politics and the law, or of social economics and education, but the basic program has remained as crude and as earnest as it was at the turn of the sixteenth century. Insisting that women cover their breasts and men cut their hair, outlawing

the Potlatch and the Sun Dance, exhorting the native people
to sustain habits of industry and thrift, lamenting the sea-
sonal congregation of so many Indians on the skid rows of
the towns and cities, calling for policies of assimilation,
termination or even extermination—all of these display a
pattern of enthusiastic misunderstanding against a background of non-native expectation, the product of relentless
civil and religious aspiration.

The basic issue was deceptive, for it appeared to rise
above that sordid desire to acquire land for its own sake
which was such a common denominator during the early
years of white settlement, and instead to concern the proper
preparation and cultivation of the native seed bed from
which the fruits and flowers of civilization might eventually
rise. One of the more common arguments, based on reasonably well-accepted theories of autochthonous native culture
and of environmental determinism,[2] was that if the native
people were to be expected to transcend their savage
"state," and to flourish in splendid civility and righteousness, it might therefore be necessary that the traditional
native environment, including the habits which were presumably adapted to that environment, would have to be
itself transcended or destroyed. And the land (as well as the
native people) would therefore have to be brought within
the orderings of civilized existence. The logic, especially to
minds schooled in the truths of the eighteenth century, was
compelling. After all, that there must be a beneficent and
civilizing effect from pleasant and stable surroundings—and
in particular from that most cultivated (if sometimes figurative) of environments, the landscaped garden—was a central belief informing eighteenth-century canons of taste and
sensibility. Could any rational man doubt that, if such an
ordered environment was a sufficient condition for civilized
existence, it must also be a necessary one.

The concern to create the proper conditions for a civilized
existence and the nervous desire to emphasize the limitations (as well as the seductions) of a primitive one were tied

together like sheaves of grain, the picturesque product of
the land—land that was, after all, a prerequisite for any sort
of cultivated product or garden, even the most metaphori-
cal. In fact, the Indians themselves were often brought into
the metaphor and harrowed according to the best civil and
religious procedures. The general scheme, however, was
not at all figurative: "those who come to Christ," remarked
the Moravian missionary David Zeisberger, "turn to agriculture and raising stock, keeping the cattle hogs and
fowls." It was a convenient equation, providing not only a
ready gauge, but a steady supply of land surplus to the
newly sedentary needs of the native people.[3] For in the
primer of civilization, "A" represented agriculture, which
conveniently presupposed a pattern of land use that allowed
for non-native encroachment on traditional (which is to say,
"idle") native lands.

Coming to Christ, and turning to agriculture, represented
a drastic change for the native people. Those who thought
about such things were convinced that this change or "progress"

must be gradual, continuous, and in accordance with Nature's
laws. The history of nearly every race that has advanced from
barbarism to civilization has been through the stages of the
hunter, the herdsman, the agriculturalist, and finally reaching
those of commerce, mechanics, and the higher arts.[4]

One of nature's stimuli in the encouraging of her species
to progress was starvation; and this particular law of nature
was seen as a useful device. It was only a matter of defining
quite clearly those to whom it should apply. Daniel Buck, in
a book entitled *Indian Outbreaks* and written out of his
experience in and knowledge of the West as a Judge of the
Supreme Court of Minnesota in the latter part of the
nineteenth century, put the case plainly.

The Indians should be made to work for a living. Their land did
not cost them anything . . . The protection of all people in their

just rights and privileges is axiomatic, but neither humanity nor justice demands that the Indians should be the pampered wards of our national government. If they will not work, let them starve . . . The Caucasian has made marvellous strides in national greatness by reason of toil and thrift, and if the Indians can possibly save themselves from a fatal destiny, they must labor and save to deserve it.

Others, often in positions of much greater influence, were even blunter: "I believe," remarked C. H. Burke, the United States Commissioner of Indian Affairs in 1923, "in making the Indian take his chance."[5] All of which meant, in all too many cases, that the Indian was perfectly free to choose to starve to death, since his "chance" was circumscribed by bonds of sword and steel rail, and by equally rigid definitions of who he was and what he should be, as well as by a population well schooled in a game to which he was little accustomed and little inclined.

In particular, a strong element in the assertion of non-native rights to native land, which was given quasi-judicial status by various writers such as the Swiss jurist Emmerich de Vattel in the eighteenth century,[6] was the argument that possession of property entailed an obligation to cultivate such property; and that "nations cannot exclusively appropriate to themselves more land than they have occasion for, and which they are unable to settle and cultivate." Since it was obvious that the natives were, by and large, doing neither, the exercise of this right was strenuously urged. In addition, the intimate association of land with private property, and of property with political responsibility and power, which was such a fundamental concept to the eighteenth and nineteenth-century European, was quite foreign to the native attitude and put them beyond the pale of even the most generous political theorist.

While H. H. Brackenridge expressed his views (in 1782) in an extreme form, they were not rarely held:

What do these ringed, streaked, spotted, and speckled cattle make of the soil? Do they till it? Revelation said to man, "Thou

shalt till the ground." This alone is human life. It is favourable
to population, to science, to the information of a human mind in
the worship of God. Warburton has well said that before you
can make an Indian a Christian, you must teach him agriculture
and reduce him to a civilized life . . . I am so far from thinking
the Indians have a right to the soil, that not having made a
better use of it for many hundred years, I conceive they have
forfeited all pretence to claim, and ought to be driven from it.[7]

Warburton's advice was basic eighteenth-century dogma,
but it did not die with the century; and by the second half of
the nineteenth century the basis of the present native condition had been well and truly laid.

Traditional and native lands, and the possibilities of their
continued use and occupancy by their indigenous inhabitants, had been reduced to small, neat splotches on the national map. The illusion of native tribal sovereignty, which
had earlier been entertained, was rudely shattered. The new
and non-native social and economic structures were inexor-
ably established throughout the continent. Land became a
commodity, something that belonged to someone, and the
Indian became a somebody, and eventually a nobody, like
everybody else. The idea of a usufructuary right (or a right
of use and occupancy) of land, an idea which had been
brought over from England with the Royal Proclamation of
1763, was obliterated not so much by treaties, though they
were a crucial factor in the process, as by one of the most
misunderstood of the engines of progress—the modern governmental state, with its righteous conviction and inordinate
power to do anything at all, to anybody, if it is convinced or
convinces itself that this is for the common good. Such a
sinister machine was the product of the political thinkers of
the late eighteenth and early nineteenth centuries and its
awesome consequence is just beginning to be felt by the
non-native citizens of Canada and the United States. But it
has long been a part of the life of the native peoples of those
lands. It was for the common good that the western lands

were opened up for settlement, even as the eastern lands had been settled; it was for the common good that treaties were signed, and often broken, and that provision was made in these treaties for roads, way stations, trading houses and forts, which could be built at governmental whim on lands reserved for Indians; it was for the common good that rail and road links were established through Indian lands to link east and west; it was for the common good that Indian hunting and fishing rights, guaranteed by treaty or solemn promise, were revoked to make room for people, or things (such as dams) to serve people, or programs (such as conservationist schemes) to satisfy people; it was for the common good that the Indians were herded like cattle, treated like children, swatted like flies and quarantined like animals suspected of having rabies. Meanwhile, it was little wonder that the cry of lamentation was everywhere heard, above the hum of the engines of civilization:

> Our inheritance is turned to strangers, our houses to aliens. We are orphans and fatherless, our mothers are as widows. We have drunken our water for money; our wood is sold unto us . . . They took the young men to grind, and the children fell under the wood. The elders have ceased from the gate, the young men from their musick. The joy of our heart is ceased; our dance is turned into mourning.[8]

When the Honorable S. H. Blake wrote a *Memorandum on Indian Work* for the Board of Management of the Missionary Society of the Church (of England) in Canada in 1909, he included as two of the mottos for his discussion the following enigmatic but apparently contradictory passages:

> It is singular how long the rotten will hold together provided you do not handle it roughly . . . so loathe are men to quit their old ways, and conquering indolence and inertia, venture on new.
>
> (Carlyle's *French Revolution*)

> Precept must be upon precept, precept upon precept; line upon
> line, line upon line; here a little and there a little.
>
> (Isaiah 28:10)

Certainly"line upon line, here a little and there a little" is how the Indians were gradually removed from their traditional lands and ways, and how they lost the use and right of occupancy of their land. This "little," of course, was sometimes quite a lot; for example, Cadwaller Colden wrote in 1764 that he knew of three tracts, each of over a million acres, ceded by the Indians; and the Ohio Company of Associates bought one and a half million acres of very recently ceded Indian land in 1787 from the federal government. Later, treaties were the instrument: between 1853 and 1856, some 52 treaties with various Indian tribes were entered into by the United States, resulting in the acquisition of 174 million acres of Indian land.[9]

The conquering of the "indolence and inertia" of the native people of North America resulted in some notoriously rough handling. How fortunate it was that the new ways upon which the native Americans were persuaded or forced to venture were civilized and Christian, for they might otherwise have had very dubious advantages.

CHAPTER TWO

To Lyve
More Vertuously

What was done becomes clear enough. What people thought
that they were doing is much less clear, but often much
more important. The attitudes toward the Indian and "the
Indian problem" of generations of explorers, traders, missionaries, settlers, military personnel and government administrators are as critical as the actions which these attitudes precipitated. The idea of the noble savage and the
idea of progress together conspired to create a very confused and ambivalent response to the native, combined as it
was with personal and national ambitions and dreams.
There was, in addition, a very strong element of evolutionary determinism implicit in the attitudes of the time, which
was especially attractive to the soldier and the missionary,
and according to which it was concluded that the Indian was
either doomed to extinction or assured of Christian eleva-
tion, if only the wheels of change could be kept properly
greased.

There is undoubtedly a certain fascination to be found by
the modern reader, blissfully unaware of his own limited
perspective, in a reading of the bizarre attitudes and responses of previous generations, which were circumscribed
by doctrines of native origin and speculation on the ultimate

destiny of the native race. One of the earliest such comments is also one of the most typical:

> And what a great and meritoryouse dede
> It were to have the people instructed
> To lyve more Vertuously
> And to lerne to knowe of man the maner
> And also to knowe of god theyr maker
> Which as yet lyve all bestly.[1]

To John Rastell, writing "A New Interlude and a merry, of the nature of the Four Elements" in London around 1520, the natives of the New World presented an orthodox missionary problem (with its equally orthodox solution). "To lyve more Vertuously" was, in general, to live less "bestly"; and, in particular, to live according to non-native standards of propriety. "To knowe of man the maner and . . . of god theyr maker" was to receive instruction in the blessings of civilization and Christianity and to become compelled by their respective verities and institutions.

The instruction was in "precepts," and the compulsion was "line upon line, here a little and there a little," in the language of the passage from Isaiah with which the last chapter closed. It is a passage which is especially appropriate, for the biblical argument which precedes this verse speaks of "their untowardness to learn," and asks:

> Whom shall he teach knowledge? and whom shall he make to understand doctrine? them that are weaned from the milk, and drawn from the breasts.[2]

The process as well as the metaphor of weaning the Indians from their attachment to nomadic ways, and from their uncivil and irreligious habits, was an indispensable one, and constituted a central part of the history of relations between the native and non-native peoples in Canada and the United States, though it was never intended that this process should be accomplished quite so literally as that the Indians would be weaned onto a whisky bottle. Yet in the minds of many, whisky quickly replaced other and more indigenous attachments as a condition of "the Indian problem."

Of course, there were almost as many perceptions of this problem as there were interested parties. For some, the difficulty was that the Indians were *so* Indian—they even spoke differently. As one zealot suggested, "the Indian tongue is the great obstacle to the civilization of the Indians [and] the sooner it is removed the better." For others, the difficulty was that there *were* Indians at all, and one such enlightened soul fumed that he "would as soon admit a right in the buffalo to grant lands as . . . any of the ragged wretches that [were] called chiefs and sachems." Still others lamented the sometime practice of treating them *as* Indians and decided that "treaties with the Indians [are] an absurdity not to be reconciled to the principles of our government."[3]

One thing that was generally agreed, as Lewis Cass remarked in *The North American Review* in 1830, was that

> the Indians themselves are an anomaly upon the face of the earth; and the relations, which have been established between them and the nations of Christendom, are equally anomalous. Their interest is regulated by practical principles, arising out of peculiar circumstances.[4]

And just who were these anomalies? It was something of a puzzler.

> How the people furst began
> In that countrey or whens they cam
> For clerkes it is a question.

Not a simple question, to be sure, but the discussion which surrounded it had important consequences, as the fictions which it generated became continuous with those of the "great and meritoryouse" mission of instructing the natives of the Americas in the proprieties of civil and religious conduct and belief. Obviously, John Rastell's "clerkes" were not the only ones who entertained the question.

In the first place, of course, the native people were the people who were already there. There was not much room for disagreement about that, though there certainly was disagreement as to their origin, and explanations varied widely. Some argued that the Indians were descended from the Hebrews, by various lines, and supported their arguments by evidence as different as the report that Columbus had identified Española as "the Ophir of which the third book of Kings speaks," or by the apparent Indian attachment to idolatries and superstitions, "living by them as did their ancestors, as David said in Psalm 105."[5] The beginning of the nineteenth century, in particular, saw a proliferation of books[6] purporting to prove that the Indians were descended from the ten lost tribes of Israel; and this belief is maintained by many to this day.

It would be wrong to suppose that such theories had only an esoteric appeal. In fact, they were used to a surprising extent to reinforce local prejudices, such as that entertained by James Mackenzie of the Northwest Company who, glibly echoing such popularizers of the Judaic theory as James Adair, could assert that "the Israelites were ungrateful, so are the Indians."[7] More significantly, men such as Thomas Jefferson were convinced that an understanding of the native's past might help in the development of strategies for ensuring their future. The abuses of this kind of intellectual enterprise were distressing, and transformed the conscious or unconscious ambitions of those who formulated policies and who established practices with respect to native affairs into the treaties and laws in which these were enshrined.

For example, it was by such a light that Mr. Justice Johnson wrote his concurring opinion in the 1831 Supreme Court case *The Cherokee Nation v. The State of Georgia,* where he argued that the situation in Georgia was in effect a state of war, in which Georgia could if it wished enforce its will. The story there was fairly straightforward. An agreement which had been reached between commissioners representing the United States and Georgia in 1802 provided that the "United States shall, at their own expense, extinguish, for the use of Georgia, as early as can be peacably obtained, on reasonable terms," Indian title to the area within the present limits of the state. This had not been done; and although the theory (propounded by George Washington from the beginning of the union, and picked up by most of his successors) taught that the Indians would, as settlement approached their lands, naturally wish to move on, flowing easily ahead of successive waves of settlement, this had not happened in practice as hydraulically as might have been wished. Relying on the theory, Presidents Monroe and Adams waited for and did something to encourage voluntary emigration; but by the time Jackson took office, there was no longer time to allow for native inertia. Georgia wanted the land for settlement and was proceeding to do everything it could to force the Indians out. The status of Indian tribal nationhood within the larger framework of a sovereign nation was at issue, though it was not decided here.[8] But Johnson himself addressed this issue squarely and compared the Indian tribes to the Hebrews of ancient times, wandering the desert, anticipating the exercise of sovereignty over "their" land but not yet invested with it.

> What does this series of allegations exhibit but a state of war, and the fact of invasion? They allege themselves to be a sovereign independent state, and set out that another sovereign state has, by its laws, its functionaries, and its armed force, invaded their state and put down their authority. This is war in fact; though not being declared with the usual solemnities, it may perhaps be called war in disguise. And the contest is distinctly a contest for empire. It is not a case of meum and tuum in the judicial but in the political sense. Not an appeal to

laws but to force. A case in which a sovereign undertakes to assert his right upon his sovereign responsibility; to right himself, and not to appeal to any arbiter but the sword, for the justice of his cause. If the state of Maine were to extend its laws over into the province of New Brunswick and send its magistrates to carry them into effect, it would be a parallel case . . . In the exercise of sovereign right, the sovereign is sole arbiter of his own justice. The penalty of wrong is war and subjugation.[9]

This was a devastating species of argument, for it turned the theory of the quasi-sovereignty of the states of the union against the interest of the native people of the United States by distorting the importance of an independent native heritage. Combined with a theory which assigned a kind of convenient sovereignty to the Indian tribes, it quickly became catastrophic, especially when reinforced by the generally accepted (though not entirely accurate) view of these tribes as essentially nomadic. The premises of Vattel's *Law of Nations* were brought to bear on the situation; and those who pursued an "idle mode of life" and "roamed over" rather than "inhabited" the land were considered expendable. Removal to land as yet unrequired for settlement or cultivation therefore emerged as the only available alternative to extermination in this scheme; and the two together defined one aspect of Indian administration. Reflecting on this "humane policy," Commissioner of Indian Affairs Elbert Herring suggested in 1831 that it

is progressively developing its good effects; and it is confidently trusted, will at no distant day, be crowned with complete success. Gradually diminishing in numbers and deteriorating in condition; incapable of coping with the superior intelligence of the white man; ready to fall into the vices, but unapt to appropriate the benefits of the social state; the increasing tide of white population threatened soon to engulf them, and finally to cause their total extinction. The progress is slow but sure; the cause is inherent in the nature of things; tribes numerous and powerful have disappeared from among us in a ratio of decrease,ominous to the existence of those that still remain, unless counteracted by the substitution of some principle sufficiently potent to check the tendencies of decay and dissolution. This salutory principle exists in the system of removal; of change of residence; of settlement in territories exclusively their own, and under the protection of the United States; connected with the benign influences of education and instruction in agriculture and the several mechanic arts, whereby social is distinguished from savage life.

A year later, Herring waxed increasingly eloquent:

It was evident, that they must either be left to the fate that was gradually threatening their entire extinction, or that the Government, by some magnanimous act of interposition, should rescue them from approaching destruction, and devise a plan for their preservation and security. From such benign considerations arose the generous policy of transferring their residence, and congregating their tribes, in domains suited to their condition, and set apart for their use. In the consummation of this grand and sacred object rests the sole chance of averting Indian annihilation. Founded in pure and disinterested motives, may it meet the approval of heaven, by the complete attainment of its beneficent ends![10]

In short order, the next act was played. Further removal became impossible because there was no land left to remove the Indians to. The Indian lands themselves became desired for settlement and cultivation—in Oklahoma, for example, which was, as one enthusiast declared, "the garden spot of the United States lacking . . . the garden."[11] Or, more ambitiously, as a writer in the *Kansas City Times* in 1880 envisaged the process,

ten millions of acres of the finest agricultural public lands on the continent . . . awaiting . . . the hardy pioneer who would soon turn up the virgin soil, subdue the waste places, and make the land . . . blossom as the rose.[12]

Clearly, the Indians must either be ploughed under along with their land, or else must turn to the cultivation of civilized habits and ambitions.

For the Indian hunting grounds were seriously restricted and depleted, and the nomadic ways of many native groups could no longer provide them access to enough food. The great American desert, to which so many of the Indian tribes had been assigned, had become needed for expansion and the United States was called upon to develop the corollaries of its grand axiom regarding the native people and their destiny. And so the native was to learn to settle and to cultivate the land. The step was, at least in principle, an easy one. Because of the bias toward viewing the native as essentially nomadic, and because of the enthusiasm for maintaining the fiction of tribal nationhood or quasi-sovereign status, the American authorities had never really identified the Indian with his tribal lands in any case. The theory did not allow for that, since it assumed his eventual assimilation in the larger community itself already engaged in settling and cultivating; and although such assimilation was contradicted by an unsettling reluctance on the part of some native groups, most felt that this was merely a temporary aberration, the product of ignorance and superstition. Those who disagreed made a curious company, of the worst and the best of men: the former wanted to exterminate the Indian, the latter to preserve for him an inviolable homeland.

The idea of assimilation was always the practical end envisaged by the Canadian government as well, though it was not incorporated into any theoretical structure which might direct its policy for Indian affairs at any particular time. Rather, as we shall see, the emphasis in Canada was on attachment to lands reserved for them, from which they might be weaned by slow degree, and in good time. There was, however, an additional factor which, especially in the United States, militated against the permanent identification of the Indian with his lands, especially when his lands were desired for development. "Common property and civilization," remarked Commissioner of Indian Affairs T. H. Crawford in 1838, "cannot co-exist."

At the foundation of the whole social system lies individuality of property. It is, perhaps, nine times in ten, the stimulus that manhood first feels; it has produced the energy, industry, and enterprise that distinguish the civilized world, and contributes more largely to the good morals of men than those are willing to acknowledge who have not looked somewhat closely at their fellow-beings. With it come all the delights that the word *home* expresses. The comforts that follow fixed settlements are in its train; and to them belong not only an anxiety to do right, that those gratifications may not be forfeited, but industry, that they may be increased. Social intercourse and a just appreciation of its pleasures result, when you have civilized and, for the most part, moral men. This process, it strikes me, the Indians must go through, before their habits can be materially changed; and they may, after what many of them have seen and know, do it very rapidly. If, on the other hand, the large tracts of land set apart for them shall continue to be joint property, the ordinary motive to industry (and the most powerful one) will be wanting. A bare subsistence is as much as they can promise themselves. A few acres of badly cultivated corn about their cabins will be seen, instead of extensive fields, rich pastures, and valuable stock. The latter belong to him who is conscious that what he ploughs is his own, and will descend to those he loves—never to the man who does not know by what tenure he holds his miserable dwelling. Laziness and unthrift will be so general as not to be disgraceful; and if the produce of their labors should be thrown into common stock, the indolent and dishonest will subsist at the expense of the meritorious. Besides, there is a strong motive in reference to ourselves for encouraging individual ownership. The history of the world proves that distinct and separate possessions make those who hold them averse to change. The risk of losing the advantages they have, men do not readily encounter. By adopting and acting on the view suggested, a large body will be created whose interests would dispose them to keep things steady. They would be the ballast of the ship.[13]

It would be a mistake to assume that the non-native population was quite so confident of its apparent certainties as it sometimes appeared. Much of the ruthless and precipitate earnestness which characterized native affairs, particularly during the nineteenth century, was the product of a disarming insecurity, just as many of the mistakes and tragedies which occurred were the sad consequence of simple ignorance or benign incompetence. On the uncertain seas upon which civilization tossed, private property provided the most sturdy sheet anchor, but many other and somewhat less awkward devices were also employed. Among the most basic were the more or less informed opinions regarding the disposition and character of the Indians, especially insofar as these were determined by his environment or by his occupation. In this tradition, Philip Turnor of the Hudson's Bay Company reported that "it has been found that the farther North, the more Peaceable the Indian"; and the more cultured explorer Radisson added a novel element, noting that "those that liveth on fish uses more inhumanities than those that feed upon flesh."[14] Almost everyone agreed that the Indians of the great basin, so-called Diggers, were inferior; that one descended anthropologically as well as physically as one moved from the mountains to the sea; and that isolation encouraged an inconvenient (to the white man) independence if the climate were suitably mild. Ethnography and orthography were not Peter Pond's line, but his remarks on the Yankton Indians are fairly typical: "[Thay] are faroshas and rude in thare maners perhaps oeing in sum masher to thare leadg an obsger life in the planes."[15] Even Edward S. Curtis, the great American photographer and ethnographer, was moved to comment that "it is scarcely an exaggeration to say that no single noble trait redeems the Kwakiutl character."[16] This, at the beginning of a volume devoted entirely to them!

Such responses had one feature in common, however certainly or uncertainly they were based; and this was the passion with which they were defended and upheld, and the influence which each had on the minds of believers and unbelievers alike. For the most significant thing by far was not that everyone in the non-native population who had any contact whatsoever with the native presence on the continent had a differing attitude towards the native people, but that everyone had *an* attitude, which influenced his response at however apparently insignificant a level. No one was without a viewpoint; it was a question upon which one had to make up one's mind, and the curious yet common character of such questions is not often recognized.

For one thing, the tradition of the naturalness of native hostility and treachery was very firmly established. It had some basis in fact, however understandable, and early government policy and practice were premised upon this notion. It was not only a question of tradition, however, though it was the orthodox view that

> the relations into which the first Europeans entered with the aborigines in North America were very largely influenced, if not wholly decided, by the relations which they found to exist among the tribes on their arrival here. Those relations were fiercely hostile.[17]

Even more influential than historical traditions was the idea that, as Edwin Denig remarked (admittedly with reference to the Arikaras, the "Horrid Tribe" whom almost everyone, both native and non-native, disliked), "Indians to be Indian must have war."[18] Even if one did not go so far as Denig, most observers in the nineteenth century were of the opinion

> that the sons of the forest will continue to seek occasions of disputing and fighting with each other, while the savage notion subsists in full force among them, that war furnishes for their young men the only road to distinction.[19]

As a consequence of this general attitude, it is little wonder that a nervous uncertainty was implicit in even the most confident of prescriptions or schedules for the improvement of the Indian, and that in the presence of an alien culture the

non-native inhabitants of North America reacted with ob-
sessively defensive zeal.

It is a source of continued frustration to native people that
histories of Canada and the United States, even histories of
the native people of these lands, tend to concentrate much if
not most of their attention upon non-native responses. And
while it is certainly true that many such histories are deplor-
ably lacking in sensitivity or attention to native situations
and attitudes, it nonetheless holds that history involves the
discovery (or imaginative invention) of significant initiatives, whether they be personal or national; environmental
or international; economic, social or religious; cultural or
cyclical. In North America, for reasons that were tragic
perhaps but basically inescapable, the initiatives were for
the most part non-native. The native people, of course,
were an inseparable part of the story and in fact took the
earliest, and often hospitable, initiative. But almost from the
moment they welcomed the first settlers, or cooperated with
the early explorers and traders, or massacred some poor
wretched little party with undisguised glee, they became
part of a process over which they had no control. Later native
initiatives were consequently in the main either deter-
minedly warlike or in recent times militant in a more so-
phisticated (and essentially non-native) way, employing
legal means, the possibilities of the media, and some of the
confrontation techniques which have shown dramatic results in the past several decades. These native initiatives
have been reasonably well catalogued, though not by any
means always with the sympathy or imaginative understanding which they deserve. Yet they have been, however compelling, still a reaction to situations which were created by
forces beyond their control, and to white attitudes which
were both cause and effect of these initiatives. The most
impressive force by far was the central government and the
bureaucratic structure which it created, and of which it at
times lost control. These bureaucratic structures were inseparable from the compelling fictions that informed the

changing times of which they were the stolid monuments; and it is to these monumental structures that we must in due course turn our attention.

Societies are curious phenomena and rely to a surprising degree on definitions and distinctions in terms of which their formulas can function. Kin and class provide the most convenient of these, though they are hardly separable; and race has provided some societies with another critical element, in which color may or may not play a part. South Africa provides what is possibly the most grotesque example of this, with its Britishers and Boers and Blacks, but the Netherlands and Canada, New Zealand and the United States, embody versions and variations of the same social structure. The great revolutions of the eighteenth century—the American, the French and the Industrial —changed many of the patterns which had defined social ordering in Europe and the New World and provided many of the initiatives which would be of influence in effecting social continuity. It is probably not an exaggeration to say that we are now in the midst of a change of similar consequence, in which the imperatives of ecological balance are becoming significant, but their importance in defining social priorities is not yet apparent.

A pattern emerges much more clearly, however, in the two centuries preceding our own. In France under the *ancien régime,* for example, there were the classically ordered estates of the realm, of which the third (the bourgeoisie) was a cruelly picturesque background decoration in the pattern of French social dynamics. This changed after the revolution, not because of the Declaration of the Rights of Man, but because of a single political act— the confiscation of the immense property holdings of the Church and their sale to the highest bidder. The result was, as one writer has recounted it,

> not only an enormous shift in the distribution of wealth, but also a great number of new owners whose property was protected by

law. The concept of private ownership with unlimited rights of disposal was one of the achievements of the French Revolution. It made the purchasers of nationalized land into the staunchest supporters of the new regime. At the same time, the redistribution of property meant a reordering of society . . .

The effect of these changes was that society emerged in a new way as a historical potency and a determining factor. It was no longer a rigid body of estates, but one that had become mobile through money. The spread of the Industrial Revolution from England to the continent hastened this process. Society, its patterns of movement and its laws, was discovered . . . as a vital force.[20]

This discovery was not made by the architects of the American constitution, but it certainly was not lost upon subsequent generations of American statesmen, legislators and scoundrels. And since it had long been a principle informing British social and political structures, it was an inevitable part of the developing pattern of Canadian civil design. For one thing, it provided the basis for that old argument which we have heard so many times already, that "the absence of the *meum* and *tuum* in the general community of possessions, which is the grand conservative principle of the social state, is a perpetual operating cause of the *vis inertiae* of savage life."[21] For another, it gave *practical* significance to what might otherwise have been seen as a theoretical issue regarding co-existence and co-extensive rights, particularly rights in land, and the political consequences which accrue from the possession of such rights.

Throughout the nineteenth century, there was a progressive codification of various social tendencies and fashionable enthusiasms as "movements," a term which was first used in France after 1830 to denote events of a political or social character. It would be wrong to underestimate the importance of such "movements" in the history of relations between native and non-native peoples in North America, because in a very real sense it is the *only* such history which is available to comprehension. Furthermore, since such movements can be interpreted in either a mechanistic or a teleological fashion—that is, as operating "from some beginning" or "to a particular end"—they form the basis for a remarkably flexible kind of history.

It has been common for writers on Indian relations to see the development of the story as defined by the development of "ideas," such as the idea of the savage or the idea of progress. But these ideas were in many ways little more than rationalizations for or objectifications of social or political movements, which were themselves defined not so much by minds versed in intellectual discrimination as by conditions which appeared to the political minds of the time to call for or indeed create certain social discriminations. Thus, the idea of the savage provided an easy discrimination for the likes of Hudson's Bay Company trader Sir George Simpson, who made the honest admission that "philanthropy is not the exclusive object of our visits to these Northern Regions," for it exempted the fur traders from many of the indiscriminate (which is to say, philanthropic) obligations which might otherwise have constrained them.[22] It was also useful, indeed necessary, for the missionaries, who could use it to argue both specifically for their own philanthropic conversion of the natives, and more generally for humanitarian treatment of a people who had once lived in Edenic innocence. And it was useful for those who saw advantages in a continued isolation of the natives from normal political processes. The idea of progress, on the other hand, fitted naturally into expansionist movements and civilizing programs, and provided a convenient basis for models both of separate and of integrated native status, depending on the particular conditions and prevailing moods that together defined the direction in which progress was understood to lie.

The literature of the time, which many writers have read as providing almost a sacred text, is less a testament of ideas than it is a fiction based upon social facts, a fiction which eventually became, as fictions sometimes tend to, more real than the reality from which it derived its life. It is often so, of course. The imaginative constructions of Marx, Lenin, or Mao Tse-tung created a reality of which social change became more a cause than an effect, and in which a policy of removal and demographic shift was imposed which was not much different (particularly in China) from that which was applied to the Indians of North America. And these constructions were, in each case, the defining feature of a social movement bolstered by that anomalous logic of ideas, an ideology.

The most important and in some respects the most absurd of these imaginative constructions in North American native affairs were the legal (initially, treaty) definitions which were created by the governments in order to expedite civil and religious "movements" of particular periods and to particular ends. In the United States, these definitions were initially devised to provide for the orderly carrying out of trade, settlement and the process of civilizing a raw land and its rude indigenous inhabitants.[23] In the British colonies after the turn of the nineteenth century, when a kind of stability was established, and then later in Canada, a sense of messianic responsibility was more apparent; and there was a strenuous attempt (which was facilitated by a much simpler political structure at that time) to coordinate theoretical and practical considerations by the simple expedient of combining them. As an ironic consequence, the actions which were taken on behalf of the Indians had neither a clear theoretical nor an effective practical relationship to the needs they were intended to serve, *even when* by accident those needs were well served, as in the case of the sending of the Royal Northwest MountedPolice to end the whisky trade and ensure peace on the western prairies in the 1870s. There is a distracting irony behind this apparent enigma, which is intimately connected with the differing political structures and traditions of the United States and

Canada, and with the different relationship between theory and practice upon which the ordering of Indian affairs by governmental authorities in both countries has long depended. In Aristotle's parable, the house is there so that people may live in it; but it is also there because the builders have laid one stone on top of another. Both the product and the process of Indian affairs, no less than of house building, admit differing interpretations; upon one's choice depends one's response to the condition and the validity of either.

The American revolutionary thinkers were, predominantly, convinced of the superiority of theory. They had a profound respect for ideas and ideological concepts, and they generally proceeded from a desired effect to imagine possible causes, or means, which would lead to the accomplishing of that end. They tended to consider the Indian, when they thought of him at all, as a problem to be solved; and even the notorious removal policy of Andrew Jackson, which has often been cited as a setting aside of the principles of the founding fathers, is perfectly consistent with the theoretical basis for Indian affairs which had been established by the time of the Continental Congress in 1787 and incorporated into the acts promulgated by the First Congress in 1790. As a rather wry addition, it is worth noting that nothing characterizes the champion of theory more exactly than his enthusiasm for engaging with other theoretical structures; and Jackson's acquiescence in the desire of the state of Georgia to remove the Cherokees from lands occupied by them within their borders was spurred by nothing so much as by Chief Justice Marshall's theoretical defense of their rights in the various cases on the matter which were brought before the Supreme Court. Jackson had his own theoretical premises ready at hand, and they were of course continuous with his theory of the eventual social structure which would define the United States. To this end, civilized settlement was of course the appropriate means. The needs of the Indians, the natural concern of those for whom practice should transcend theory, were entirely secondary;

theory is not a response to needs, but to ideological desires, or to the purposes by which those desires are compelled. When such desires become creative principles, informing the pseudo-practice—the fiction applied to fact—by which the theory is effected, then the opponents of such actions accuse its architects of self-interest. They are right, but usually for the wrong reasons.

CHAPTER THREE

Them
and Us

In 1914, the Director of the Board of Indian Commissioners appointed his Secretary, Frederick H. Abbott, to do a study of the Administration of Indian Affairs in Canada. The Board had originally been proposed by Henry B. Whipple, Episcopalian Bishop of Minnesota, in 1862, and was finally established in 1869 (under President Grant's "peace policy") to advise the government of needed changes in Indian policy and in particular to oversee Indian appropriations and agency conduct. The members of the Board, who were to be "men of high character" with no political ends to serve, were nominated by various religious denominations. Initially, they exercised joint control with the Secretary of the Interior in the disbursement of two million dollars recently (in 1869) appropriated by Congress for "keeping the Indians at peace and promoting self-sustaining habits among them."[1]

By the first decade of the twentieth century, however, they had become a rather inconsequential crew of clerics and other righteous folk, but they were still a fairly vocal group, and still saw it as their mission to analyze the ever-changing state of Indian affairs. Abbott had the full cooperation of the Canadian government in his investigation and his report was an interesting one, reflecting more credit on the Canadian than on the American principles and methods of administration, though some of this credit was no doubt owing to the chagrin of the Board at no longer being of much influence in American Indian affairs. At one point, Abbott commented on the policies of enfranchisement, or relinquishment of special Indian status, in the two countries, and the differing approaches were directly addressed:

> Canada's approach to enfranchisement, as to many other policies of dealing with her Indians, has been diametrically opposite to that of the United States. She has been preparing her Indians for full citizenship by letting them exercise extensive powers of local self-government, but has stopped short of conferring upon them the title of citizenship for which her scheme of training has prepared them. On the contrary, in the United States we have been prompt to confer the title of citizenship upon our Indians and to extend to them the right of franchise while we have almost wholly neglected the training in self-government necessary to prepare them for an intelligent and helpful exercise of that right.[2]

What Abbott was saying, in effect, was that the Americans had been too ready to create theoretical structures within which the Indians would fit—in this case, the structure of a relatively homogeneous society—and had neglected to adapt the theory to the appropriate practice. In Canada, on the other hand, the social determinants of a property-based civil structure had been recognized in practice, but the theoretical basis of this structure, and the necessary sense of how these determinants might in fact be expected to function, was sadly lacking, or else equally sadly (albeit unconsciously) inappropriate.

It would be an oversimplification to say that in the United States the end was kept clearly in mind but the means wallowed in murky waters, while in Canada the means were consistently applied yet the end never properly perceived—but it would not be an atrocious oversimplification. What such a statement ignores is the subtle relationship between theory and practice which does not permit us simply to match them up with ends and means, or effects and causes. For practice and theory are discontinuously related, as are facts and fictions.

In both Canada and the United States, after the initial period of discovery and early settlement in which it was simple enough to distinguish between Them and Us, the problem of defining rather precisely who was entitled to, or (within the structures of civil and religious prerogatives that were current) who needed, the special attention which was to be bestowed upon the benighted native inhabitants of the land became significant. In the United States, an Indian is defined in law, and with respect to his responsibilities and privileges, on a racial basis. A quarter-blood criteria is generally applied; and consequently a non-member does not gain membership by marriage to a member, and the third generation of mixed marriages produces children who do not have membership. However, certain classes of non-members—spouses of members and their non-member minor children—have rights to reside on reserve lands. Behind this definition, which although purely administrative does have a significant role in determining Indian identity, there lies the assumption that an Indian's "way of life" is a temporary feature and should not be taken as identifying his uniqueness, but rather that the blood line is the determining factor. Membership is distinguished from residency on Indian lands, and implicitly from adoption of an Indian way of life, for the non-member spouse will be permitted to live on the reserve but can never become a member of the tribe. Miscegenation becomes a possible, but not generally discussed instrument of assimilation, though many observers felt that mixed bloods represented progress, both genetic and socio-political. "Wherever there are half-breeds," remarked Timothy Flint, "there is generally a faction, a party; and this race finds it convenient to espouse the interests of civilization and christianity. The full-blooded chiefs and Indians are generally partisans for the customs of the old time, and for the ancient religion."[3]

The more usual instruments for effecting the transformation of Them into Us have been legal ones, however, and have included various "extensions" of civil responsibilities and privileges to native individuals and groups, to make Them more like Us, with the corresponding destruction of native structures of allegiance and responsibility, and of special privileges which correspond to those structures. One critical difficulty is that this procedure assumes that We know who We are, and are happy that this is so. At times, the whole exercise has taken on a depressing resemblance to the game of trying to find a steer that is lost after summer pasturing; slowly, one realizes that the steer is not lost at all—it is only that we cannot find him.

The system of definition which has been applied in Canada is different from that in the United States, but equally arbitrary, and almost equally destructive of indigenous cohesion and responsibility. What was the alternative to this haphazard attempt to draw strict lines of demarcation? Whatever it was, neither the Americans nor the Canadians discovered it. The American practice of native administration developed in a manner that was compelled by an energy that was fascinating and irresistible. The Imperial, and later the Canadian, response was in principle almost exactly opposite, though the actual policies were often very similar.

> The radical principle underlying [the Canadian] policy of Indian management is to keep the Indian community attached to the land, at the same time giving the greatest freedom to individuals to secure their livelihood far and wide by any honest endeavour.[4]

The instrument of this policy and this attachment to the land has been the Indian Act, a piece of legislation which was first passed in 1876, as "An Act to amend and consolidate the laws respecting Indians." Essentially, the Act gathered together all the laws respecting Indians, and removed the distinction which had previously applied between Indians and their lands. A Department of Indian Affairs, which would be responsible for every aspect of the life of its clients, was created, and these clients were in turn defined in specific and exclusive terms. The intention of the Act was oddly inconsistent with its provisions, however, for the intention was to provide the means and a coherent process by which Indians might become assimilated. Much care and attention was given to defining Indian status for the purposes of the Act and to distinguishing the Indian from other members of society. (One of the definitions in the 1876 Act, for example, was that "the term 'person' means an individual other than an Indian.") The first step was to identify the Indian community by its attachment to the land and to maintain this attachment as a defining condition, by identifying band membership with specific reserve lands.[5]

For purely practical reasons, the Canadian government did not proceed to subvert the tribal structure as a means of effecting native conversion to civilized habits, but saw that as the inevitable (and desirable) end of the process. It chose instead to rely on the supposed temptations of enfranchisement, which is the process by which "registered" or "status" Indians in Canada—which is to say, Indians who are defined as such (through band affiliation) for the purposes of the Indian Act—give up that status and become full members of the non-native community. In fact, it could fairly be said that the interest of the Canadian legislators of the 1850s and 1860s was not with the creation of a legal Indian status, though much trouble was taken over this, but with a way to effect its end. The logic, roughly speaking, was that the more specific the status, the more impressive would be the relinquishing of that status and the amelioration of the condition of Indianness. Who, after all, would choose to be an Indian, now that the new dispensation had arrived?

It should, however, be noted that the status provisions had a more positive purpose as well and were designed to ensure that Indian lands would be employed for the exclusive benefit of Indians, that as few as possible (within reason) qualified, and that the number would remain relatively static. For this purpose, and reflecting both the non-native and what were taken to be the native social structures, an 1869 Act declared that when an Indian woman married a person not of Indian blood, she and her descendants lost their status, as well as any interest whatsoever that they might have had in the lands or property or treaty provisions belonging to the tribe. In fact, the provision was insisted upon by the Caughnawaga band of the Six Nations, who were fiercely anxious to protect their corporate identity. It was therefore provided in the legislation affecting Indians

> that any Indian woman marrying any other than an Indian, should cease to be an Indian within the meaning of this Act, nor shall the children issue of such marriage be considered as Indians within the meaning of this Act.

This has been a very contentious point and the provision was recently challenged in the Supreme Court of Canada as being contrary to the Canadian Bill of Rights. The challenge was unsuccessful, but the issue is still very much alive.[6]

The persons entitled to use reserve lands therefore formed a peculiar sort of charter group, membership of which was (and continues to be) based partly on a "style of life" criterion. The historical importance of these distinctions relates very clearly to the question of these protected Indian lands and to the exclusion of a group of "halfbreeds" (a legal term in the 1876 Act), many of the descendants of whom with the passing of years have suffered all of the discrimination which has unfortunately been practiced upon Indians, and have enjoyed none of the benefits of special status. Their numbers in Canada are today variously estimated at between a quarter and a half-million, and they are referred to, or refer to themselves, as non-status Indians or Métis. They have, with minor exceptions, no reserve land and their condition is dismal. Their history, on the other hand, is stirring, as we shall have occasion to see.

The idea of defining an Indian for the purposes of legislation affecting Indian lands was a curiosity which grew out of both the nature and the purpose of the Canadian legislation. The spirit of the time favored a policy of assimilation for the Indian, with the instrument being the concept of private property; but the pressures to achieve this end and to employ this instrument were not nearly as great in Canada as they were in the United States; and there was for a time a fairly desultory discussion of alternatives. In this regard, the Canadian commissioners who reported on Indian affairs in 1858 remarked that

> various schemes have from time to time been proposed for the apportionment of land to the Indians. An examination of these several suggestions will show that they may be divided at once into two classes, the one advising the total seclusion of the Aborigines from contamination by the white settlers, the other hoping by constant intercourse to assimilate the habits of the two races.

For pressures aside, the differing principles were obvious. The Imperial, and later the Canadian, governments focussed their early legislation respecting Indians on Indian land; the Americans, on trade and intercourse with the native peoples. The attachment to the land was never a critical element in the definition of native identity in the United States, and the government authorities consequently felt not only free but compelled to deal with Indian land as an instrument of change. Both traditions included a devotion to the civil stability provided by private property, but saw this stability in rather different perspectives. In both countries, of course, romantic or ignorant delusions about "Indianness" resulted in grotesque misinterpretations of Indian pride and authority, and the meaning of the land in Indian life and tradition. But the specific absence of a legislative context identifying the Indians with their communal lands in the United States was significant for the simple reason that a consciousness of the civil responsibilities which pertained to the enjoyment of private property was not a quality of the native intelligence, and certainly not of the tribal perspective, and had to be instilled in both before either would function as useful elements of the new and non-native socio-economic structure with which they were to be integrated.

In Canada, there was more flexibility to provide for this process of native transformation, since the country had an enviably simple political structure when compared to that which applied in the United States during the mid-part of the century, a structure which was complicated only by the cabalistic machinations of Imperial diplomacy. Furthermore, while Canada was fairly smoothly accepting a transfer of colonial authority and responsibility for Indian affairs, the United States was in the midst of a Civil War. As a consequence of having a number of options still available, the 1858 report was able to recommend that

> the preferable course to be adopted in Canada must partake both of the separatist system, and also that in which the Indians are located with the white population. Which of these elements will predominate must depend upon the locality of the band.[7]

Nonetheless, while recommending a consolidation of legislation regarding Indians (which was partially effected in 1859 with "An Act respecting Civilization and Enfranchisement of Indians"; and in 1860 with "An Act respecting the Management of Indian Lands and Property"; and fully in "The Indian Act" of 1876), the Canadian commissioners advocated "the gradual destruction of the tribal organization"; and suggested some provision such as that which was included in Article V of the Treaty signed in Detroit on July 31, 1855, between the United States and the Ottawas and Chippewas.

> The Tribal organization . . . except so far as may be necessary for the purpose of carrying into effect the provisions of this agreement, is hereby dissolved, and if at anytime hereafter, further negotiations with the United States, in reference to any matters contained herein should become necessary, no general convention of the Indians shall be called, but such as reside in the vicinity of any usual place of payment or those only who are immediately interested in the questions involved, may arrange all matters between themselves and the United States, without the concurrence of other portions of their people, and as fully and conclusively and with the same effect in every respect as if all were represented.[8]

Tribal organization was clearly recognized as a defining feature of native identity; destroy it, the argument ran, and you would destroy the coherence of the native way of life and reduce native recidivism. The argument itself was astonishingly stubborn. Much later, when the concept of Indian self-determination and cultural autonomy was given its first institutional go-round by the New Deal administrators under President Roosevelt, it was still to be hampered by rigid guidelines which followed from the premises of this argument: specifically, by provisions which often resulted in the dictating of tribal constitutions by federal administrators; and by suspicious collusion between tribal governments, their lawyers (who had to be approved by the Secretary of the Interior), the federal government (and especially those of its agencies with an interest in Indian land, water and mineral resources), and non-native concerns. And yet the Wheeler-Howard Act of 1934, which provided legislative formulation for New Deal pieties and enthusiasms, was criticized by Flora Warren Seymour, a former member of the missionary Board of Indian Commissioners, as "the most extreme gesture yet made by the administration in this country toward a Communistic experiment," and as fostering paganism. Another critic of the bill, Ray Kirkland, wrote an article which appeared in the *New York Herald Tribune* under the heading "Commissioner of Indian Affairs Urges Tribesmen to Accept Soviet Type Rule."[9] Progress takes strange forms, and few stranger than those which have been defined by competing forces in Indian affairs, and conflicting theories as to what constitutes amelioration of the native condition. Whatever the specific issue, the presence of a native "tribal" consciousness was sure to emerge as of importance.

In general, the process of ameliorating the native condition was gradual. In the United States, it culminated during the latter part of the nineteenth century, in legislation specifically designed to force the civilization of the Indian, and to conquer the "indolence and inertia" which appeared to characterize his condition by altering the social and economic environment which appeared to sustain that condition. A central aspect of this, it was agreed, was the presence of a native tribal consciousness.

The General Allotment Act of 1887 was one of the most comprehensive programs ever devised to destroy this tribal consciousness and to replace it with a consciousness of the importance of private property and national aspirations.

The Act, which was stewarded through the House by Senator Henry L. Dawes, provided that the President, at his discretion and without Indian consent, could break up the reservations and thereby make all reservation Indians landowners in severalty and citizens of the United States, with all attendant privileges and responsibilities, including the suffrage, instead of landowners in common and members of the tribe, with all the contrary allegiances which that implied. (The citizenship provision was changed by the Burke Act of 1906, which withheld citizenship until all land titles in which an individual had interest had become alienable, it being assumed that civil responsibility presupposed the possibility of personal irresponsibility.) Furthermore, the federal government, with tribal consent, could sell "surplus" land to white settlers and hold the money in trust for the Indians.

Nothing was withheld for future allotments, to take account of increasing population, because it was assumed that in a generation or two the end of Indian separateness would be accomplished by the working out of the accepted principle, enunciated by Secretary of the Interior Carl Schurz in 1877, that "the enjoyment and pride of the individual ownership of property is one of the most effective civilizing agencies."[10] The allotment scheme was, in fact, a far more effective agency at getting lands away from Indian control than it was at civilizing the Indians. In fact, the allotment provision which was included in many treaties which had been signed since 1854 contained a clause that permitted the revoking or cancelling of assignments to "any such person or family [who] shall at any time neglect or refuse to occupy and till a portion of the land assigned, and on which they have located, or shall rove from place to place."[11] Obviously, the idea was to discourage nomadic habits, but also to encourage an acceptance of the socio-economic imperatives which defined non-native society and without an acceptance of which it was earnestly believed that the natives could not survive. Furthermore, these imperatives were, to the non-native, clearly superior; and therefore acceptance of them was a necessary condition of progress towards civilized existence. There is little reason to doubt that this policy was conceived in good faith and out of a belief that the civil and religious betterment of the Indians might thereby be achieved. Once again, however, theory and practice failed to cooperate.

The Act was a disaster for a number of reasons, not the least of which was that it was introduced without any legislation to effect changes in native conditions or adequate provision to educate Indians in new habits. Impatience, and a sense that a trial by the fires of individual entitlement and responsibility would be beneficial, resulted in one of the most depressing depletions of a cultural resource in the history of native affairs. From another point of view it was even more of a disappointment, for it simply did not work. In most cases, native tribal allegiance stubbornly persisted.

The supporters of the Act formed a curious compact, divided between earnest zealots and avaricious scoundrels; the former wanted the Indian's soul, while the latter wanted his land. But that is perhaps too clever. Basically, the Allotment Act was designed to accommodate the well-intentioned missionary enthusiasm and benign faith of men such as Alfred Riggs and the American Board of Commissioners for Foreign Missions,[12] with practical advice of the kind that was supplied by Charles Painter, a lobbyist in Washington with the Indian Rights Association, who cautioned that unless reform legislation could be seen to serve the interests of the white citizens, it would not pass.[13] It passed all right, but so did much of the Indian heritage. The Indians themselves had little to say about the entire process, for the very simple reason that there was no political structure within which they could effectively operate.

In the final analysis, all of the legislative evangelism which accompanied this "civilizing agent" was but a pious candle in the greedy wind which blew across the Indian territory, as surplus lands not needed for allotments at the time a particular reserve was allotted were sold to non-native settlers in 160-acre tracts. The proceeds were kept for the benefit of the Indians, but this in itself was little comfort, for the Indians were becoming increasingly dependent upon the charity of the central authority as their estate and their capacity for self-support diminished. Already, the eleemosynary function of government, so contrary to the principles of free and self-sufficient enterprise which were supposedly to be inculcated into the native consciousness, was becoming an increasing part of the scheme. The tentacles of the welfare system slowly encircled the Indian nations, at the same time as the octopus was being put (by Congress) on shorter and shorter rations. In addition, this was the period when the church groups were charged with responsibility for Indian education, but Congress was unwilling to vote sufficient funds for subsistence, much less for education. Where allotment was opposed by traditionalist members of the tribe (this was particularly so in the south), many individuals of very questionable and far-fetched Indian heritage lined up for their parcel of land, while the full-bloods refused to sign away their lands, but lost them by *fiat* anyway. One of the chronic problems in Indian affairs became acute, as the identification of tribal leadership grew increasingly difficult, a natural consequence of the stated policy (though not always the actual practice) of the government to discourage traditional tribal governing bodies.

Lands went out of tribal hands at an alarming rate; and by 1934, when allotment was ended, a total of 246,569 allotments had been made of 40,848,172 acres of land on about 100 reservations. Of course, some of this land still remained in individual Indian control, but much of it had been alienated despite the provision that 25 years from allotment should elapse before this would be possible, and despite an Appropriation Act of 1906 which permitted the extension of the period of restriction on the sale of Indian lands beyond 25 years. Taking into account the surplus lands which were sold to non-natives, about 90 million acres were lost. Furthermore, although the domestic matters of tribal members (such as marriages and adoptions) were retained by tribal governing bodies, the descent of real property was within the jurisdiction of state inheritance laws, so that the ownership of the land was divided as shares among the heirs of the allottee. The present result is Byzantine; and since the land itself is not divided but shared, in differing proportions, it becomes very difficult to get consent to do anything with the land, such as leasing, developing or otherwise putting it to profitable use.

It took a long time for the lessons to be learned; and when they were the theoretical premises still did not change, though the practices certainly did. In the early years of the twentieth century, experienced men such as Francis E. Leupp, a former United States Commissioner of Indian Affairs, was advocating (in *The Indian and His Problem*, 1910) a further development of existing government policies leading towards assimilation and soundly attacking what he felt were "uninformed" reform movements and proposals. Leupp, who justly claimed when he took over the position of Commissioner of Indian Affairs in 1905 that he had "twenty years' study of the Indian face to face and in his own home," asserted in his first report that "the field of Indian affairs is presenting every day fresh problems for solution, and, there being no precedents to guide us in solving these, we are necessarily driven to experiment." It is a rather startling admission, especially after a century and a quarter of Indian administration. In fact, what Leupp suggested was a strenuous and imaginative application of the policy of his friend and mentor (to whom he later dedicated his book) Theodore Roosevelt, who had referred in his first annual message in 1901 to the Dawes Act as "a mighty pulverizing engine to break up the tribal mass. The Indian," continued Roosevelt, "should be treated as an individual—like the white man."[14] In this vein, Leupp argued that

> our aim ought to be to keep [the Indian] moving steadily down the path which leads from his close domain of artificial restraints and artificial protection toward the broad area of individual liberty enjoyed by the ordinary citizen . . . One day must come to the Indian the great change from his present status to that of the rest of our population, for anomalies in the social system are as odious as abnormalities in nature. Either our generation or a later must remove the Indian from his perch of adventitious superiority to the common relationship of citizenship and reduce him to the same level with other Americans.

It is some small comfort to see the word "reduce" thus used, but the nature of the experiment was clear.

A great deal has been said and written about the 'racial tendency' of the Indian to squander whatever comes into his hands. This is no more 'racial' than his tendency to eat and drink to excess or to prefer pleasure to work: it is simply the assertion of a primitive instinct common to all mankind in the lower stages of social development. What we call thrift is nothing but the forecasting sense which recognizes the probability of a to-morrow; the idea of a to-morrow is the boundary between barbarism and civilization, and the only way in which the Indian can be carried across that line is by letting him learn from experience that the stomach filled to-day will go empty to-morrow unless something of to-day's surplus is saved overnight to meet tomorrow's deficit. Another sense lacking in primitive man is that of property unseen.[15]

As always in Indian affairs, the appeal to professional experience with Indians was either ignored or used to substantiate doctrinal considerations. And it was becoming clear that even the most well-intentioned social experimentation of the sort that Leupp advocated—and Leupp himself was surprisingly sensitive to native cultural priorities—could no longer be condoned in the face of the depressingly obvious predicament of the Indians. The experience of both the government administrators and the missionary workers did little more than reinforce old pieties. Both were absolutely incapable of dealing with the theoretical possibilities raised by plural cultural values in the midst of a singular national dream; and although their practice was earnest and dedicated, its effects were not related to the causes which had produced the situation in the first place.

By the 1920s, government policy and administration were under constant attack by organizations and individuals concerned about the welfare of the Indians. The allotment in severalty policy was being harshly criticized and the criticizers in turn were condemned: Commissioner of Indian Affairs Cato Sells spent a large portion of his 1920 annual report defending the policy against an attack by the San Diego Women's Civic Center, under a heading in the report which referred to "Obstructive Propaganda." And Francis Leupp's book was filled with denunciations of uninformed reform groups and their proposals. Nonetheless, there was no escaping the fact that while the Indian population was increasing—in 1915-1916, for the first time in fifty years, there were (according to the rather haphazard statistics compiled by the Bureau of Indian Affairs) more births than deaths among the Indians of the United States—yet this population was not being well serviced by health and education facilities, nor was it developing those habits of self-reliance and self-sufficiency which the government was so anxious to promote.

It is difficult to assess accurately the situation during these years, since the statistics are so curious and unreliable; and it is all but impossible to compare the situation in Canada and in the United States, both because of the inadequacy of statistical information and because the Canadian definition of Indian status was so different, and excluded almost as many as it included (of those who would, for instance, be counted as Indians under federal supervision in the United States). Thus much of the dramatic increase in native population in the United States during the 1930s was accounted for by an increase in mixed bloods—of 22.5 per cent from 1930-1932, for example, while full bloods increased only 3.5 per cent.[16]

There was one specific problem which was sufficiently common and sufficiently intractable to receive general attention and that was the high incidence of disease, and especially infant death, among the Indians. It was recognized that a solution to this problem would have to be at least partly educational, for it was not easy to inculcate throughout the native community those non-native habits of sanitation and care which were necessary for the proper functioning of non-native "medicine," of the physical, mental and spiritual varieties. Whatever the difficulties, it was easy to condemn the present state of affairs and there were many who rushed to do so. Although Frederick H. Abbott reported in 1914 to the Board of Indian Commissioners that "while tuberculosis is prevalent among the Indians of Canada, it is apparently under more effective control than it is among the Indians of this country," there were those who found little comfort in such a comparison. Dr. P. H. Bryce, the former Chief Medical Officer of Indian Affairs in Canada from 1901 to 1921, published a pamphlet in Ottawa in 1922 entitled "The Story of a National Crime, being An Appeal for Justice to the Indians of Canada, The Wards of the Nation, Our Allies in the Revolutionary War, Our Brothers-in-Arms in the Great War." It was a confused piece of work, being the product both of Bryce's outrage at what he felt to be the continued inattention to the health of Indians and of his disappointment at not being appointed Deputy Minister of Health, and being forced to an early retirement (at age 67). But it had its significant point:

> A sum of only $10,000 has been annually placed in the estimates to control tuberculosis amongst 105,000 Indians scattered over Canada in over 300 bands, while the City of Ottawa with about the same population has 3 general hospitals and spent thereon $342,860.54 in 1919 of which $33,364.70 is devoted to tuberculosis patients alone.

While lack of funds, and the absence of general interest, mitigated an energetic campaign to wipe out disease and deprivation among the native people, and while the most earnest requests of Indian agents to "renew daily our warfare against the arch foe of efficiency—disease"[17] were useless without sufficient arms, there was another, distressingly complex impediment. This was the native attachment to traditional habits, which appeared neither adequate to cope with the diseases which had been introduced by the non-native population, nor capable of being reconciled with the social and economic cures which had been prescribed for those ills. By 1920, it was possible for only the most sanguine or the most stupid of souls to be convinced that things were changing for the better. Yet some could still crow that the old barbarous customs and degrading influences with their pagan dances, their superstitious medicine men, and all the feathered and painted heraldry of wild indolence are giving way to the sure beginning of initiative, industry, and thrift, and to the desire for their children's education and social betterment.[18]

Conditions were still wretched, health still poor, education still inappropriate and often unavailable or inadequate, social and economic possibilities still disgracefully limited, and traditional native values and resources still under a constant state of siege. The solutions were not working: either the answers were wrong or the questions.

CHAPTER FOUR

Social
Credit

> The temple is holy
> because it is not for sale.
> Ezra Pound*

Although there are fairly clear examples of initiatives taken or situations created in which both the native and the non-native could be said to benefit, and be seen to benefit, it was increasingly a feature of the relationship between the two groups that the Indians were felt to be getting something for nothing. This, of course, was after the land cessions had, in the main, been completed; but this had been fairly nearly accomplished by the last decade of the nineteenth century.[1] The Dawes Act in the United States, and the rustle of papers that could be heard all over the Canadian prairies as the government rushed to sign treaties and extinguish Indian land rights, had put the Indians quite clearly in the position of wards of the government—wards who were being asked to join in a social contract with the non-native population, and especially with the government, by which the natives would be helped to help themselves.[2] Unfortunately, it was not generally recognized that this *was* a kind of social contract, and that the benefits of the novel civil and religious

---

The Cantos of Ezra Pound. © 1959 by Ezra Pound. Reprinted by permission of New Directions Publishing Corporation.

structures which were being offered to and in many cases forced upon the Indian should have had a counterpart in a sense of an identifiable benefit to the non-natives. Since the ideal was assimilation of the entire population, it is reasonable to expect that this might have taken the simple form of a commitment to the undertaking and underwriting of this process in such a way that the advantage to the natives would be both apparent and deserved.

According to one model of such social contracts,[3] the credit or benefit (which, for the Indians, is generally characterized as "advancement" or "welfare" programs) is given for one or both of two elements: what is sometimes called "cultural inheritance" and includes skills, tools, processes, designs, aptitudes; and "the increment of association," which is what men gain by not being isolated from one another, a sense of communal land (family, tribal, provincial, state or national) and the advantages of collective effort. The two, obviously, are interdependent and not simply distinguished, but they do provide a useful scheme. (The latter enables eighty men to move a boulder to a hill near Salisbury when one could not budge it; the former enables them to build Stonehenge. The latter enables a nation to wage war; the former provides the rationale for doing so. In a nomadic group, the two are intimately related; the more sedentary the group becomes, the more the division becomes obvious and falls into social and economic patterns which we tend to call "civilized."

It has been the sad story of native affairs over the past century that the interdependence which sustains such a system of social benefits, along with the importance of ensuring that such benefits are seen to be given as some kind of cultural or "social credit," are almost entirely ignored. This becomes an especially significant failure when it is not immediately apparent to the recipients that the benefits are indeed such and when the initiative is exclusively on the one side. The degeneration of native response from insolently active to the most depressingly passive is some measure of the seriousness of this failure; and although militant (if not military) action appears once again to be a part of this response, it is depite and not because of the sustaining structures of native and non-native relationships.

From the first contact between the indigenous inhabitants and the newcomers, a rather more strange and less workable compact was established. It depended neither on civil nor on religious proprieties, but on the assumption that credit would be given for that which was accepted as of value. In the beginning, both sides found valuable that which the other had little use for or a surplus of. The receipt of presents of very dubious worth was important to the native; it is futile to pretend that it was not, or that a simple fraud was perpetrated in the giving of such gifts, because an abundance of contemporary testimony exists which clearly indicates the socio-economic importance to the Indians of such ceremonial exchanges. On the other hand, furs, advice and to a certain extent land were of almost obscene importance to the greedy settler. Land, of course, was quickly recognized as a finite and non-renewable resource and the Indians eventually balked at ceding it with quite the generosity they had previously displayed. But then again, the increasing obligation which the colonial and Imperial governments were under to make their annual presents to the Indians became extremely burdensome and with the passing of years the generosity of previous generations began to wane. Liquor and firearms, but especially liquor, were more problematic; but even then their mutual usefulness was for a time at least accepted, though that usefulness was to the one side economic and to the other social.[4]

Everywhere, particularly in the nineteenth century, the mutual satisfactions to be gained by such relationships were foremost in the arguments of those non-natives advocating them. For the missionary, there was a rich harvest of souls and the glory of working for God and civilization. The satisfaction for the Indian, in the missionary view, would be "the complete development of the tender affections, and the institution of those associations [such as 'chambers of commerce, insurance companies, banks, joint stock associations'] by which men express their interest in one another, and aid one another," a blessing which "depends almost entirely upon the diffusion of Christianity."[5] Not to forget, of course, the salvation of his soul.

> Let then, missionary Institutions, established to convey to them the benefits of civilization and the blessings of Christianity, be efficiently supported; and, with cheering hope, you may look forward to the period when the savage shall be converted into the citizen; when the hunter shall be transformed into the mechanic; when the farm, the work shop, the School-House, and the Church shall adorn every Indian village; when the fruits of Industry, good order, and sound morals, shall bless every Indian dwelling; and when throughout the vast range of country from the Mississippi to the Pacific, the red man and the white man shall everywhere be found, mingling in the same benevolent and friendly feelings, fellow citizens of the same civil and religious community, and fellow-heirs to a glorious inheritance in the kingdom of Immanuel.[6]

For the trader, the Indian was indispensable, though often a nuisance. As one writer on the fur trade expressed it, "two things about the natives especially warmed the trader's heart—his furs and his absence, particularly the latter."[7] Nonetheless, even in a time of crisis such as that following the War of 1812, when American traders were struggling fiercely to keep out foreign traders from their territories, Ramsay Crooks, a senior officer of the American Fur Company, could write to J. J. Astor that the Canadian *coureurs-de-bois,* who were mainly Métis or half-breeds of partly French extraction, should be exempted from any such restriction. (It had, of course, been a similar principle which had resulted in the curious provisions of the Jay Treaty.)

> It will still be good policy to admit freely and without the least restraint the Canadian Boatmen: these people are indispensable to the successful prosecution of the trade, their places cannot

be supplied by Americans, who are for the most part too independent to submit quietly to a proper control, and who can gain
anywhere a subsistence much superior to a man of the interior
and although the body of the Yankee can resist as much hard-
ship as any man, 'tis only in the Canadian we find that temper of
mind, to render him patient, docile and persevering, in short
they are a people harmless in themselves, whose habits of submission fit them peculiarly for our business.[8]

Everyone, perhaps naturally enough, could be seen to be
acting out of some form of self-interest. For example, the
most stirring question in Indian affairs in the years following
the Canadian Confederation in 1867 involved the complex
system of enfranchisement, by which it was intended that
the Indian would be seduced from his traditional ways and
urged into an acceptance of the habits of civilized life, and
of the responsibilities as well. Specific qualifications regarding enfranchisement had been included in the various Acts
relating to Indians since 1857, but success was not spectacular; as one wit remarked in the House of Commons in 1880,
"at [the present] rate, five persons every two years, it
would take 36,000 years to enfranchise the Indian population of Canada." One of the difficulties was that enfranchisement was made contingent upon the breaking up of
the reserves.

> An Indian could not become enfranchised unless he separated his
> holding from the common property of the band. The object of
> the Act was to break up the tribal system, but that system was
> endeared to the Indian by many associations, and it was the last
> remaining protection they had against the capacity of the white
> man. They were attached to it because it was inherited from
> their ancestors, because it had become a part of their very
> nature and entered, in all its ramifications, into their everyday
> life. They would never cease to adhere to the tribal system until
> they ceased to be Indians.[9]

And so, discovering that "all we can hope for is to wean
them, by slow degrees, from their nomadic habits, which

have almost become instinct, and by slow degrees absorb them or settle them on the land,"[10] the Conservative government of Sir John A. Macdonald still saw other advantages to a limited form of enfranchisement such as the extending of the vote to the (male) Indians who had possession of tracts of reserve land, even though such land was inalienable, and such Indian were wards of the government, unable to do much more than spit without the approval of the Superintendent-General. Writing to Macdonald in January, 1879, one progressive Conservative tied together several strands:

> A few days ago I took the Liberty of writing to you with reference to redeeming this county from Grit Rule. At that time I had not consulted any one on the subject. Since then I have explained the matter to Mr. A. Watts and Chief Johnson and there is no doubt if you can see your way to Franchise the civilized Indians in this county for which there can be shown good and cogent reasons both ridings in this county will be redeemed.
>
> Chief Johnson informed me that as a *matter of justice* the civilized Indians should be Franchised; also that he can show that there are over 1400 Indians over 21 holding land in this county *Every One* Conservative.[11]

The legislation which resulted was the Franchise Act of 1885, but it proved to be not a great success and continued in effect only until 1898. It was a complement to the Indian Advancement Act of 1884 which had provided for limited forms of self-government. There were obvious advantages which the Conservative government of the time may have hoped to gain from the extension of the franchise to the Indians, but the major issues were more basic and controversial and were intimately associated with the very nature of civil responsibility and with the extent to which the Indians could and should be expected to participate in social, economic and political processes by which they were inevitably affected, and in which they had a mutual interest with the non-native community. Not unexpectedly, the Canadian government intended to exercise a certain element of control over the composition of the semi-autonomous elected band councils for which there was provision in the Indian legislation of the 1870s and 1880s. Section 11 of the Advancement Act, which referred to the fitness of the council members for office, eventually precipitated a dispute which was closely analogous to that which was prompted by the extraordinary powers of approval given to the American Secretary of the Interior under the Wheeler-Howard Act of 1934. It also gave rise to some amusing yet quietly instructive exchanges in the debates in the House of Commons.

> Mr. Edward Blake: Why should not this be extended to the whites? It is an admirable clause: 'Any member of a council elected under the provisions of this Act who shall be proved to be a habitual drunkard, or to be living in immorality, or to have accepted a bribe, or to have been guilty of dishonesty, or of malfeasance of office, shall be disqualified from acting as a member of the council.
>
> Sir John A. Macdonald: It would be a very good clause for the whites.
>
> Blake: Why should we be more moral with our Indian friends than with ourselves?
>
> Macdonald: It might diminish the members of the Opposition.[12]

Yet the principle at stake was anything but trivial, even though it received a rather glib defense by Macdonald with respect to the Indian's capacity for accepting responsibility.

> Yes; and perhaps the Indians are liable to lose their money in gambling. Then there was Sheridan and William Pitt, and other great men, who not only exercised the electoral franchise but governed nations victoriously. They were incapable, however, of attending as individuals to matters of their own concern. And

so it is with particular races. In my own country there are two great nations, the Lowland Scotchmen and the Highlanders. The Lowland Scotchmen are known to be saving and industrious. The Highlanders are impulsive, not so industrious and certainly not so saving; but equally intelligent, equally possessing a right to vote as free men, and equally exercising that right. So I say that the Indians living in the older Provinces who have gone to school—and they all go to school—who are educated, who associate with white men, who are acquainted with all the principles of civilization, who have accumulated round themselves property, who have good houses, and well furnished houses, who educate their children, who contribute to the public treasury in the same way as the whites do, should possess the franchise.[13]

For all of his bombast, Macdonald could usually be relied upon to deflate the pompous platitudes of his opponents. But neither he nor his opponents, nor indeed anyone in or out of authority on either side of the border, was adept at illuminating the fundamental questions which needed to be asked as well as answered before particular changes were effected, and before the question of Indian responsibility and perception of self-interest was resolved.

Important issues in the discussions which characterized native affairs in North America during the last decades of the nineteenth and first decades of the twentieth century were all too often obscured by the dust raised by the wheels of "progressive" legislation and by the dirt thrown by its retrograde opponents, as well as by those interested parties, both native and non-native, who had so much at stake. Distinctions between individual and collective responsibility were never clearly established; and, even more critically, the nature of the authority which was to prevail over the native people was never properly appreciated. As one writer has remarked,

Authority should not be confused with either leadership or power. The essence of authority consists in the fact that it operates without conscious exercise and without challenge. It springs up mysteriously and is then simply there as by a natural process of development. Leadership is striven for and striven against. Will and resistance are of its essence. The leader acts, authority rules. It rules in the sense of "le roi règne, il ne gouverne pas." The monarchy is the archetype of all genuine authority.[14]

As the native people were ushered into the stadium of late nineteenth-century enthusiasms, and as the banners of self-sufficiency and individual enterprise were waved before them, somebody forgot to mention that the rules of the game had changed. For so long in native affairs, an heroically "authoritarian tradition" had prevailed, in which the indigenous inhabitants were encouraged to pay respect to the Great Mother or the Great Father who supposedly ruled the society that was being established in their midst. All of a sudden this situation was altered; quite different skills from those of obedience or unquestioned respect were called for, and a quite different concept of self-interest and mutual responsibility was expected. The exercise of choices and of responsibilities was urgently demanded; and when it was not forthcoming, the illusion was fostered that choices had been made and responsibilities accepted. But it was nothing more than an illusion; and when the illusion was shattered, a deep disillusion set in, which in many cases continues still. For those who were in authority over the Indians never stopped reigning, and never began to govern. They were and continue to be exempt from most of the usual forms of civil responsibility, for they never have been a part of any organically constituted political process which the native people can affect. Yet the native people have been encouraged to think otherwise and to proceed as though the various bureaus and departments of which they are the subjects were something other than intrinsically authoritarian.

One of the simplest ways in which this illusion has been fostered is by providing a certain amount of local autonomy or control to the native people. The concept of local autonomy was, of course, a paramount consideration when the relationships between the state and federal authorities were being established and enshrined in the constitution of the United States. Insofar as it is a matter of concern for any federated organization, it was also an issue in Canada, though fierce conflicts over federal and state rights —conflicts which appear to take on an almost religious importance in the United States—have not been a feature of Canadian federal-provincial relationships until very recently, and then only in a few specific areas. The United States also dealt for a time with the Indians as semi-independent nations and allowed them great latitude in their choice of civil structures. The demise of the federally controlled factory trading system in 1822, the troubles in Georgia, and above all the spread of settlement and the difficulty of maintaining law and order on the frontier, interfered with what might otherwise have been an interesting republican experiment. Instead, the Indians themselves were caught in the midst of a welter of judicial disputes. In the first place, there was conflict between civilian and military jurisdictions, even after the Department of the Interior took over responsibility for Indian affairs from the Department of War in 1849.

This was a serious matter, for whatever autonomy and scope for self-government and initiative the tribes had depended upon the cooperation of the Indian agent and the department which he served. Neither the Indian nor the agent, nor indeed the military, could count on any help from state authorities, and this was a particular difficulty when it came to the prosecution of cases against those who were interfering with the Indian's welfare, usually by selling him liquor and buying (or stealing) his land. For his troubles, the conscientious Indian agent, anxious to protect the Indian from trespass or unlawful encroachment, could expect to be sued for false arrest and be vilified by local interests. The Indian was not always the victim, of course, and horse-

stealing by Indians was one of the most troublesome problems on the prairie lands during the middle part of the last
century, as the references in the treaties to reparations
make sufficiently clear. But the Indian, encouraged on the
one hand to be self-sufficient, was prevented from being so
by almost every civil function—judicial, administrative,
political—that was operative. His only alternative, for a
time, was military, to which a generation of Indian wars are
bloody testament.

The Indian was slowly being deprived of his cultural inheritance and was given little sense that he had any control
at all of the process of change. It was, in fact, not so much
that he was being deprived of control—though he certainly
was—but that no one had any control: neither the federal
nor the state or territorial governments, neither the military
nor the civil authorities, neither the educators nor the missionaries, neither the politicians nor the trading companies.
Every now and then alliances would be formed, between the
politicians and the business interests, for example, or between the politicians and the civilian authorities, for the Indian agents became effectively political appointees. As
drastic events and fashionable enthusiasms moved inexora-
bly on, there were periodic attempts in the United States to
establish more local control by Indians themselves. But
control of what? The Indian police bill of 1878, which provided for the organization on reserve of constabulary forces
under the supervision of Indian agents, had dramatic success in some areas,[15] but it was rather like allowing a caged
animal to clean up his own manure, or providing hospital
benefits for conscripted soldiers after an unpopular war and
then allowing them the privilege of doing the ward work.
The Indian was given no sense at all that he was anything
but an at times picturesque impediment, a momentary stut-
ter in the otherwise smooth flow of western expansion; and
those who were set or who set themselves in authority were
obsessed with their particular solutions and with the deli-

ciously frustrating intractability of the problems facing them. Former Commissioner of Indian Affairs Francis Walker, writing about "the Indian Question" in 1873, suggested that

> so long as the attention of the executive department is occupied by efforts to preserve the peace; so long as Congress is asked yearly to appropriate 3 millions of dollars to feed and clothe insolent savages; so long as the public mind is exasperated by reports of Indian outrages . . . so long will it be vain to expect an adequate treatment of the question of Indian civilization.[16]

The "peace policy" of those years, to which Walker was referring, was instituted by those who, in the words of a recent historian of the time,

> were aware that the great hope of the red race lay in the education of Indian children. Its administrators learned quickly that the most effective method was through their enrollment in industrial boarding schools. The environment of an Indian village could not be overcome by any other means.[17]

Whether "aware" that the great hope lay in education, or "aware" of the need for coercion, the non-native line was straight and very, very narrow, and most often lay between two conditions, the Scylla and Charybdis of nineteenth-century native affairs.

> Unused to manual labor, and physically disqualified for it by the habits of the chase, unprovided with tools and implements, without forethought and without self-control, singularly susceptible to evil influences, with strong animal appetites and no intellectual tastes or aspirations to hold those appetites in check, it would be to assume more than would be taken for granted of any white race under the same conditions, to expect that the wild Indians will become industrious and frugal except through a severe course of industrial instruction and exercise, under restraint. The reservation system affords the place for thus dealing with tribes and bands, without the access of influences inimical to peace and virtue . . .

In the two hundred and seventy-five thousand Indians west of the Mississippi, the United States have all the elements of a large gypsy population, which will inevitably become a sore, a well-nigh intolerable, affliction to all that region, unless the Government shall provide for their instruction in the arts of life, which can only be done effectively under a pressure not to be resisted or evaded. The right of the Government to do this cannot be seriously questioned. Expressly excluded by the Constitution from citizenship, the Government is only bound in its treatment of them by considerations of present policy and justice.[18]

Given such premises, it was impossible for the Indians to have any effective local autonomy, or even to be honestly encouraged to recognize their interest in the changes that were taking place, for it was not a part of the accepted scheme of things for them to possess any recognizable resources, whether civil or religious, material or organizational. They were, *sui generis,* Indians; as such, they were incapable, and had no legitimate interests. Becoming other, they might possibly become capable, but only then—and only then, of course, would their unique interests no longer exist.

Variations of this sentiment can be found in innumerable documents of the time; for example, in the report of the Chippewa Indian Commission investigating the dispute which arose in 1892 following the passage by Congress of a bill providing for the relinquishment by the Turtle Mountain Band of Chippewa Indians of about nine million acres of their land in North Dakota:

The segregation of the Indians and keeping them separate from white men on reservations is another great hindrance to civilization. In the reservation the Indian children see only a dull sameness in the culture of their surroundings. No man has a better home than the other . . . The only thing they could find on which their ambitious desires can feed is some useless sport of the pony race sort. Thrifty white settlers should be scattered

among them; and the rearing of beautiful homes, with their
carpeted rooms, their cosy furniture, their pictures, and the
many articles of art and refinement, not forgetting cleanly and
well-dressed families, will have a greater civilizing effect, at
least on the younger members of a tribe, than anything that has
ever been attempted with the Indian.[19]

It makes chilling reading, but it was a logical consequence
of the assumption that the Indians were without resources—without anything to give in return for the benefits they were receiving. Relations became hopelessly
perverted, in large measure because of this theoretical premise. Land was taken, not so much out of sheer greed,
though there was much of that, but because the Indian did
nothing with it that fitted into any pattern of land use that
was accepted at the time. His culture was not valued and his
habits were neither apparently industrious nor obviously
thrifty. That he simply had his own mode of conspicuous
consumption was not recognized by a generation that had,
like most generations, scarcely any perspective on its own
habits. And, indeed, there was enough truth in the response
of the non-native to make his remedies for the Indian problem seem at least possible, if not entirely plausible. Such
stress needs to be laid on the basic insufficiency of a response which did not recognize the *need* for an imaginative
insight into the possibilities of indigenous cultural and material resources which could be turned to new uses by a
process that was organically continuous, because it was an
insufficiency that created the conditions for the spirals of
welfare dissolution down which the native people have been
spinning for a hundred years.

The predicament in which the native people were placed
was nonetheless a desperate enough one and the need for
some sort of change was not manufactured by non-natives
of the time. They simply could not see, and had not the
imagination, or the prescience, or in many cases the interest, to discover or invent future possibilities which would

be consistent with past and present indigenous resources. Or perhaps it would be more accurate to say that they could not or would not try to discover or invent an interest—an interest which would be practical as well as theoretical—in such possibilities. And so they would not give the Indian any social "credit" because he could produce no collateral that was acceptable; and instead they extended to him a different and perverse sort of credit, at usurious interest, to be repaid in a new, and not in his own, currency. The new currency was, of course, stamped out of entirely European civil and religious dies.

CHAPTER FIVE

Indian Giving

The intention of the legislators, and certainly of the missionaries upon whom much of the burden of responsibility of dealing with Indians lay, had always principally been to prepare the basis for the civilizing of the Indian (though there was some dispute as to whether the civilized chicken or the Christian egg should come first). There were innumerable other non-native interests which converged upon this one, of course, but it is roughly true to say that the native concern was not irreconcilable with such general intent. At the very least, by the last decades of the nineteenth century, many of the Indian leaders recognized the inevitable, which was to say the certain spread of non-native standards of civil conduct. Non-native religious conduct and belief was not so certainly spreading, despite the outlawing of particular native ceremonies such as the Potlatch and the Sun Dance; and the following half-century would witness a complex array of messianic movements which bear witness to the inter-relationship of the new civil and religious impulses,[1] and to the deep roots which the latter had established in the native consciousness.

There were, as we have suggested, many differences in the methods of civil conversion that were applied in Canada and the United States. For example, if we consider the problem of liquor abuse, which provided in miniature the kind of problem which the contact between the two races precipitated, we discover quite distinct approaches. In both countries, the earliest legislation concerning Indians dealt with liquor and in both cases it was protective. But the ineffectiveness of such legislation prompted the Canadian government to proceed much further to enforce the pattern of coercive restrictions of which such legislation was a part, and to reinforce the standards of order and the rule of law which were under such constant siege in the West by establishing a federal rather than a military police force there.

The "gypsy" population of Indians west of the Mississippi was a source of continual concern to the authorities, as well as to the local non-native population, in the middle of the nineteenth century. For the Canadians, the example of widespread native discomfort south of the border was comfortably instructive up to a point, but that point was soon reached; and from then on the awkward confusions of frontier social and economic structures, and the much more awkward methods which were available for preserving civil order in the hinterland, became urgent considerations. The turning point was reached in 1873 on the occasion of a massacre in the Cypress Hills of Assiniboin Indians by a group of American hunters who (mistakenly) thought the Indians had stolen their horses. This was, in a sense, the last straw. When the Hudson's Bay Company relinquished its control of Rupert's Land in 1869 by selling it to the Canadian government, the strong central authority which had prevailed for so long in the Canadian West disappeared. The newly formed Dominion was anxious about establishing rail and communications lines to the West, thus avoiding the traditional detour into the United States. It was anxious to secure, and, when it had secured, formally to control the great northwestern lands. It appeared anxious to spread British (which meant Ontarian) domination to these lands. But at the same time it appeared completely disinterested in the well-being of the ten thousand whites and Métis living in the Red River valley and the thirty thousand Indians living further west. The result was a growing disaffection and crisis in the Red River country in 1869–1870 that culminated in the Manitoba Act, which gave the small colony the status of a province, with (rather illusory) recognition of the equal rights of French and English inhabitants, and (similarly in-consequential) recognition of the legitimacy of Métis land claims. Before the crisis was resolved, however, the Métis leader Louis Riel had established a provisional government, and, to demonstrate its authority, had stupidly ordered the execution of one Thomas Scott, an Ontarian Orangeman whom he had taken prisoner for failing to recognize his "government." The combination of this act, and residual Protestant distress at the support given Riel in his challenge to Ottawa by the Catholic clergy, resulted in the sending of a military expedition, under Colonel Garnet Wolseley, to the Red River. The rebellion was quelled without active military intervention, but the division between French and English, Catholic and Protestant, and colonial (hinterland) and Imperial (metropolitan) interests, continued to plague the West and to define eastern Canadian sympathies.[2]

The American pattern of frontier violence seemed to be threatening to engulf the Canadian West at the time of the Cypress Hills Massacre. It was therefore decided that if not a military, at the very least a coercive presence was neces-sary there. As a consequence, the Royal Northwest Mounted Police force was established in 1873; and, in 1874, some 300 men mounted their horses and rode from Fort Dufferin to establish the Royal authority in the Northwest. The idea of such a force had originally been considered by Sir John A. Macdonald as an instrument of the transfer of authority from the Hudson's Bay Company to the Canadian government, and in case of Indian troubles. It appears that at one point Macdonald had a concept of a force composed partly of Métis, but the 1869 rebellion quashed that idea. And the fear of antagonizing the United States by sending a permanent military force determined almost by accident the eventual character of the RNWMP.[3]

The new police force was quite effective in certain ways.

Among other things, it contributed to the solution, one that the United States had been constitutionally incapable of discovering, of the problem of liquor peddling to the Indians. Instead of fumbling about for almost half a century with trade and intercourse acts, as the United States had done from 1790 to 1834, the Canadian government established a federal agency with summary powers and gave magisterial jurisdiction to its Indian agents, who became *ex-officio* justices of the peace, competent to try any case of infraction of the legislation regarding liquor traffic with Indians. Liquor itself, of course, continued to be present, but those abuses which interfered with trade had at least been minimized. Those that interfered with the health and happiness of the Indian still survive, defying such crude responses.[4]

Most significantly, the police force prevented the widespread establishment of vigilante groups to deal with Indian troubles, and it was remarkably effective in gaining the respect of the Indians themselves.[5] The most significant consequence of the Mounted Police presence, moreover, was that they insisted upon the rule of Canadian law in all aspects of affairs, both native and non-native. This was in marked contrast to the practice in the United States, where the tribes were implicitly encouraged to conduct themselves as they might wish provided they did not interfere with non-natives (and, initially, they were empowered within certain limits to deal as they saw fit with non-natives who had wronged them if they were discovered on Indian lands). The intention on the Canadian plains was not only to maintain peace, but to instill in the Indians a sense of British justice and law, so that, by a kind of cultural osmosis, the transition to civilized forms of life would be much simpler and indeed natural. The men who furthered this knew nothing about theories of acculturation, but a great deal about the practice of British Imperial discovery and settlement; and they had an absurd faith in the universality of concepts of the law and property upon which British society was based.

For civilization was, to such men, quite definitely a British invention—or, if one felt generous, Anglo-Saxon. The missionary conflicts between Protestant and Catholic provide perhaps the most histrionic statement of this attitude, but it was one that was widely prevalent in most of the West and in Upper Canada (Ontario), with parts of Manitoba and Lower Canada (Quebec) being looked upon as areas of very uncertain stability. The Reverend George McDougall, who with his son John was one of the most prominent of the Methodist missionaries in the Canadian West in the latter part of the nineteenth century, gives a fairly typical summary:

> The man of sin is powerfully represented in this country. There are five priests to one Protestant missionary; they are anti-British in their national sympathies; and if we may judge the tree by its fruits, anti-Christian in their teachings. Their converts have a zeal, but their fervour prompts them to propagate a system, not a Saviour. By them the Sabbath is desecrated, polygamy tolerated, and the Bible ignored. Their churches are the toy shops where the poor heathen get their play-things, such as idols, beads, and charms, and where the Anglo is denounced as no better than a brute beast, or, to quote from one of their sermons, 'no better than the buffalo that herd on the plains.' They carry with them large pictures, representing two roads, one terminating in Paradise, the other in a bottomless pit; on the downward track, all Protestants are travelling surrounded by demons and lost spirits. One of the tricks of these gentlemen is, when a child is born in a Protestant family, a female agent enters the tent, fondles the infant, and then, professing to show it to their friends, carries it to the priest, who baptizes the babe. The policy of the Protestant missionaries has been to avoid controversy and simply to preach Christ. The very opposite has been the practice of the Priest. And if trouble should arise between the tribes of this country and the White, the cause, in a large degree, will lie at the door of the Papacy.[6]

This, of course, is an extreme view, though not that of an extreme man; and it would be a grotesque mistake indeed to assume that the Catholic missions did not serve as well and as faithfully as the rather more nervous Protestants. For one thing, the Hudson's Bay Company had for a long time adopted the policy that the French half-breeds or Métis were the responsibility of the Catholic church, and the factors of the western posts traditionally requested that priests be sent to serve the Métis who gathered around the Hudson's Bay Company forts. The most famous of these was Father Albert Lacombe, who succeeded Father Thibault at Lac Ste. Anne, about 45 miles northwest of Fort Edmonton, in 1852, and who ministered to the natives of western Canada until his death in 1916.

Lacombe was a powerful force in the West during the years which followed the coming of the railroad and his influence has been properly recognized. But it was the civil and political agitation of men like the McDougalls that caught much of the attention of those who were charged with responsibility for Indian affairs in Ottawa. John McDougall, for example, figures prominently in the reports quoted by M. C. Cameron in the House of Commons in the course of his long and specific attack on Indian administration in the Northwest. Cameron quoted McDougall, "who has devoted his life to the service of elevating, educating, civilising and christianizing the Indians," as

> urg[ing] a change, and the Indian given a fair chance; he wants the Government's Indian policy—to make the Indian a responsible citizen—carried out in its true spirit. To do this he asks for employees of the Indian Department who will be true to their country if not to their God, who will refrain from licentiousness, blasphemy, drunkenness and laziness, who will have force of character enough to command special respect, and who will by precept and example teach the Indians industry, thrift and obedience to the law.[7]

In another interview also reported by Cameron, McDougall was even more outspoken:

> The "Government is false to the treaty, the white men have lied to us, we are deceived," the Indians said, and it required the

services of loyal old-timers to point out to them why, through unavoidable delays, lack of speedy transport, etc., the obligations of the Government were sometimes unfulfilled. But Mr. McDougall says: "We could not find, nor did we try to find, any excuse for the promises made but not fulfilled, for the cutthroat policy often exhibited and sometimes enforced by officials of the Indian Department, for the shameful and immoral lives of many of the employees of the same. Some of these were a disgrace to the lowest barbarism, let alone civilisation. Now how could we, when earnestly trying to teach Indians habits of industry and thrift, be expected to excuse the laziness and incompetency of many sent into the country to teach the wards of the Government those lessons we have been working for them to acquire for so many years. Moreover could we be blamed when we felt strongly that something was wrong in the system which allowed such men in its branch of the service. The inconsistency has often times appeared to us very glaring when we looked at a department claiming to have a certain object in view, set aside by the country at large, whose servant it is, to attain this object, and yet within its own grasp and power doing those things and adopting those methods which are defeating their object. Very little rebellion in these men ten or fifteen years ago . . ."[8]

Was this situation the product of negligence, or incompetence, or stupidity? Certainly the criticism has an eponymous and ubiquitous quality about it and could as easily be taken to refer to American as to Canadian Indian administration in the nineteenth century. In defense of their practice, the Canadian officials turned to friendlier testimonials—for example, that of Rev. Alfred Andrews, Methodist minister at Lethbridge in the 1880s, who suggested

that the Indians seek things in garbage heaps, not because they are starving but because they are curious and not over particular . . .

that Mr. Robertson's statement that the majority of the Indians were ready to rebel is untrue.

that Mr. Robertson's statement as to the failure of missions was very incorrect.[9]

To which the Rev. James Robertson replied:

> Mr. Andrews asks, where are the Indians starving, searching
> refuse heaps and swill barrels, and ravenously devouring crusts
> of bread and scraps of meat? At Minnedosa, Birtle, Broadview,
> Fort Qu' Appelle, Prince Albert, Battleford, Moose Jaw,
> Medicine Hat, and the rest, I have seen them doing this. It
> might have been because they were very curious or preferred
> dirty crusts and decaying meat to tender, well bled beef, but I
> did not think of accounting for their action that way. I know the
> eager look, the shrunken form, and the wolfish face that speak
> of want in the adult, and the wan, pinched face that speaks of
> starvation in the child; and I have seen them near Fort Ellice,
> Fort Pelly, the File Hills, and other places, and have had my
> sympathies drawn out towards the owners. I have seen Indians
> eating horses that had died of disease, when the flesh was half
> rotten. I have seen them picking up the entrails of animals about
> slaughter houses—when these entrails were fast decom-
> posing—aye, and eating them without cooking, or even wash-
> ing. They may prefer such carrion to good beef, well bled and
> cool when killed, but I doubt it.[10]

As for the question of a general native rebellion which opponents of the current administration rather gaily predicted,
and for a model of which they pointed south of the border,
once again the government would admit none of this, though
in 1886 it was somewhat unduly fortunate in being able to
lay the blame for the recent trouble in Manitoba on the
unusually hypnotic attraction of that traitor Riel, recently
executed; and they could, at least in a fashion, gloss over
the genuine complaints, and the disgraceful neglect of those
complaints, which had given rise to the second Red River
rebellion in fifteen years. The matter was difficult, but there
were some simple issues. Riel had sent a bill of rights on
behalf of the mixed bloods to Ottawa in 1884, urging the
government to confirm their land claims, to sell land for the
building of schools and hospitals, to establish an *effective*
local government which would serve all local interests
equally, and to give direct aid. The request deserved a response, but got none.

In asserting its righteousness, the government had an unlikely ally in Father Lacombe, who wrote to the Indian
Commissioner (Edgar Dewdney) in 1886:

> Let the Indians alone with the Government officers appointed
> to look after their welfare and there will be no trouble with
> them.[11]

Asked for advice on how to prevent future troubles such as
the Riel uprising, Lacombe had advised the government
(the previous year) to "consider the Indians in all respects
and everywhere at least for many years as real minors. Consequently they are not at liberty and are under the tutelage
of the government."[12] To ensure this relationship,
Lacombe suggested that the Indians' horses should be con-
fiscated and replaced by cattle, as a first step in forcing them
from a nomadic to a sedentary existence. Dewdney, to his
credit, responded that the government did not have the right
to take Indian property without their permission.

Lacombe was a complex man, trying to deal with a complex problem. At the time of the rebellion, which was *the*
Canadian crisis in the West at a time when the Americans
were winding up a rather long run of Indian wars, Lacombe
attempted to convince both the public and, one suspects,
the Indians themselves, of the loyalty of many of the western Indian tribes (such as the Blackfoot) to the Crown when
there was a general threat of widespread native support of
Riel. But he recounted later that

> among the Indians of the North-West there was a kind of gen-
> eral feeling, with the old and the young, that the time was at
> hand to finish with the white policy. Many influential Indians
> were at the time fomenting the fire of rebellion.[13]

No one would pretend that these were easy times. Both
nations were, during the 1870s and 1880s, experiencing
acute national stresses; and both were, although for differing reasons, engaged in a program of industrious, beaver-

like activity, in the course of which the Indians were in large measure a nuisance, to be cut down and hauled into convenient piles, or left as a testament to the value of the pure exercise of civilization's rodent teeth. The Americans were rather precise about the native situation: a report for 1872 noted that

> as to civilization, [the Indians] may, though with no great degree of assurance be divided, according to a standard taken with reasonable reference to what might fairly be expected of a race with such antecedents and traditions, as follows: Civilized, 97,000; semi-civilized, 125,000; wholly barbarous, 78,000.

The same report, signed by Commissioner of Indian Affairs Francis Walker, warned that

> no one certainly will rejoice more heartily than the present Commissioner when the Indians of this country cease to be in a position to dictate, in any form or degree, to the Government; when, in fact, the last hostile tribe becomes reduced to the condition of suppliants for charity. This is, indeed, the only hope of salvation for the aborigines of the continent. If they stand up against the progress of civilization and industry, they must be relentlessly crushed. The westward course of population is neither to be denied nor delayed for the sake of all the Indians that ever called this country their home. They must yield or perish; and there is something that savors of providential mercy in the rapidity with which their fate advances upon them, leaving them scarcely the chance to resist before they shall be surrounded and disarmed. It is not feebly and futilely to attempt to stay this tide, whose depth and strength can hardly be measured, but to snatch the remnants of the Indian race from destruction before it, that the friends of humanity should exert themselves in this juncture, and lose no time. And it is because the present system allows the freest extension of settlement and industry possible under the circumstances, while affording space and time for humane endeavours to rescue the Indian tribes from a position altogether barbarous and incompatible with civilization and social progress, that this system must be approved by all enlightened citizens.

Whenever the time shall come that the roving tribes are reduced to a condition of complete dependence and submission,
the plan to be adopted in dealing with them must be substantially that which is now being pursued in the case of the more
tractable and friendly Indians . . . This is the true permanent
policy of the Government.[14]

The Canadian government was not quite so well armed
with a "true permanent Indian policy," largely because it
was a little less certain that the "complete dependence and
submission" of the Indians was something which its coffers
could deal with, depleted as they were with the costs of
building a national railroad. It adopted a scheme for educating the Indians in the West in church-run industrial boarding
schools, similar to the model which had been imposed in the
United States under the "peace policy" of President Grant.
As with a distressing number of such experiements, the
Canadians embarked upon it (in the 1880's, following a report on Indian schools in the United States submitted to the
Canadian government by Nicholas Flood Davin in 1879)
just as the Americans were recognizing its limitations and
going off at full speed in the opposite direction. But the most
pressing interest was not in educating the Indians of the
West, but in pacifying them; and although the subtle propaganda of the recent "pacification" programs of benighted
indigenous folk was not fully developed, the techniques
were already finely tuned to the situation.

In Canada, for example, the loyalty of some of the western tribes such as the Bloods, the Piegans and the Blackfeet
during the Riel rebellion was ensured by a simple device
—the placing of trusted and reliable agents in authority during difficult times. Governor Dewdney appointed Cecil
Denny, who had been an original member of the Northwest
Mounted Police force that came West in 1874, and who had
served as Indian agent to the Blackfeet, Stonies and Sarcees
in 1882–1883, as his special representative to the Treaty
Seven tribes in 1885.[15] Denny was trusted by the Indians,
though not always by the Ottawa officials, and his response

to the critical situation was simple: increase the rations of beef and flour. His counterpart in the United States was perhaps Major James McLoughlin, who was agent to the Sioux at Standing Rock, North Dakota, and who attempted to pacify his charges according to somewhat different, but nonetheless sincere, methods and with drastically inadequate funds. Both made mistakes, though Denny's mistakes were curious: he apparently approved some sub-standard shipments of flour for the Indians during his early years as an agent and was harshly condemned for his action in debates in the House.[16] McLoughlin's errors were more spectacular: he sent his native lieutenants to arrest Sitting Bull in 1890; and in the ensuing tragedy, Sitting Bull and his son Crow Foot were murdered by Indian police. But both agents tried honestly to keep the Indians content and friendly to the government. Their instrument was both humane and valuable, as welfare schemes always are, but it was intended only to relieve the immediate distress in which the native people found themselves.

There was one other device which the Americans in particular employed, and that was the federal commission, of which the most significant in the troubled second half of the nineteenth century were the Peace Commission of 1867 and the Sioux Commission of several years later.[17] Each of these, and their lesser cousins, advanced a policy of selective pacification, by means of increasing the benefits which the Indians were to receive. The argument was simple: if the native people were to accept the advantages of civilization, they must first be made aware of them and be convinced that immediate needs would be satisfied. The first need of a destitute man is food, clothing and a sense that his physical requirements are being properly and fully attended to and are the object of the interest of whoever claims to be his guardian. The relationships of colonial wardship were called into play, while their limitations were conveniently ignored by the civil, or as conveniently exploited by the military, authorities of the age. The concentration on temporary solutions was a product both of the urgency which was felt and of the widely held belief that it would assuage the unrest of a native population which was culturally predisposed to ignore, or incapable of thinking about, the future.

It was, depending on one's perspective, crude bribery or wise diplomacy, but it brings to a focus two rather critical issues, one practical and the other basically theoretical. The first is obvious enough and received much theoretical and some practical attention by administrators and concerned individuals: how does one provide for a service of responsible Indian agents and supervisors? In the United States, the Indian service was notoriously corrupt, the agency appointments being the zealously held prerogative of the local politicians, and the office of agent providing ample opportunity and indeed encouragement to the ambitious for the lining of their pockets and those of their friends. One of the difficulties was that supplying the Indians with annuity goods and rations was big business—indeed, for some suppliers, their only business. There were two temptations for the agent: one was to give the contract either to friends of the politician who had appointed him or (in some cases) to the politician; the other was to profit from arrangements made with the supplier himself.[18]

The tradition that the agent's salary was only a small part of the material rewards he might expect had been of long standing, especially in the United States, from the time of Sir William Johnson. In 1762, Attorney-General Kempe wrote to Johnson for assistance in purchasing land from the Iroquois, and although he eventually deleted the following stuttering remarks they give some indication of his thinking on the matter.

> It is the only way I can have of making my office of any advantage to me, especially, when it is considered that as a public officer, in this way only, I can make my office . . . because I . . . am but illy supported in my office, have no other way.[19]

Though Johnson was no friend of Kempe's, he well understood the "ill support" given to the officials of colonial Indian affairs; in one case, the New York assembly had granted him £5,800 to cover expenses of £7,100. In his case, the insufficiency was eventually recognized and on August 24, 1767, the Board of Trade recommended that George III bestow on Johnson a grant of 66,000 acres from the Mohawks as a mark of his favor and "as ample and Sufficient Compensation for all such arrears and deficiencies on account of his pay as in Justice it may be incumbent on the Crown to make good."

Such official generosity was, however, very much a thing of the past by the mid-part of the nineteenth century. The salary of the agent was absurdly low,[20] and the position often attracted men either of meagre abilities and doubtful character or those with a shrewd eye for the main chance and of more doubtful character still. In many cases, the most responsible agents came from the military in the United States, and from the police force in Canada, and the agitation by the military authorities in the United States after the Civil War to return the administration of Indian affairs to military jurisdiction was prompted not only by the desire to find jobs for military personnel, but by a genuine belief that the job would be better done.[21]

One of the staunchest advocates of this view was Brigadier General Ely S. Parker, who was a Seneca Indian. He had been an aide to General U. S. Grant during the Civil War and had written the surrender terms which were handed to Lee at Appomattox in 1865. In 1869, he was appointed by Grant as the first Indian to head the U.S. Indian Bureau as Commissioner, a post which he held until 1871. During this time, he spoke out strongly in favor of the transfer of the Bureau back to the War Department:

Treaties have been made with a very large number of the tribes, and generally reservations have been provided as homes for them. Agents appointed from civil life, have generally been provided to protect their lives and property, and to attend to the prompt and faithful observance of treaty stipulations. But as the hardy pioneer and adventurous miner advanced into the inhospitable regions occupied by the Indians in search of the precious metals, they found no rights possessed by Indians that they were bound to respect. The faith of treaties solemnly entered into was totally disregarded, and Indian territory wantonly violated. If any tribe remonstrated against the violation of their national and treaty rights, members of the tribe were inhumanly shot down, and the whole treated as mere dogs. Retaliation generally followed, and bloody Indian wars have been the consequence, costing many lives and much treasure . . .

I would provide for the complete abolishment of the system of Indian traders, which in my opinion, is a great evil to Indian communities. I would make government the purchaser of all articles usually brought in by Indians, giving them a fair equivalent for the same in money, or goods at cost price. In this way it would be an easy matter to regulate the sale or issue of arms and ammunition to Indians, a question which of late has agitated the minds of the civil and military authorities . . . Indian trading licences are very much sought after, and when once obtained, although it may be for a limited period, the lucky possessor is considered as having already made his fortune. The eagerness also with which Indian agencies are sought after, and large fortunes made by the agents in a few years, notwithstanding the inadequate salary given, is presumptive evidence of frauds against the Indians and the government. Many other reasons might be suggested why the Indian department should altogether be under military control, but a familiar knowledge of the practical working of the present system would seem to be the most convincing proof of the propriety of the measure. It is pretty generally advocated by those most familiar with our Indian relations, and, so far as I know, the Indians themselves desire it.[22]

Though Parker was intimately familiar with eastern Indians, both from his own background and from his collaboration with Lewis Henry Morgan in gathering information for the latter's classic study, *League of the Iroquois* (1851), he knew little about the western natives. And his plans for eliminating corruption in the Indian Bureau came to nothing: in fact, he himself was blamed for much of it and he was tried for malfeasance by the House of Representatives in 1871. He was acquitted, but resigned shortly after.

Instead of turning to military supervision, however, the Indian administration was to adopt a novel approach: reservations were divided up among various of the religious denominations, whose members were appointed agents to the Indians under their supervision. This was the basis of President Grant's "peace policy," promulgated at a time of unprecedented Indian warfare. By the time Carl Schurz was appointed Secretary of the Interior under President Hayes in 1877, the limitations of extensive denominational influence in Indian Affairs were apparent; and Schurz attempted to establish a government-appointed merit system for the assignment of officials in the Indian service. The consequence of his efforts was the Pendleton Act of 1882, but by this time the political influence had so successfully reestablished itself that it would be a long time before the kind of civil-service appointments that Schurz envisaged were the rule. In fact, from the frying pan of moral righteousness and Christian zeal, after an intermission of political hackery, the effective control of Indian agency appointments descended into the fire of educational earnestness and progressive betterment through the obliteration of native traditions and the celebration of institutional learning. In 1893, as part of another attempt to wrest control of the Indian service from political influence, and having a year earlier provided that army officers could be appointed to vacant agencies, the Congress of the United States authorized the Commissioner of Indian Affairs to give control of agencies to school superintendents. Over the next couple of decades the Superintendent of Indian Education (an office which had been created in 1882) became a central force in the administration of Indian affairs.[23]

The problem of corruption was, in a sense, replaced by

the problem of sheer though earnest incompetence, but the result was little better. Traditional education (whether vocational or academic) was, long before Coleman and Jencks,[24] patently a failure in effecting social change. And the new agents were little more responsive to the Indian's real and genuine, as well as his imagined and yet no less urgent, needs. The failure of the agent meant the failure of the policy, because the agent was the *only* contact which the Indian generally had with the bureaucracy responsible for his welfare. The client departments of Indian affairs in Canada and the United States forgot to attend to their reason for existing, and their clients went without services to which they were entitled as citizens (and as human beings), as well as those which they had been especially promised as Indians in exchange for the cession of the lands which were their traditional resource and heritage. By far the most common and most universally heard complaint in Indian affairs over the past century and a half has centered on the inadequacy and malevolent negligence of Indian agents; and almost the first words of the British crown on this matter concerned the necessity of ensuring the competence and suitability of those charged with the responsibility of dealing with the Indians. But they were, in large measure, words to the wind. While the senior officers of the Bureau and the Department of Indian Affairs in the United States and Canada have often been unusually talented and of rare sensitivity and intelligence, many of the local agents have been men of numbing mediocrity or in some cases of sinister greediness. Even those least sympathetic to the Indians recognized their legitimate desperation; for example, the Canadian Farmers Union, during the time of the Riel Rebellion, pointed

> with a sorrowful pride to the fact that whilst we are trying to secure considerations and justice our sons and brothers have left their farms to grow weeds while they are away in the North-West Territory, risking and laying down their lives like

loyal sons to Canada to defend the supremacy of the flag of our forefathers from the contaminating touch of half-breeds and savages driven to despair by misgovernment, and by the acts of incompetent and dishonest Government officials.[25]

The Indians themselves, of course, protested bitterly against the incompetent management of their affairs, but this was easily dealt with.

It is true that they complain. Mr. E. McColl [Inspector of Agencies], as has been seen [in correspondence previously quoted, from the year 1878], says that 'to complain is a chronic feature of their nature.' And there is too much reason to think that they have been encouraged to complain by men who had the interest of the Indians less in view than the political effect of Indian dissatisfaction and even Indian warfare.[26]

Nonetheless, the Indian agent became something of a macabre figure of fun in the literature of the succeeding century and not without good cause. Many of them had authority far beyond what they were reasonably competent or at all trained to handle, and yet the centralized structure of both federal departments mitigated against the exercise of initiatives and imagination, the possibilities for which might have attracted individuals of the caliber that the service deserved and desperately needed. There were, of course, notable exceptions, but they were in large measure hamstrung by a bureaucratic organization which was paralyzingly complex, and by local pressure which, particularly in the United States, could be distressing and overpowering.

The second issue to which I referred earlier, as raised by Cecil Denny increasing rations to pacify the Indians, was in fact *the* issue of Indian affairs throughout the nineteenth century and up to the present day. How does one encourage habits of industry and thrift and at the same time maintain a measure of stability and continuity among the Indians themselves, and provide reasonably for their welfare and protection? Putting them on the dole, while humane and

in many cases absolutely necessary, was scarcely conducive to the inculcation of habits of self-sufficient enterprise.
The giving of alms may be government's most compelling
function, but it is seldom its most constructive—unless, of
course, one takes a radical approach and assumes that at the
base of it all it is the *only* function of a central government,
whatever the masks it puts on. Whatever the case, the patterns of social coherence and economic reward upon which
the non-native civil *and* religious orthodoxies were founded
were foreign to most, though not all, of the Indian cultures.

Yet from the beginning, the Indian was a necessary part
of the economic structure of the New World; consequently,
he was an inevitable part of the system of government responsibility which became inseparable from this structure.
The importance of the Indian in the fur trade, though sometimes exaggerated, was indisputable. This cooperation
could not entirely be seen as an instrument of civilization,
however, for it was very easy

> to argue that the advance of civilization entailed the debase-
> ment of the native [which] logically implied the obligation of
> preserving a primeval state in which Indians perpetuated their
> virtues, trapped fur-bearing animals, and sold them to traders.[27]

Nonetheless, the inevitable effect of the fur-trading system
was to increase contact between the native and the non-
native groups and to make the Indian at least somewhat
aware of the things which compelled the white man. The
early traders on their part became convinced, almost to a
man, of what compelled the native and called it "self-
interest." The concept of "Indian-giving," or giving which
is motivated by self-interest, has a long history. William
Byrd of Virginia, on refusing an offered gift, explained that
he knew

> that an Indian present, like that of a Nun, is a Liberality put out
> to Interest, and a Bribe plac'd to the greatest Advantage.[28]

And Edwin Denig, a shrewd and observant trader, remarked upon several occasions that the Indians

> appear to look upon every person as a source from which
> benefit is to be derived, [and] care but little for individuals or
> principles if some gain is realized. This runs through the whole
> course of their operations . . . It is more or less the great mo-
> tive of all savage nations. It forms the basis of all their
> transactions.[29]

One would have thought, if this were true, that the history
of the New World would be a history of harmony and of
mutual advantage gained. Such was, of course, not at all the
case, partly because Denig's statement was no more universally true of the Indians than it was of the whites, and
partly because the advantage to be gained by the natives on
the one hand, and the non-natives on the other, was in many
cases almost completely opposed.

The traders differed in their suggestions as to what might
be done about or with the Indian about as much as they
differed in their personalities, but they generally agreed that
there was a need to work towards the transforming of the
Indian so that he might better be able to cope with the new
order which was encroaching upon his domain. There were
exceptions to this response, especially among the earlier
traders. David Thompson, for example, envisaged the establishment of inviolable havens or "reserves" in the north
of what is now Canada, where the Indian might continue to
lead a free and nomadic life. But most advised either that
the Indian should be, to the greatest degree possible, exposed to the economic activities which sustained the fur
trade, on the assumption that trade was a fairly basic instrument of civilization—something like the assumptions
surrounding wage employment during the middle decades of
the twentieth century; or that the Indian should be encouraged, and if necessary forced, to turn to agriculture. Many
doubted that this was possible; but most preferred that the

attempt be made since, so far as they could see at the time, eventual extermination was the only alternative. Charles Larpenteur phrased the typical view reasonably accurately when he noted that

> from what I have seen, and knowing him as I do, I would say it cannot be done; yet there is nothing like trying.[30]

Yet he ended his memoirs, *Forty Years a Fur Trader on the Upper Missouri,* with a comment reflecting the other side of the story, recorded during a conversation with the great Sitting Bull:

> I don't want to have anything to do with people who make one carry water on the shoulders and haul manure . . . The whites may get me at last, but I will have good times till then. You are fools to make yourselves slaves to a piece of fat bacon, some hard-tack, and a little sugar and coffee.[31]

CHAPTER SIX

Constructing the Unreconstructed

By the 1870s the good times were running out, even for Sitting Bull. The "civilizing" programs of both governments had been fairly haphazard and almost entirely unsuccessful. For one thing, the Americans had effectively decided that it was to be farming for all, and very few of those in authority recognized the limitations of such a policy. One who did, though he was almost ignored, was General John Pope, commander of the Missouri military department, who strongly recommended that the interdependence of environment and culture be taken into fuller account, and that a program of study be instituted to determine appropriate occupations which might lead to Indian "advancement" in particular cases. In addition, he suggested that Congress should appropriate more money for Indian administration, since the army was being asked to keep the Indians on reserves while there were insufficient rations allowed to keep them from starving there.[1]

An indication of the kind of thinking which informed even the most generous of programs may be gotten from this comment by a Canadian missionary in 1847:

It has passed into a proverb, that a fisher seldom thrives, a shooter never, and that a huntsman dies a jovial beggar. How then is it to be expected that the Indian, who can have no motive to a settled and laborious agricultural life, but the persuasions of the Missionary and Superintendent, will, in favourable situations for success, relinquish his former employment of hunting and fishing, for those which are less profitable to him, and attended with, to him, much greater fatigue.

It is necessary the Indian youth should be prevented becoming hunters or fishers, and this can be alone done by locating [his] village where there are no facilities for either.[2]

The idea of fitting the occupation to the individual, rather than the reverse, has never really appealed to the architects of western society and it certainly made little headway in the nineteenth century. Indeed, it is making little headway even now, for the story is being rewritten in the north of Canada at the present time. In the late eighteenth century, when the federal government of the United States was trying to accomplish several things at once in its relations with the Indians, it attempted to ensure that over and above treaty provisions securing Indian lands for the natives, the government would have the option of acquiring at any time lands for military posts, agencies and trading factories, and for roads connecting what were considered important settlements of the non-native population, or major areas of American territory. With the former there was little problem, but the Indians were not anxious to have their territory divided and subdivided by roads and other transportation corridors. As an inducement, it was the government's practice to suggest that the Indians themselves could profit by running the rest houses for the travelers (land for which was requested along with that for the road).[3]

Almost two hundred years later, the government of Canada is playing the same game and promoting the idea that increased wage employment for the native people in the north will be a sufficiently attractive benefit to ensure their support of resource-exploitation projects which may destroy their muskrat marshes, or pipeline corridors which will certainly change their way of life beyond recognition, and subdivide their lands. Only rarely, and usually rather shyly, does one hear alternatives to wage employment advocated, to return to the Indians and Eskimos something of the self-sufficiency which they have lost as a result of forces beyond their immediate control. Wage employment, and the style of life which it inevitably creates and in turn supports, is the new tool and mark of civilization, much as agriculture was during the past century. The difficulty is that the kind of self-sufficiency it sustains is a very slippery achievement, both because it is dependent upon the sufficiency (and the economic necessity) of the venture which provides the employment; and because it is not at all obvious, in these times of dramatically increased government involvement in every aspect of the lives of its citizens, that self-sufficiency has much, if anything, to do with what we like to think of as civilized existence. However, it has very much to do with the fictions we have created about the progress of developing cultures and of the individuals who together keep a culture alive; and it is a goal which certainly the Protestant missionaries have advocated with zealous enthusiasm and have bound together with the progress of civil structures to create an interwoven design of civil and religious self-sufficiency which is often grotesquely inappropriate and anachronistic.

One of the earliest of such schemes was that established by Henry B. Whipple, who was appointed (in 1868) supervisor of appropriations for the Sisseton and Wahpeton Sioux—who had been removed after the Minnesota massacre of 1862 to Dakota Territory. The Indians under his charge were in extreme want; and because Congress was loath to approve sufficient monies for the agencies to look after their responsibilities properly, Whipple decided to put into practice a principle he had been enunciating for some time. At Lake Traverse, he promoted an agricultural enterprise which he hoped would become self-sufficient, and to this end he provided a simple alternative for the Indians there: either work the land or receive no rations. Since no buffalo had entered the region that summer, and the ducks and geese which had flocked into the area in the fall could not be preserved for winter use, the second alternative was quite simply to starve.

Whipple's approach, and the experiment itself, were praised mightily, but a few minor details should perhaps be emphasized.[4] Whipple's simple incentive was, as we have seen, by no means novel. Nor, indeed, was his lack of foresight. The Lake Traverse region which he chose was not particularly suited to agriculture; the crops were destroyed annually by drought and grasshoppers for a decade; by that time the metropolitan influence of St. Paul had effectively encompassed most of the region; and the economics under which Whipple had inaugurated the experiment had become complicated beyond measure. So had the social pressures, which were exaggerated by the intrusion of the railroad;[5] and by 1880 a corridor of continuous settlement had been formed from Lake Traverse, the source of the Red River, down to its delta at the south end of Lake Winnipeg. Not intensive cultivation, but cattle ranching, was the business to be in if one was to participate in the development of the West, though the irony was that much of the beef market existed to supply treaty Indians in the southwestern Canadian plains.

It is not so much that some of the Indians should have turned to cattle ranching rather than farming, though this was in many cases true for cultural as well as economic reasons, but that "solutions" to the "problem" of civilizing the Indian have invariably been unimaginative and almost totally lacking in a sense of future possibilities or developments. For the nineteenth-century administrator, missionary or politician there was some justification for this situation, since orthodox thinking of the time tended to view the evolution of everything, and particularly the evolution of cultures, as taking place in stages and defined by *activities;* and agricultural activity was the stage which followed the nomadic according to this scheme. But there is much less excuse for those who, for example, have had charge of the administration of the Eskimo people in the north of Canada and in Alaska. The most withering indictment of those who have affected the native situation there is to be found in the series of books on *Eskimo Administration* written by the eminent anthropologist Diamond Jenness.

Initially, the story was fairly typical. The Canadian government took an interest in the Eskimos at the same moment as it took an interest in the land on which they lived. It was not so much that it wanted the land itself, but that it did not want anyone else to have it; and so in order to establish sovereignty in the far North in the face of American and Norwegian pressure, police posts were established at various locations. At first, these posts were ill-equipped to provide the natives with anything other than emergency rations and, of course, police service, which they did not need. But little by little the once widely nomadic Eskimos became concentrated in particular areas, in order that the instruments of civilization might work more effectively.

> It was the white men who chose the sites, most of them for three reasons: because they were readily accessible by sea, possessed safe anchorages, and centred in areas sufficiently well populated to yield the trader an abundance of furs and the missionary a bountiful harvest of souls. But should fate ever cut off the villages from the civilized world and compel their inhabitants to rely once more on the local resources only, one and all would have to be wholly or partly evacuated, because their immediate environments cannot provide enough fish and game to support their populations more than a few days or weeks.[6]

Dependence upon the central administration—and in this case, on the charity of the government—replaced an independence which was surely one of the wonders of environmental adaptation, but which was becoming less and less possible as the impact of non-native goods (in particular rifles) made it so much easier to kill the game that the annual harvest became seriously depleted; and the impact of non-native luxury items seduced many of the natives from the rigors of their former nomadic independence. The traders were, of course, generally the first to move into an area, except in those few outlying regions where police detachments were established to maintain Canadian sovereignty.[7] They were closely followed by the missionary, and then by the police, the visible and for many years the only arm of government in the North. The trader and the missionary did much to ensure that the Eskimo had his physical and spiritual needs provided for, insofar as those needs could be ascertained by those who were frantically busy with the practical matters of operating a trading post or blinded by the spiritual truths shining forth as the light of God. Nonetheless, were it not for these people, the Eskimos would most likely have perished much more quickly than many of them did, sadly enough. Of course, if the whalers and later the fur traders and the missionaries had not entered into those northern lands at all, it might be that the Eskimos would still be pursuing their old and primitive way of life. But that is beside the point: for at least two hundred years, and much longer on the Labrador coast, there have been contacts between the Eskimos and the European, in some cases accompanied by groups of Indians for whom the Eskimo provided an exercise in butchery, which compliment the Eskimos returned as often as they were able.

The government was a long time realizing its responsibilities. By an Imperial Order in Council of 1880, the Dominion of Canada officially assumed title and ownership of all British possessions to the north of what was then Canada. The Canadian government did in a manner accept one of the responsibilities of sovereignty, a continued interest in the territory, though it took a quarter of a century for her to do even this. Yet it was not until after the Second World War that the welfare of the Eskimo was seriously considered, and then initially only by including them in the family-allowance scheme to which all Canadian citizens had recently (1945) become entitled. It was a grotesque beginning, for what the Eskimos desperately needed was a sense of possible independence. What they were offered, after the barbarous luxury and waste of material possessions had passed before their eyes during wartime, and during the construction of the D.E.W. line, was a meagre dependence upon government handouts and upon decisions concerning their welfare and their livelihood (for example, new fish and game regulations) made in somewhere called Ottawa, or (more recently) in an equally remote swamp called Yellowknife.

As a further impediment, though some might think it something of an advantage, the Eskimos were specifically excluded from the Indian Act. Indeed, for a number of years, until 1939, the larger federal responsibility for "Indians, and lands reserved for Indians," which is defined in Section 91 (24) of the British North America Act, was not extended to Eskimos. A dispute with the province of Quebec over the payment of welfare to Eskimos within that province's jurisdiction reached an impasse, and

Ottawa in 1935 referred the matter to the Supreme Court of Canada, and asked that august body to decide, once and for all, whether the framers of the British North America Act had or had not grouped the Eskimos with the Indians. In the fullness of time the Supreme Court examined many witnesses, whose evidence it studied long and patiently.

Parturiunt monto: nascetur ridiculus mus
[The mountains are in labour. From their womb will issue an absurd little mouse.—Horace]

At last, in 1939, its labour ended—*Eskimos are Indians.* The Northwest Territories Council mistook the puny mouse for a raging lion. Panic-stricken at the consequences, its Minister of the Interior wrote to the Minister of Justice, and the Department of Justice wrote to Dr. O. D. Skelton, then Under-Secretary of State for External Affairs, asking him to lodge an appeal with the Privy Council in London to have the verdict reversed. But Skelton gently pointed out that a world war was raging too, and suggested that it might be advisable to leave the

'lion' undisturbed until the other conflict ended. The conflict
did at last end, but by that time a new Minister of the Interior
and a new Northwest Territories Council had discounted the
fears of their predecessors and quietly accepted the verdict.

Thus from the late 1920's right through to the mid 'forties, the
Northwest Territories Council and its allies unweariedly fought
the dragon of Eskimo status.[8]

What the verdict meant was, however, more than a little
unclear. The virtue of the Indian Act is that it functions as a
kind of parliamentary and administrative primer and outlines quite specifically the responsibilities which both the
government and the Indian can assume. There is at least the
fiction, though many take it to be far from the fact, that the
government knows what it is doing merely because it is
doing something, and that very earnestly and deliberately.
From its initial promulgation, there have been those who
have questioned the sanity of a piece of legislation which
actively discouraged, and indeed in some areas positively
prohibited, the assimilation of the Indian into the social and
economic life of the non-native population, while at the
same time being the centerpiece of a broad policy of moving
the Indians towards full citizenship and full participation in
Canadian life. By existing to regulate and systematize the
relationship between the Indian and the majority society,
the Act codifies and often exaggerates the distinctions
which it is its function eventually to eliminate. The terms
have changed slightly over the years: where once the Indian
was to be "assimilated," later he was to be "integrated";
and where he was once to be "civilized," now he is to be
brought into the "mainstream" of Canadian life and to
"participate fully in its social and economic advantages."
Yet all of the time the regulations governing his activities,
and the distinctions which were a necessary part of those
regulations, became ever more complicated, and the entire
game, for which the Indian Act was a book of instructions,
began to take on a life of its own.

And so the Eskimos were not the object of even such

mixed blessings as the Indian Act might afford. The continued use and occupancy of their traditional lands was not guaranteed, nor was any step taken to extinguish their rights in land in exchange for the kind of special attention and reserve land provided to treaty Indians. In fact, there was until very recently a great deal of doubt whether the government would recognize *any* aboriginal rights in land in the North.[9] For there has never been a sense of policy or any broad administrative direction for the Eskimos, and the results have been predictably confused. For so many years, the government did not know what it wanted to do and was very busy with other matters in any case. The missionary groups which had taken responsibility for much of the education and health service were insufficiently organized, and had too few funds, to do the job properly. The economic base which had sustained many of the Eskimos for a long time and which, though it had not been truly "primitive" or traditional for many years, had been reasonably consonant with a semi-independent and semi-nomadic life, had cracked and was already disintegrating badly. Trapping became unprofitable; the price of white-fox furs, for example, dropped from $38.82 in 1920–1924 to $8.88 in 1948–1949, and at one period in 1949–1950 fell as low as $3.50,[10] and this was roughly synchronous with a shattering increase in the cost of the white man's goods upon which the natives were increasingly relying, both materially and psychologically. Muskrat furs were much more stable in price, but were rare outside the Mackenzie Valley Delta; and even there the problems of conservation and protection of the trapping community against further expansion became acute. The wage-employment activities which had provided a boom during the construction of the Crimson Air Staging Route fell off, and the Eskimos were forced to rely more and more on government relief.

The situation for the Eskimos was not unlike that which the Indians in the United States had faced during the years following the Dawes Act, when occasional periods of devastating prosperity with which the native social structure was incapable of coping were followed by scandalous deprivation and disorganization. The government was unsure of its policy and vacillated between energetic meddling and culpable disinterest in the state of native affairs. The dogmatic non-native civil and religious verities of the age continued to be preached at the native people, in defiance of their pleas for a recognition of their own cultural heritage and resources. These resources, in particular, were being assiduously alienated or devalued, and those which were maintained were set outside the scheme of non-native enterprise which the native people were apparently supposed to be adopting.[11] Finally, during the administration of President Coolidge, Hubert Work, the Secretary of the Interior, requested (at the urging of John D. Rockefeller, Jr., who contributed much to the cost) that the Institute for Government Research (later known as the Brookings Institute) conduct a survey of the situation facing the Indians and recommend a program of government action. Lewis Meriam supervised the investigation and the Meriam Report, naturally enough entitled "The Problem of Indian Administration," was published in 1928. It contained valuable statistical information, as befitted an early "futures research" study, and advised that in the past "too much reliance was placed on the sheer effect of individual land ownership and not enough was done to educate the Indian in the use of land." The Dawes Act failed, in the opinion of Meriam, because of a faulty government education program.[12] Basically, the report suggested a holding action to re-establish or in some fortunate cases maintain a measure of cultural and economic stability among the Indians, and a redevelopment plan to prepare the Indians to take advantage of the wonderful social and economic opportunities which America had to offer. The availability of unearned income (from leases, annuities, natural resource royalties, and the like) was particularly censured, since it was felt by Meriam to permit and indeed encourage the continuance of a "life of idleness." The traces of the old enthusiasm for the encouraging of "industry" and "thrift" are clearly apparent, for Meriam's report was about as theoretically conservative as it could possibly be. Like Edmund Burke, he advocated the vital necessity of the "little platoon," or in this case the tribal group, for the maintaining of an organic pattern of civic responsibility and benefit; and he saw in native traditions the crucial vitality and stability which would be necessary if the native people were to respond to the changing times. Yet he also affirmed the inseparability of rights and duties; and what this was to mean so far as the Indian was concerned would necessarily be established by the nation as a whole, for there was no longer any question of the Indian tribes having sovereign status. Their duty, basically, was to become self-sufficient, or else to become dependent *in the same way* as others were becoming dependent, with the spread of social security and welfare schemes.

The report was hailed as "a masterpiece of reform propaganda in the best sense of the word."[13] Aside from the curiosity of deciding *which* word, the report was not quite the masterpiece it has been celebrated as being. It was, however, a landmark in American Indian policy, if only in that it *appeared* to recognize the importance of the group as well as the individual. But this was to some extent subverted by the obsession with making "choices" available to the native people, and providing for a process of exercising those choices which depended very heavily on non-native political structures and on the availability of non-native resources, particularly those which were effectively appropriated by Congress, and which included bureaucratic personnel and tagged funds.

In 1934, the Indian Reorganization Act (or the Wheeler-Howard Act) was passed and it incorporated many of the features recommended in the Meriam Report. It was

An Act to conserve and develop Indian lands and resources; to extend to Indians the right to form business and other organizations; to establish a credit system for Indians; to grant certain

rights of home rule to Indians; to provide for vocational education for Indians; and for other purposes.

President F. D. Roosevelt grandly declared that the time
had come to

> extend to the Indian the fundamental rights of political liberty
> and local self-government and the opportunities of education
> and economic assistance that they require in order to attain a
> wholesome American life.[14]

The chief architect of the new program was John Collier,
appointed Commissioner of Indian Affairs in 1933, who
contended that

> *assimilation,* not into our culture but into modern life, and
> *preservation and intensification of heritage,* are not hostile
> choices, excluding one another, but are interdependent through
> and through.[15]

Collier was sure that he knew what was best for the Indians,
and although the reorganization which the Act proposed
was opposed by 73 tribes (out of a total of 245), according to
the referendum procedure which the Act incorporated, Collier extended the provisions of the Act to include all tribes
by a series of administrative maneuvers.

The difficulty was that tribal self-governance and
economic self-sufficiency were, in the final analysis, so dependent upon non-native standards and decisions that they
quickly became little more than a disarming daydream
which created a dangerous illusion of stability among some
of the native groups. And it was dangerous quite simply
because it was an illusion and eventually resulted in a repeti-
tion of the pattern of defeated expectations and feelings of
bad faith which had been the sad story for so many years. In
a sense, while the civil authorities were generally sold by
the pious promises which the Act implied, the religious
leaders were much nearer to identifying the difficulties. Dr.

C. C. Lindquist, a former member of the Board of Indian Commissioners, remarked hysterically that "Collier's plan is socialism and communism in the rankest sense."[16] While one would hardly wish to join hands around the burning pyre with Lindquist, and while many of the programs of Roosevelt's New Deal came in for a similar sort of criticism, it was nonetheless true that the new Indian social and economic structures were extremely vulnerable. They were established in order to effect the assimilation of the native people "into modern life." Yet they were in many ways in direct theoretical opposition to the immensely powerful ideological forces in American society which defined modern life and the liberties it allows, as well as the kind of happiness it envisages, in quite different and inexorable terms. Even John Collier, despite his sensitivity to native values, ran afoul a number of times, and in one case dramatically.

> [He] had two loves—soil conservation and Indians; when he pushed soil conservation too fast on the Navajo reservation the Navajos, the largest and most 'Indian' of all tribes, rejected his reorganization plans. The story of this great man in his moment of self-inflicted tragedy some day will produce an epic chapter in the history of Indian-white relations.[17]

In spite of all this, the Act accomplished several notable changes. Tribal organization was reinforced—apparently a far cry from several decades earlier. In fact it was not such a far cry, except that the group rather than the individual was now being harrowed and cultivated, in an attempt to make it blossom into an instrument of change. That wonderful fertilizer, money, was available, for the government was spending freely in order to try to counteract the effects of the depression, itself a rather disconcerting aspect of nonnative economics to hold up as a model to a people who were to be tempted *away* from a way of life which occasionally exposed them to drought and starvation. But the climate was unpropitious in more than one way during these years; and all the earnest harrowing could not produce the flowering which the dreamers hoped for in a region where the winds blew so interminably, and the words on the wind spoke of capital and individual enterprise. The native people did not have the first, and so were impaired in developing the second.

However, the Indians had little choice, for such extraordinary powers were vested in the Secretary of the Interior that it mattered little what the Indians felt either about the basic shift (in gears rather than in direction), or about the particular changes which might be encouraged under the new legislation. The Secretary was instructed to prescribe rules under which tribal elections were to be held, to approve tribal constitutions before they became effective, to make rules for the management of Indian forests and grazing lands. In addition, and most curiously, the choice of tribal legal council and the fixing of his fees were subject to the approval of the Secretary. The Act excluded from many of its provisions all of the tribes of Oklahoma, many of whom no longer retained a tribal organization. The governments of the Five Civilized Tribes had been dissolved in 1906, as the logical conclusion to the work of the Dawes Commission which had been created in 1893 to extinguish title to all remaining lands in Indian Territory.[18] (In the same year, of course, the two territories of Oklahoma and Indian Territory were combined to form the state of Oklahoma, which joined the union in 1907.) Those who supported the exclusion of the tribes of Oklahoma from the crucial provisions of the Reorganization Act argued that to revive Indian communities and re-establish tribal organization there would be a retrograde step, "back to the blanket." The compromise which was eventually reached resulted in the Oklahoma Indian Welfare Act in 1936.

There was still much dissatisfaction with the state of Indian administration, particularly over redress for past expropriations and other grievances. A decade later, in 1946, the Indian Claims Commission was established to expedite Indian claims against the government. But it was a two-edged sword, for in making final settlement of injustices and claims it was also intended to hasten the end of special status for tribes. The wheels were rolling quickly again and extra momentum was added by the desire of the federal government, which had recently financed a war effort, to divest itself of the heavy financial burden of Indian administration. The Social Security Act of 1936, which had universal application and involved Indians with the States, had reduced certain areas of special federal relationship; and this movement was accelerated by Public Law 280, enacted in 1953, which gave permission to state governments to assume, under certain conditions, civil and criminal law-and-order jurisdiction on Indian reservations (though it excluded the special hunting and fishing rights which had been secured by certain of the treaties). The House Concurrent Resolution 108, passed in the same year, was even more definite, expressing it as the sense of Congress that the unique relationship between Indian tribes and the federal government should be "terminated" at the earliest possible date, though the rhetoric of the time spoke of "freeing" the Indians, members of a "captive nation." The Bureau of Indian Affairs was directed to prepare a list of tribes which could be considered "ready for termination" and to draft appropriate legislation. The development programs of the federal government were slowed down except insofar as they would assist in effecting the policy of termination, and other programs were directed towards relocation of individuals and families from reserves to urban areas.

Throughout these years, there was a progressive disengagement by the government. In 1949, the Commissioner of Indian Affairs noted that

> it is not the intention of the Federal Government to continue in the role of trustee of the Indians' property. The role was not

assumed arbitrarily but devolved upon the United States out of historic antecedents. Colonial law generally guaranteed the Indians protection in their land holdings. The Royal Proclamation of October 7, 1763, was a declaration by the King of England that the several nations or tribes of Indians 'who live under our protection should not be molested or disturbed in the possession of such parts of our dominion as, not having been ceded to, or purchased by us, are reserved to them'. The United States incorporated similar policy into its basic law, declaring in the Northwest Ordinance of 1787:

> The utmost good faith shall always be observed towards the Indians; their land and property shall never be taken from them without their consent.

The protective role was dictated as a matter of public policy; moreover, it was most often the direct result of a treaty provision between an Indian tribe and the United States, in which the tribe requested protection for its members and property. It is realized, however, that protective guardianship, if pursued without regard to the welfare of the person protected, can defeat its purpose. Development of the property to full utilization and encouragement of the owner to accept responsibility for management—these are the proper goals of Indian administration. They are the means by which the United States may, within a reasonable time, withdraw entirely from its historic role and turn over its trusteeship to a trained and responsible Indian people.[19]

A year later, a program of "withdrawal" was proposed; and by 1953 the cycle had completed itself, as the policy of "termination"—the new euphemism for "withdrawal" —was explicitly described by, naturally enough, the Assistant Secretary (in the Department of the Interior) for Public Land Management. Once again, land was at the center of the scene, where it had always belonged and usually had been, except that it had sometimes been upstaged by clever actors and shrewd stage managers.

Federal responsibility for administering the affairs of individual Indian tribes should be terminated as rapidly as the circumstances of each tribe will permit. This should be accomplished by arrangements with the proper public bodies of the political subdivisions to assume responsibility for the services customarily enjoyed by the non-Indian residents of such political subdivisions and by the distribution of tribal assets to the tribes as a unit or by division of the tribal assets among the individual members, whichever may appear to be the better plan in each case. In addition, responsibility for trust properties should be transferred to the Indians themselves, either as groups or individuals as soon as feasible.[20]

It is not easy to characterize the attitude of the white to the native population during these years. Progressively, natives were looked upon quite simply as instruments of government policy; the native policy came first, the native people followed after. "If the Indians were to disappear from the continent," noted John A. Macdonald in 1880, with stolid common sense, "the Indian question would cease to exist." To make the Indian "disappear" has always been one basis for Indian policy, described variously as extermination or termination. On the other end of the see-saw have been those who wished to reinforce native identity, however temporarily, and to deal with the native people either as protected wards of the state or as sovereign groups. Some form of arbitrary separation has always been an aspect of attempts to integrate the natives with the majority society or with the landscape. Behind all of this are some implicit assumptions: that to be an Indian is to be something different; that to change an Indian into a white man is to do something important; and that to remain an Indian is to remain unreconstructed. From time to time, being unreconstructed has been fashionable, but not often, nor for long.

An Anomaly
Upon the
Face of the Earth

The United States administration of its Indians has always been conditioned by the theoretical premise that a single, complete and final solution could be found for the problem which they present; and that this solution would be continuous with the social, economic and political structures which define the Union and which contain its ideological intentions. In other words, some form of assimilation has always been envisaged as the end, while the means have changed with the fashions—from religion, to close association with civilized societies, to the possession of private property, to education, and eventually to the exercise of normal civic responsibilities (such as voting and paying taxes).

The latest, and most fashionable, example of such means is provided by the Alaska Native Claims Settlement Act, which was put into effect in 1971. The natives of Alaska had, from the beginning, been specifically excluded from most legislation which involved Indians. Neither the Russians nor the Americans had ever entered into treaty with the natives; and the status of the lands occupied and used (primarily for hunting, fishing and berrying) for the roughly 30,000 Indians, Eskimos and Aleuts had long been a matter of controversy, both in Congress and in the courts. Although the Indians were assured (in 1884, and again in 1900) of the undisturbed "possession of any lands actually in their use or occupation," the legal status of such lands was left unclear from the Treaty of Cession of 1867 to the Settlement Act of 1971. The Statehood Act of 1958 recognized native rights of use and occupancy, though precisely what this meant was dubious, since in the celebrated Tee-Hit-Ton case of 1955 the Supreme Court had ruled that the acquiring by the United States of native lands held under claim of aboriginal right was not such an acquisition as to require compensation under the fifth amendment.[1]

The critical point was reached when oil was discovered, for

> despite all of the pious sentiments expressed in the Treaty and in the several Acts of Congress, active consideration to settle the Alaska Native Claims did not begin until almost nine years after the adoption of the Statehood Act, and then not until oil was discovered in vast quantities on the North Slope. Thus settlement became an economic issue as well as a legal and moral one.[2]

If there were a scenario which could be said to apply to nearly all of such extinguishments of native title and eventual land settlements, it is surely this. Even the most certain of theoretical experts on the future of the Indian has tended to find the problems of reconciling native and non-native civil structures intractable, and the desirability of obliterating one by enforcing the other fairly difficult to establish until such time as economic interests interfered. At that point, the Americans in particular have been inclined to invent or discover final solutions which reflected theoretical models of current social expectations, and the Alaska act is certainly in this tradition.

Thus it provides for the setting aside of 40 million acres, to which the native will get legal title with both surface and sub-surface rights, plus nearly a billion dollars, derived from $462.5 million from the federal treasury, payable over 11 years, and $500 million from 2 per cent of the (non-retroactive) revenues from mineral-leasing activities on both state and federal land. The act extinguishes all native claims based on aboriginal use and occupancy of lands and adjacent waters, including aboriginal hunting and fishing rights. It sounds marvellous, and so it may prove to be, but there are some immediate twists which are rather distressingly consistent with the confusions that beset previous legislation enacted during the preceding two centuries.

In the first place, the number of people who are to benefit from the settlement will be much larger than expected. The original estimate of 53,000 may be out by 100 per cent, for the "one-quarter blood" provision, and the inclusion of non-resident natives—both familiar enough criteria—will in all probability bring over 100,000 people within the fold. The location of the land which the natives may select is fixed by the sites of their (not always, in non-native economic terms, well-placed) villages, yet the intention is that these lands be turned to productive use. The money which is forthcoming is tied to its use by about 220 villages and 12 regional corporations, of which the former may be non-profit, but the latter (which receive the sub-surface estate on all 40 million acres, though title to only 16 million) must be business-for-profit entities. Thus the possible financial benefits are very closely tied to orthodox non-native economic ventures. In addition, the money both from the federal treasury and from the resource-revenue sharing provision will be a long time coming. In 11 years, that $462.5 million from the federal treasury may be worth somewhat less; and the 2 per cent royalties on mineral revenues will require $25 billion in realized returns to add up to $500 million. For instance, if the natives had realized 2 per cent on the $900 million which the federal government received from the sale of leases on the North Slope—a very exciting and dramatic oil bed—they would only have received $18 million. The organizational difficulties, and costs, will be formidable, and much may be lost in the process.

In particular, the familiar confusion of non-native and native patterns of group action and decision-making will undoubtedly cause disruptions. The intention is that the provisions of the act will ensure the individual welfare of the native people of Alaska. The result may be to tie the individual natives to group structures which are neither informed by indigenous values nor responsive to non-native criteria. These are not so much failings of the act, but inherent limitations which attend schemes such as this which try to solve group necessities by appealing to individual sufficiencies. Native people throughout North America have *group* needs, closely tied to the patterns of belief and habits of life, as well as visible racial features, which distinguish them from the non-native population. Yet an inattention to these needs is general where aboriginal and (generally) European cultures have come into permanent contact, as a writer on the Australian situation has aptly pointed out.

> The aim of "assimilation" has been to winkle out the deviant individual from the group, to persuade him to cut the ties which bind him and his family to it, and to set him up as a householder in the street of the country town. But policies which aim to change social habit by educating individuals, while ignoring the social context which has made him what he is, can have only limited success. A program involving social change must deal with the social group.
>
> The welfare of an individual is worth while for its own sake, and properly regarded as an end in itself. Welfare means nothing except in terms of individual satisfactions. But national policies should utilize the most effective and the quickest means. The most effective methods will be found from an analysis of the *whole* situation; and when we look at the situation of the Aboriginal as a whole, he is a member of a special group united at least in the beliefs held about the white majority. Moreover, the cause of the individual's special handicaps is related to his membership of the group. To ignore such a causal connection is to deal with the symptom while ignoring the cause. In this way also policy can be bogged down and lost in the welter of individual needs. To meet these is certainly the

object of the whole effort; but to assume that they will be most effectively met only by dealing with individuals, as 'ordinary Australians,' while ignoring the effect on their attitudes and beliefs of membership of a special sub-group, is to concentrate on the part to the neglect of the whole.[3]

It is here, really, that the crux of the matter lies, and it is very closely linked to the "definition" one gives of the member of any such group and the sense one has of what it means to be an individual within and without that group. The fairly precise definitions which are part of native administration in both Canada and the United States constitute an implicit recognition of this fact and of the attachments to land and tribal structures upon which the native sense of individual identity depends. But while static conditions are managed moderately well by this scheme, both countries have displayed a remarkable insensitivity to the need to provide for a redefinition of individual and group status that is organically related to any process of social change which is contemplated. In this respect, the Alaska Settlement Act appears little better than the grand schemes of several decades earlier to shift reservation Indians to urban centers.

One of the chief difficulties is that most programs of radical social change are informed by conventional civil and religious pieties, rather than by a perceptive concern for the needs and the reasonable expectations of those who are being transformed. Instead of a cautious hesitation, there has usually been an earnestly righteous and headlong enthusiasm for the latest route to the promised land. Jerusalem underwent a number of transformations in this scheme; and while it began by looking suspiciously like an English country estate of the eighteenth century, with a nicely savage grotto as a reminder of one's origins and other self, and a large wall topped with broken glass beyond which the happy and primitive impulses roamed at will, it ended by resembling a very neat office and apartment complex, cooperatively owned, and presided over by a board of very worldly wise directors, who make decisions quickly and efficiently after hearing all sides of every argument.

A nice scheme, perhaps, but what of the people who are to live on the estate or inhabit the board room? Secondary considerations, obviously. Fortunately, these things are never as neat as the planners would wish, and often the saving grace for the native people has been the simple impossibility of these wonderful programs, or the utter incompetence of those who would put them into effect. Efficiency is a marvellous attribute; but inefficiency is sometimes more marvellous still.

All too often, however, and particularly with fragile cultural institutions such as the family, much damage can be done even by the inefficient. During the 1950s there was increased concern in the north of Canada over the health of the natives. Disease has long been one of the scourges of the native people since the white man brought his blessings to the New World; smallpox and other epidemics have probably taken the greatest toll, followed by tuberculosis, venereal diseases, whiskey and attendant dissipation, removals, starvation and subjection to unaccustomed conditions, low vitality due to depression, and wars.[4] Smallpox alone, which was brought to America in the early seventeenth century, swept away from one-quarter to one-third of the Indians of the New World before the land was half explored. In 1837, for example, smallpox first came to the northern plains, carried to the Upper Missouri by the American Fur Company's steamer *St. Peter*. The disease nearly obliterated the Mandan tribe, then spread to the Arikaras and north to the Assiniboins.

At the mouth of the Little Missouri, a Blackfoot Indian was allowed to board the disease-ridden steamer; when he left he became a messenger of death. Although the traders knew they had made a mistake in letting the Indian on board, they did not stop him from leaving.

For two months, no Blackfeet came to trade at Fort McKenzie on the Upper Missouri River. Finally, the chief trader, Alexander Cuthbertson, went to look for them. After travelling for a few days, he found a camp of about sixty lodges from the Piegan tribe. There was no sound and as he approached, a horrible stench permeated the air. When he came to the first tipi, he saw the grim results of the white man's disease. 'Hundreds of decaying forms of human beings, horses and dogs lay scattered everywhere among the lodges,' he recorded. 'Two old women, too feeble to travel, were the sole living occupants of the village.'

During that year, an estimated six thousand Blackfeet, or two-thirds of the whole nation, perished from smallpox. Never again were they quite as numerous as they had been before that tragic year.[5]

Thirty years later, a second epidemic was spread in almost the same way, and with nearly as devastating results. As one contemporary newspaper remarked, with enigmatic gusto,

the dreaded disease broke out among the copper-coloured devils, and spreading like wild-fire from tepee to tepee and from camp to camp, has made a great havoc in their strength and numbers—sending them to perdition in quicker time than bullets and bad breath could do the work.[6]

In the lands north of the forest edge, there were few Europeans who stayed around long enough to report on the extent of the diseases which were spread there. Certainly, measles took its toll; and one disease remained, to become endemic. By 1950, tuberculosis was estimated to affect 15 to 20 per cent of the Eskimo population in the Arctic; and, as we have seen, its incidence among the Indians in the South, in both Canada and the United States, was startling. Poor housing, and the inevitably confined conditions; poor clothing, with the decline of available caribou (a partial consequence of the concentrating of Eskimos in settlements, and the discouraging of a life of following the migrating herds) and the use of alternative, inferior-quality, store-bought clothing; and malnutrition, as country food was slowly replaced by food purchased at the local trading post, but without any sense of the proper way to balance such a diet—all of these exaggerated the problem; and the consequent high infant mortality rate was appalling.[7] It was the latter which finally caught the conscience of the public and the attention of the government administrators. A booklet was published in 1960 by the Canadian Departments of Health and Welfare and of Northern Affairs and Natural Resources, which had joint responsibility for native health services. It was entitled *Eskimo Mortality and Housing* and provided a pictorial look at the squalor and wretchedness of much of the housing that served as temporary or permanent shelter for the northern natives.[8] It is a distressing book to look at, not only because of the conditions which are so graphically displayed, but also for the notes and comments on many of the illustrations which give evidence of a frightening ethnocentricity and plain insensitivity on the part of its authors, and of an implicit policy which would soon be foisted on the Eskimos of the North, for their own good and in order to improve the health statistics. Under one picture, of a very neat and tidy shelter, there is the following inscription:

> The owner of this tent at Resolute [Bay] was able to get a proper bed and bedding. Eskimos stabilized in one place soon try to acquire better furniture, bedding, utensils and even phonographs and radio receivers. They seem to enjoy collecting bottles and odds and ends—note the badminton bird![9]

Another photograph is underlined by this comment:

> A clean tent interior, Lake Harbour. Why two clocks? Note the store seal oil "lamp" and the wooden frame above it on which pots and kettles are suspended.

To the badminton bird and the two clocks as clear evidence of cultural idiocy, there is added a tacit argument for the "ordering" and "stabilizing" of the lives of the Eskimo people. It would be a small matter, in a small publication, were it not that this pamphlet was one of the key instruments of an orchestrated program of cultural change. The cure which was administered for these medical ills and cultural disabilities was, in many respects, much worse than the disease, for the government embarked upon a massive (and very expensive, though poorly designed) housing program as part of a stategic plan to force the Eskimo people "to gain experience in new forms of social organization necessitated by settlement living and the influences of modernization."[10] In addition, it was intended that the new houses would introduce the Eskimos to, and instill in them a sense of, that "pride of ownership" upon which North American non-native social and economic structures so largely depend.

It was a new page in an old book. For almost the whole history of relations between native and non-native, the condition of the native people has excited the anxiousness of those who cared about the welfare of all of God's creatures. To some, this condition was wretchedly uncivilized; to others, it was impoverished or unhealthy; and to still others, it was wonderfully picturesque, like a romantically fading ember. Each group has tended to confuse material culture and traditional social values, or more usually to concentrate its attention on one to the neglect of the other; and to bring its earnestness to bear on changing conditions so as to ensure the survival of that which it most valued, or thought most worthy of preservation. Native people have been forced to farm or to take wage employment in order to become civilized or to learn the sense of dignity that grows from ownership of property and personal possessions. They have been flooded with (impatient) money for improvement or self-improvement projects and brought into the purview of social assistance schemes in order to decrease their poverty and destitution. They have been exposed to the most advanced medical treatments and transported to hospitals and medical centers to better their health; and they have had new houses provided for them, so that the conditions in which they lived might be more conducive to the maintaining of good health and the prevention of disease. The children (though seldom the adults) have been educated to the advantages of being and doing all the things that they are and have not, and often have been taken away from their families to lessen the danger of "backsliding." They have been separated and isolated from the non-native community and provided with rigidly protective legislation in order to preserve their native culture and traditions. Always, however, they have been protected most zealously neither from poverty nor disease nor outside influences, but from themselves.

Even the Canadian Indian Act, which has operated to preserve much of the native heritage, including token parcels of their land, and much of the disillusionment and poverty which are also their genuine heritage from the nineteenth century, still has its part in this pattern. Generally, such protective legislation, which includes the series of trade and intercourse acts passed in the United States between 1790 and 1834, has had as its central focus the warding off of the influence of unscrupulous non-natives, and of non-native instruments such as liquor and fire-arms, as well as moral depravity and viciousness, against all of whose seductions the natives apparently had little defense. Occasionally, however, protecting the property and the person of the native from outside influences was felt to be insufficient, and certain native customs and traditions were then explicitly forbidden. This was, distressingly often, a feature of American legislation; most usually, it was part of a broad scheme of cultural obliteration which pretended to be nothing else. Canadian reaction, though not quite so thoroughgoing in this respect, was occasionally rather similar. In response to difficulties in the Northwest—difficulties which would lead to the second Riel rebellion in Canada and had already led to the Indian wars in the United States which Canada was desperately anxious to avoid—the Canadian government amended the Indian Act in 1884. This was not unusual, since it was always tinkering, but what was noteworthy was one of the prohibitions amended. In addition to going slightly beyond the Criminal Code and providing that

> whoever induces, incites or stirs up any three or more Indians, non-treaty Indians, or half-breeds apparently in concert, (a) To make up any request or demand of any agent or servant of the Government in a riotous, routous, disorderly or threatening manner, or in a manner calculated to cause a breach of the peace; or (b) To do an act calculated to cause a breach of the peace, is guilty of a misdemeanor, and shall be liable to be imprisoned for any term not exceeding two years, with or without hard labour;

the Act also stated that

> every Indian or other person who engages or assists in celebrating the Indian festival known as the "Potlatch" or in the Indian dance known as the "Tamanawas" is guilty of a misdemeanor, and shall be liable to imprisonment for a term of not more than six nor less than two months in any gaol or other place of confinement; and any Indian or other person who encourages, either directly or indirectly, an Indian or Indians to get up such a festival or dance, or to celebrate the same, or who shall assist in the celebration of the same is guilty of a like offence, and shall be liable to the same punishment.[11]

This provision may have been in response to the complaints of some missionaries in British Columbia that they were unable to counter such barbaric customs even with the powerful Truth which they announced. More likely, however, the Potlatch, which involved the giving away or destruction of property, was simply too much for those who

believed in the virtues of thrift and industry to accept in
their midst, aside from the awkward fact that some of the
property which was disposed of was part of the currency
which sustained the fur trade. Whatever the motive, it was
certainly true that many who worked with the Indians found
it very difficult to deal with, or to overcome, the traditional
ways and values to which many of the native people clung
so desperately. And in many of the comments of such people there is a mixture of honest concern for the welfare of
the native and righteous indignation at his recalcitrance.
The principal of a Manitoba School, for example, wrote at
the end of the last century to his superiors that

> it is criminal for our Government to allow bright young
> Indians—many of them well-educated, lost by the score
> —simply because they will not use compulsion if necessary to
> make the older Indians conform to proper modes of nursing,
> isolation and sanitation. Most of those who die do so because of
> Indian prejudice against White methods, to pure pigheaded-
> ness, and to gross negligence. A few sharp squatters upon each
> Reserve would mean the salvation of many of the race.[12]

The problems which are condensed in this cry of honest
outrage have been the bane of native affairs in North
America for two centuries. But they have been complicated, if that is possible, by a further one: the question of
who is to pay, and how much, for this process of whipping
the indigenous population into some sort of civilized shape
and making them productive members of society.

The
Indian
Question

The issues, and the real costs, have changed very little in the years since Columbus stumbled greedily into history, and since men first spoke seriously of "the great and meritoryouse dede" of "having the people (which as yet lyve all bestly) instructed to lyve more Vertuously," or sought answers to the question of "how the people furst began in that countrey or whens they cam." The ubiquitous and ambiguous Indian Question which encompassed such intentions was, in so many ways, *the* public question in North America during the following centuries. It engaged the attention at the same time as it confused the ambitions of the civil and religious leaders; and it enraged the sensibilities at the same time as it diffused the energies of the scoundrel and the philanthrope alike. In addition, it exposed the settling foundations of political structures in the United States and Canada.

There is no easy way to an understanding of this question, though one device which has often been employed is to start with the answer. There is much to be said for this strategy; it produces neat policies, comfortable satisfactions, readable books. But it bears about the same relationship to its subject as a piece of string does to a complicated tapestry.

And it is an immensely complicated fabric which has been woven out of the aboriginal woof and the European warp, even though as one moves along the tapestry to the present day the same story is repeated time and again. It is not so much to the story itself, but to the fabric, that our attention needs to be turned. This is not nearly as much fun, unfortunately; but it is necessary. Ears that are deafened by the sound of teeth righteously gnashing, and eyes that are blinded by the spectacles which moral indignation parades before its eager audience, need to be re-educated to the subtle complexities that native affairs and the process of its development present; and they also need to be made aware not only of present exasperations but also of the various assumptions about what it is to "lyve more Vertuously," and the various responses to "lyving all bestly," which have from the beginning influenced the serpentine course of white attitudes toward native North Americans.

The specific question about the ultimate origin of the North American Indian,[1] which had so fascinated earlier generations for reasons which were by no means narrowly antiquarian, did not in itself lead to very productive answers. But even aside from the subject of traditional land use and corresponding rights, the manner in which the question was dealt with and used to further other debates is instructive, and the structures of fact and fiction upon which the discussion was based will become depressingly familiar as we follow the course of events in native affairs. Initially, of course, there *was* no question; and Columbus, in the letter to Ferdinand and Isabella in which he described his discoveries, did not much ponder the existence of men in the New World for the very simple reason that he did not realize that it was a New World. Slowly at first, and then quite rapidly, the light dawned, and by the time the reports of the Magellan Expedition (1519–1521) were available, the realization that Europeans had discovered both New Men and a New World was fairly complete.

The first writer to deal in any orderly way with the question was Pedro Mártin de Anglería, in a book (*Décadas del Nuevo Mundo*) published between 1511 and 1530; but Gregorio García's *Origen de los indios de el nuevo mundo,* published in 1607, was the first book which devoted itself exclusively to the subject. Through a series of indiscriminate ethnological comparisons, García presents to his reader a patchwork quilt of possibilities, each deriving from the basic assumption that the Indians are descended from the sons of Noah, with the patches put together by lining up cultural habits or traits which appear to be common between Old and New World peoples and civilizations. His method prompted an argument which carried on through the seventeenth century, and the issue around which it turned was first and best stated by Joseph de Acosta. Contradicting García, Acosta denied that it was possible to trace the original Indians by the traditional sixteenth-century method of comparing cultural traits, since he believed that the cultural characteristics of the present Indian civilizations would not have been brought with them, but rather would have been developed *in situ,* and therefore must be looked upon as essentially autochthonous. This application of the idea of autochthonous cultures and environmental influence was quite novel, and had a great bearing on the questions which the discovery of the New World had raised.

Several of these questions were of particular importance. The first was basically secular, though it often took a religious form. When the Papal Bull of 1537, *Sublimus Deus,* stated "that the Indians are truly men and are not only capable of understanding the Catholic faith but desire exceedingly to receive it," the rights of Indians to possess (and therefore to dispose of) property was being affirmed, along with their supposed exceeding great desire to be converted. The laws of the Indies, proclaimed in 1542, reinforced this principle in a more clearly civil context. But behind such statements, whether given by religious or civil authority, was an extreme and interminable ambivalence about the capability of the Indian to manage his own affairs, and about the nature and purpose of any program of change which envisaged his doing so. Most of this eventually precipitated into a specific debate about educability, and about the administrative and executive responsibilities, and particularly about the control over money and resources, which the native people could and should be expected to assume. The legislative enactments and missionary records in both Canada and the United States display a nicely schematic application of successive conclusions on this matter and an almost complete insensitivity to the intricate logical manipulations by which these conclusions were formed.

There was a second impulse, moreover, which queered the pitch for succeeding generations even more completely, and this was the insistent priority which was given, with dogmatic zeal, to theoretical criteria and expectations as the source for solutions or guidelines to the Indian "problem," and the corresponding renunciation of all but the most immediate of practical considerations. Combined with an almost religious faith in education (thereby keeping the Indian and the white within the same natural order), and in the eventual progression of mankind through successive stages of development, this predisposition to theory or ideology has determined much that has been done or undone in Indian affairs. Its earliest entry on the scene was mildly amusing; intellectual and religious authorities from Aristotle to Augustine had argued that man could not live in the Burning Zone; and now, indisputably, men were found living there. Proved experience was, in this case, incontrovertible; and some of the more empirical voices of the time, such as Amerigo Vespucci, crowed that "it is certain, that practice is of more value than theory." But this was not so certainly believed by others, and the lumbering inertia of authority and ideology still continue to determine the course of most of the thoughts and actions in Indian affairs, disturbed only by the extremest of frictions, such as war.

The history of Indian affairs in the United States and Canada has been one of conflict between the obligations and attractions of theory and the necessities and conveniences of practice, with the inventions of one (the idea that tribal allegiance defined native culture and sensibility, for example) becoming the discoveries of the other (the fact that tribal structures were in fact of sustaining importance to the native people). These discoveries and inventions, however, were generally less likely and converged only as rather crude and sometimes malignant prejudices in the mind of the zealot or scoundrel.

The New World was the obvious playground for both, and this situation has in its turn exercised the cynical wit or the righteous indignation of succeeding generations of scoundrels and zealots. And yet the general pattern of relations between the native and non-native peoples was, in the main, set by individuals and institutions acting not out of excessive zeal or blatant and cruel self-interest, but out of the accepted presuppositions and the conservative aspirations of their age and of their temperament. We tend to write and to read history according to specific structures and to concentrate on great men, or institutions, or nations, or social movements, or political processes, or economic changes, without recognizing the confusion of most of these neatly traditional categories that has characterized relations between natives and non-natives on this continent. Yet it is the same history of which each is a part, and we need to find a more accommodating framework within which to place all of the events and personalities that define this history.

Many of their problems are, quite strictly speaking, insoluble, for they are past; and they are understandable only if one takes into complete and imaginative account the fictions of civil conduct and religious belief which have informed the actions and the reactions of the people of each age. But they do, of course, have a bearing on present circumstances. And it is, furthermore, as facile and misleading to assume that the aboriginal inhabitants of this land have not responded with and to the times, as it is to see the Puritan sensibility of the seventeenth century, so hard and narrow and utterly lacking in charity, informing the philanthropic actions of men of the nineteenth. King Philip was as different from his Indian brother Chief Joseph as he was from his contemporary King George, and the latter would have understood the motives of Andrew Jackson or Henry L. Dawes very little, if at all. And Louis Riel would have scorned the lot of them.

The practical principles and peculiar circumstances which conspired to define the anomalous relations that existed between the white and the native population in the New World varied considerably between the United States and Canada and within each country, yet the basic situation was surprisingly similar. In addition, the theoretical premises upon which such practical principles were founded, or in the absence of which they were promulgated, and which in either case led to the viewing of the peculiar circumstances in particular ways, are often most clearly apparent when relations between the native and non-native populations of the United States and Canada are compared. Local and national prejudices, or what were often more like "low" and inarticulated theories regarding the relation between the individual and the state, have sometimes obscured the situation, most notably in the distrust of British motives and actions which was so central a feature of the American national consciousness during the late eighteenth and early nineteenth centuries; and in the nervous fear of American liberal enthusiasms, which were most obvious in the frontier expansions of the same period, on the part of the British and later the Canadian population. A model for these differences is, to a certain extent, found in the early disagreements which characterized the French and the British presence on the continent and in the rather different attitudes which each displayed and the alliances (or enmities) which each established with the aboriginal inhabitants. The presumed or imagined status of the Indian tribes and individuals in each country is a hard thread to pick up in the historical tapestry, but it is among the most important; and it provides one of the clearest indications of the civil and religious theories and practices which determined (or, at the very least, affected) relations between the native and non-native inhabitants. But all of this becomes apparent quite quickly if we attend more specifically than we have so far to the most troublesome strand, which has been knotted and snarled by generations of earnest apologists and facile opportunists alike, and which is intimately linked with all of the issues which have troubled relations between Indians and whites—the question of land, and of the responsibilities and rights attending to its use and occupation according to the various theoretical and practical orthodoxies which prevailed at various times, for each of the groups, in the history of the relations between them. This must involve a fairly detailed examination of the early land policies and treaty practices which were followed in both countries, for upon them these relations depended, and by them they were in many ways determined. Indeed, the deterministic bias which provided such a useful counter-balance to the exercise and celebration of free will in North America could conveniently be applied to the native people only after the basis for an Indian policy had been well and truly fixed. This fixing was accomplished in the early treaties and laws and in the specific pronouncements and proclamations which accompanied them and reinforced their certainties.

CHAPTER NINE

Alas
for Caliban

Alas for Caliban. The Thousand Islands
Were full of noises,
Landscape and history echoing back and forth
Under immense skies, till his master
Cabined his spaces in a folio
And Euclids of the tepee, leaning-to
Birch-pole isosceles in a glade of hemlocks,
Drank deafening whisky in a written treaty.

Donald Davie, from
"A Sequence for Francis Parkman"*

As early as the beginning of the eighteenth century, the patterns were already set. At one extreme, there was the action of Pierre Charles Le Sueur, an instrument of the French struggle against the English for control of North America, who had been present at Lake Pepin in 1689 when Nicholas Perrot, a trader and also the military commander in the upper Mississippi region, had proclaimed French sovereignty over the entire area occupied by the Sioux. Le Sueur wished to reduce the inter-tribal warfare among the

*From *Collected Poems 1950–1970* by Donald Davie. Copyright © 1972 by Donald Davie. Reprinted by permission of Oxford University Press, Inc., and Routledge and Kegan Paul Ltd.

Sioux, as it was interfering with French trading practices; and having decided that it was "not possible to subdue the Sioux or to hinder them from going to war, unless it be by inducing them to cultivate the ground,"[1] he attempted to make farmers out of the Indians by persuading them (through the withholding of French goods and presents) to form a sedentary village around the fort which he had built near the mouth of the Blue Earth River. Both the farming enterprise and his hope for a copper mine there came to nothing, but his attempt stands as a model for other experiments of related intent that were to follow.

At the other extreme and at about the same time, there were the fraudulent or at the very least questionable dispossessions of Indians during the early colonial period in the eastern part of the continent. Once again, trade was at the heart of the matter; but this was aggravated, so far as Indian use and occupancy of land was concerned, by the fact that land acquisition could be a key to the founding of substantial fortunes, and a rather less risky one than trade. The kind of thing that could and did happen was exemplified by the Delaware "walking purchase" of 1737, and even this was "dignified" by authority in ways that other acquisitions were not.[2] The Delaware Indians had questioned the validity of a deed for title to Indian lands which had been obtained by the Pennsylvania colonial government in 1686. The contested land was in part of what is now Bucks County and included substantial tribal land on the west bank of the Delaware River in addition to the area between the Delaware and Lehigh rivers known as the Forks. When the Indian chiefs met in Philadelphia with representatives of the province, led by Chief Justice James Logan, they acknowledged with some reluctance that the deed was legal, for it had (in the fashion of the times) been signed by a not entirely representative element of the tribe; but they insisted that the extent of the tract was undetermined, for the northern boundary was described as being "as far as a Man can goe in one Day and a half." The exact determination of this distance was left to Logan and one James Steel, both of whom were, in the words of one of their apologists, members of the Society of Friends and of unimpeachable character in the eyes of fellow Pennsylvanians. These sterling characters obtained the services of three fleet-footed woodsmen, who began on September 19, 1737, and in 18 hours covered 55 miles, a notable distance. The Indians were appalled at the trickery, but had no recourse other than the comfort that misery enjoys in the knowledge that other tribes had in some cases been much more extensively and crudely defrauded.

There were various practical matters involving land cessions which were of considerable importance at this early stage of Indian affairs and which continued to trouble relations between the white man and the Indian during the succeeding centuries. The first was basic to the situation; neither the Indians nor the European newcomers were particularly adept at or much interested in ensuring that each understood the other. There could, of course, be more than a little self-interest or self-deception in this, especially when it involved differing conceptions of land tenure and of the value of goods and presents that were given in exchange for land surrenders; but in part the difficulty was more practical. Neither the European languages, nor the systems of land measurement, were familiar to the Indians, and the early compromise of employing easily translated formulaic expressions and using natural limits such as brooks, hills and springs to define land boundaries was only partially successful. The latter, in particular, made it difficult to guard against fraud and the need for a system of surveys was recognized. But these, in turn, often seriously offended native needs and cultural habits, especially where hunting or fishing played a major part in the life of the tribe. And the use of formulaic land-petition or treaty statements, while consistent both with European legal and native ceremonial (and basically legal) traditions, did not further a clear understanding of the significance of the events which were taking place.

Finally, and in some respects most significantly, it was

always difficult to ensure that the Indian leaders who signed or nodded away their tribal lands were in any sense, whether native or European, representative of their people. This was, of course, a convenient area of uncertainty for those who were anxious to obtain the land, since it was not too difficult to find one or more persuadable or (to use the contemporary euphemism) far-sighted chiefs who could be convinced of the inevitability of European expansion. But it was a genuine difficulty and one which still plagues native affairs. The tribal chairmen who now represent so many Indian bands in the United States are democratically elected, according to the best constitutional procedures, yet are routinely vilified as "apples" (red on the outside, white on the inside) by some of their more radically conservative constituents. The confusion on the other side, about which non-native representatives could acquire native land, was also a contentious issue; and although the sovereign authority moved quickly to assert its prior right, this was not always respected, and became a major source of irritation between the Imperial government and the colonial authorities, and then between the federal and state or provincial jurisdictions.

The description that Peter Wraxall gives, in his famous *Abridgment of the Indian Affairs (Contained in Four Folio Volumes) Transacted in the Colony of New York, from the Year 1678 to the Year 1751,*[3] provides a good account of the early practices in the exercise of sovereign control and civil influence, particularly in matters which concerned land; and when he became William Johnson's secretary and aide-de-camp, Wraxall had an opportunity to observe the formulation of British Indian policy at the hands of one of its most brilliant and successful exponents. But British policy already had something of a history, which began in 1670 with the instructions of Charles II to the Governors of the North American colonies, and which was premised upon the need to ensure and maintain peace. The instructions direct, among other things, that forasmuch as most of our Colonies do border upon the Indians, and peace is not to be expected without the due observance and preservation of justice to them, you are in our name to command all the Governors that they at no time give any just provocation to any of the said Indians that are at peace with us . . . and that [the Governors] do employ some persons, to learn the languages of [the Indians], and that they do not only carefully protect and defend them from adversaries, but that they more especially take care that none of our own subjects, nor any of their servants, do any way harm them.

And you are to consider how the Indians . . . may be best instructed and invited to the Christian religion, it being both for the honour of the Crown and of the Protestant religion itself, that, all persons within any of our territories, though never so remote, should be taught the knowledge of God and be made acquainted with the mysteries of salvation.

Peace and security were obviously of primary concern, followed closely by the urgently felt need to Christianize the indigenous inhabitants in preparation for or as part of the process of their joining the civilization that was being created in their midst. This latter and specifically civil impulse, with or without its familiar religious vehicle, inevitably became confused with the question of native rights, both because of the practical difficulties of dealing in rights affecting material matters with people for whom material advantage was something of a novelty, and because of the fundamental conservative principle that, as Edmund Burke later phrased it, "men cannot enjoy the rights of an uncivil and of a civil state together." Thus native people were to be taught the value of property and the importance of the habits of industry and thrift, for otherwise they might remain insensible of the advantages—the rights and privileges—which they were being offered in the form of a new code of civil and religious propriety. This rather awkward strategy, whereby the receiver must be schooled in the proper value of and the appropriate response to the gift which is bestowed, became a feature of native relations as soon as the uncertainties of early contact were cleared away and the pressures of non-native settlement effectively ensured its stability. The contortions and gymnastics of this strategic attitude were often grotesque, but they are of great importance to an understanding of eighteenth and nineteenth-century Indian affairs in Canada and the United States, and to a proper appreciation of the transition from a military to a civil (and, for a period in the United States following the Civil War, to a partially religious) administration of Indian affairs, and of the conflict between the military and civil authorities in the effecting of government policy.

The main instrument which was employed to standardize civil as well as military relationships with the native people was that old European invention, the treaty. In general, treaties were effected either for the purpose of ensuring peace or to extinguish native rights in land, though they were often urged as devices not so much for extinguishing but rather for replacing and redefining these rights in ways that accorded with non-native habits and expectations. Various constructions were put on such aboriginal rights or title, but the basic principle was fairly straightforward.

> The fact is that when the settlers came, the Indians were there, organized in societies and occupying the land as their forefathers had done for centuries. This is what Indian title means and it does not help one in the solution of this problem to call it a 'personal or usufructuary right.' What [those who claim aboriginal title] assert . . . is that they have a right to continue to live on their lands as their forefathers lived . . . There can be no doubt that this right was 'dependent on the goodwill of the Sovereign.'[4]

It is, however, not especially easy to distinguish the specific intentions of most of the treaties, for the maintaining of peace was rather intimately associated with the orderly acquisition of land for non-native settlement.

Yet however much the Indians were subjected to a policy

of necessity, it was nonetheless a recognizable policy, aptly described by Duncan Campbell Scott, the Deputy Superintendent-General of Indian Affairs in Canada during the early years of the twentieth century:

> To keep the Indians at bay by friendship, to distrust them profoundly while cementing treaties with them, to heal each treachery with the salve of presents, to be ready with ample rewards for negative services—these were to be the actuating principles until the increase of population should abate the terror of the savage, and the pressure of civilization should turn him into a peaceful subject.[5]

An interesting guide to the principles which were implicit in early relations between native and non-native inhabitants may be found in the special medals which were struck to facilitate or commemorate certain aspects of this relationship and to further the establishing of the kind of peaceful co-existence which would lead to profitable trade. The earliest such medal, struck by the colony of Virginia in the same year that Charles II wrote to the colonial governors, was purely practical: it was to be given to the friendly Indians to identify them and allow them entrance into the settlements. (It had, on its obverse side, the head of Charles II; and on its reverse, the Royal Arms with a representation of a tobacco plant.) This may appear an excessively nervous precaution, but it should be remembered that many of these settlements were frontier towns; and the Indians were more than a little exercised at the violation of what they felt to be their obvious rights, and at the unconscionable encroachment upon their lands and interference with their hunting and fishing habits. Also they learned very quickly the advantages of taking and holding hostages for ransom; and the more northerly settlements were often the object of skirmish attacks by French and Indian parties, who would at times carry off victims to Canada.[6]

There were a number of medals given on particular occasions during the French regime, including one in 1701 to celebrate the allegiance of many of the northern tribes; this series was terminated, appropriately enough, by the issuing of a Conquest Medal by Sir William Johnson in 1761, to reward 23 Onondaga chiefs for their (essentially passive) assistance in the defeat of the French by the British at the Battle of the Plains of Abraham. (As an indication of Johnson's pre-eminence in Indian affairs at this time, it is interesting to note that while it was customary on such medals to display the arms of the sovereign, this medal was to feature those of Sir William. Unfortunately, there was some confusion when the medal was struck, and a "likeness" of Montreal—which corresponds not at all to what Montreal was like at the time—was substituted.) Most of these medals are of interest primarily in their embodiment of the interrelated concerns of the time: conflict between the European powers, trade rivalry, the allegiance (or treachery) of particular native tribes, and the ensuring of the safety of nonnative settlements.

Even after their defeat of the French, the British were cleverly anxious to cultivate their native associations, in every manner possible; and although their efforts in this regard exacerbated some of the difficulties with the rebellious colonies, it also secured a surprisingly solid native support during the years of the Revolutionary War and the later War of 1812. No single individual represented this policy more clearly or more effectively than Sir William Johnson. It was, once again, the need to maintain the security of and to promote some stability in the colonies which prompted the most important action on the part of the British authorities, the Royal Proclamation of 1763. Word reached London in August of that year of the Conspiracy of Indian nations which the Ottawa chief Pontiac was organizing; and thus a series of documents, as well as a digest of advice from colonial officials such as Johnson, were put together to form a major statement of political and administrative principles. Although it will be useful to look in a moment at the exact nature of the Proclamation, it is instructive to note once again the broad pattern of which this was merely a small part.

When a treaty of peace was finally signed with Pontiac and his chiefs in 1765, a most interesting medal was struck to commemorate it. The medal represented a lion, in the foreground, lying watching a prowling wolf, which is seeking to destroy civilization, which is in turn represented by a church and a schoolhouse nestled among the trees. This was quite specifically a peace treaty, so that its strident symbolism is perhaps appropriate. But the relationship between peace and security was always fluid and the requirements of the latter flowed easily into the necessities of civil and religious evangelism. When the danger of war abated, it was smoothly replaced by the danger of savage and primitive influence, so that the tactics as well as much of the symbolism of later attempts to "stabilize" or civilize the native population show a striking resemblance to the practices of Johnson's administration in attempting to secure peaceful co-existence. For example, later treaties, such as the eleven which were signed in Canada after Confederation, between 1871 and 1921, were quite openly effected for the purpose of extinguishing the Indians' interest in the land and encouraging their settlement in one place where they might be instructed in the mysteries of civilization and salvation. But the preamble to these treaties, while honest enough as to their material effect, still maintained the unmistakable marks of their tradition as peace agreements and ceremonial occasions the consequences of which were perhaps not quite so clearly understood by the Indians as they might have been.

> And whereas the said Indians have been notified and informed by Her Majesty's said Commissioners that it is the desire of Her Majesty to open up for settlement, immigration and such other purpose as to Her Majesty may seem meet, a tract of country bounded and described as hereinafter mentioned, and to obtain the consent thereto of Her Indian subjects inhabiting the said

tract, and to make a treaty and arrange with them so that there
may be peace and good will between them and Her Majesty and
that they may know and be assured of what allowance they are
to count upon and receive from Her Majesty's bounty and
benevolence.[7]

A sense of this bounty and benevolence, and of the
character of the treaty as a peace agreement, is further reinforced by the Treaty Medals which were given at the time of
signing. For Treaties 1 and 2, signed between Her Majesty
the Queen and the Chippewa and Cree Indians of Manitoba
and adjacent lands on the coming of Manitoba into Confederation in 1871, the government was not properly prepared,
and distributed to the chiefs stock medals, of a kind usually
awarded as school or agricultural prizes. It was felt, both by
the officers of the Crown who were sensitive to ceremonial
etiquette, and by the chiefs, that these medals were insufficiently large and distinctive, so special medals were ordered
struck to celebrate the occasion. Unfortunately, the sil-
versmith (Mr. R. Hendry of Montreal) who was given the
contract did not have large enough dies, so he took some
smaller and fairly common medals which had been struck in
1867 at the time of Confederation and fixed to them a ring 11
mm. wide, on which he soldered the letters of a short inscription; he then plated some electrolyte impressions
which he had made from the original hybrid. The result was
an enormous medal (94 mm. diameter, 10 mm. thick), which
was very heavy, and initially quite popular with the chiefs;
but when it was discovered that the medals were of unexpectedly little value when traded, the chiefs were upset
—the Indians had, after all, absorbed a fair measure of
European respect for commercial "value," though it was often applied in uniquely indigenous ways. As a consequence, by the time Treaty 3 was signed with the Saulteaux
Tribe of Ojibbeways in 1873, a new medal had been created,
which displayed on its obverse side, Queen Victoria, and
on its reverse side an Indian encampment, at sunset, on the

prairie, with an Indian chief in war costume and a British general officer clasping hands; a Tomahawk is "buried" at their feet.

It is a significant design, for it reinforces the fictions which had been used to sustain the policy of dealing with the Indians since the time of Le Sueur. Not only were the Indians at times a threat because of their intermittently warlike moods, but their very way of life—generally nomadic, in large measure communal, engagingly ceremonial, almost without exception insensitive to the European notions of the political and economic importance of property, and entirely lacking in the conventional non-native respect for habits of industry and thrift—constituted a very serious danger to the basic civil and religious, as well as the narrowly social and economic, stabilities which the European newcomers were attempting to establish or sustain. For this reason, the lion and the wolf, as well as the buried tomahawk, were indicative of a genuine concern to sustain the values by which civilization as it was understood to the non-native might survive; and these values were inseparably bound up with the notion that property is defined not only by its use but also and more materially by its ownership, and that such a definition is both a necessary and a sufficient condition for civilized human settlements. Treaties were the most important early instrument of this rigorous logic upon which civilization in the New World was felt to depend, although the United States had ironically backed itself into a corner on this matter by the same year that the new Dominion of Canada embarked on its own series of treaties.

It was during the years leading up to 1830, and the successful attempt by Georgia to remove the Cherokee nation from its lands within the boundary of the state and thereby free the area for settlement (as well as bring it under state jurisdiction), that the two major difficulties about the entire treaty process were given most attention.[8] The first concerned the status of the Indian tribes or nations with whom treaties were effected; and, as we have seen, it was out of

the tangle which surrounded this issue that Chief Justice
Marshall resolved the concept of "domestic dependent nations." The possible conflicts which might arise from an
acceptance of such status, with its corresponding confusion
of civil rights and responsibilities, were implied or explicitly
recognized by a number of individuals at the time and during
the succeeding several decades, but this recognition was by
no means universal. Asher Robbins, the Senator from
Rhode Island, remarked (on April 21, 1830) during a debate
on the Removal Bill that an Indian nation is

> *sui juris;* that is, subject, within itself, to no law but the law of
> its own making: externally it may be subject to another jurisdic-
> tion, and then it is a dependent sovereignty . . .

and he continued that

> as to the civilization of the Indian, that is his own concern in the
> pursuit of happiness; if the want of it is a misfortune, it is his
> misfortune; it neither takes from his rights, nor adds to our own.

But this was simply not true, for by the political orthodoxy
of the time rights and duties were inseparable, and the Indians had entered into the sphere where political orthodoxies prevailed by the act of signing treaties and becoming
involved (or entangled) in their Procrustean implications.
They had, and continue to have, their own equally political
orthodoxies, it is true; but in those areas where relationships between native and non-native elements have been
involved, which increasingly has included all that urgently
matters, the treaties have been taken by the non-native signatories as implying acceptance by the Indians of certain
rights, responsibilities and political prerogatives. The rights
were those of commitment to non-native standards of conduct and accomplishment, and the ultimate though not immediate responsibilities were those of replacing indigenous
political imperatives with those that the non-native world

required. For this was, and continues to be, absolutely necessary, at least for those (and this includes the vast majority) of the native people who can no longer claim that their aboriginal land rights have not been extinguished.

Friends of the Indian still glibly argue for a separation of political structures between native and non-native groups in order to protect the native culture. But such a separation places the native people at the unreliable mercy of those worthy souls who know what is best for them. We have no reason, and the native people certainly have little enough cause, to trust the charity of each new generation of enthusiasts. That the native people did not in general understand this implication, and that the non-natives did not themselves really understand the practical consequences of the rights and duties which they so glibly promulgated, and misused the political prerogatives which they claimed, was the sad and tragic situation.

For the newly United States, in particular, the making of treaties was a rather critical process. As Henry R. Storrs, the Senator from New York, remarked in May of 1830, again in the House debate on the Cherokee removal bill,

> it is well known that the disposition of the treaty-making power was one of the most difficult points to be settled in the Convention of 1787. In Europe, it was in the hands of the sovereign, and was liable to the greatest abuse . . . It was in the view of this evil that, under our Constitution, it was considered unsafe to trust it to the Executive. In Europe it was prerogative; but here it was to be limited by the Constitution, and subjected to the control of the States in the Senate, where their sovereignty was equal.

The practice of treating with the Indians to obtain cessions of land was, then, established very early in relations between the two races, and it involved a second and crucially important aspect of affairs in the New World, one which complicates and often frustrates federal Indian policy in both Canada and the United States to this day. The British crown and (in due course) the federal authorities of the Republic and the Dominion were anxious to preserve their sole pre-emptive rights to the lands which the Indians used and occupied. There is continuing disagreement as to the exact nature of the rights enjoyed by the succession of authorities which claim sovereignty over various parts of the lands of the New World, but it is clear that the British became anxious to clarify matters when they assumed control of the northern part of the continent after their defeat of the French in 1759. The premise upon which early colonial practice had been established was described in 1823 by Chief Justice John Marshall of the United States Supreme Court:

> On the discovery of this immense continent, the great nations of Europe were eager to appropriate to themselves so much of it as they could respectively acquire. Its vast extent offered an ample field to the ambition and enterprise of all; and the character and religion of its inhabitants afforded an apology for considering them as a people over whom the superior genius of Europe might claim an ascendancy. The potentates of the old world found no difficulty in convincing themselves, that they made ample compensation to the inhabitants of the new, by bestowing on them civilization and Christianity, in exchange for unlimited independence. But as they were all in pursuit of nearly the same object, it was necessary, in order to avoid conflicting settlements, and consequent war with each other, to establish a principle, which all should acknowledge as the law by which the right of acquisition, which they all asserted, should be regulated, as between themselves. The principle was, that discovery gave title to the government by whose subjects, or by whose authority, it was made, against all other European governments, which title might be consummated by possession . . .
>
> In the establishment of these relations, the rights of the original inhabitants were, in no instance, entirely disregarded, but were, necessarily, to a considerable extent, impaired. They were admitted to be the rightful occupants of the soil, with a legal as well as just claim to retain possession of it, and to use it accord-

ing to their own discretion; but their rights to complete sovereignty, as independent nations, were necessarily diminished, and their power to dispose of the soil, at their own will, to whomsoever they pleased, was denied by the original fundamental principle, that discovery gave exclusive title to those who made it.

While the different nations of Europe respected the right of the natives, as occupants, they asserted the ultimate dominion to be in themselves; and claimed and exercised, as a consequence of this ultimate dominion, a power to grant the soil, while yet in possession of the natives. These grants have been understood by all, to convey a title to the grantees, subject only to the Indian right of occupancy. The history of America, from its discovery to the present day, proves, we think, the universal recognition of these principles.[9]

Marshall's opinion is credited with establishing, "for all time," the character of the Indian title.[10] This is nonsense, both because no decisions of the U.S. Supreme Court are necessarily sacrosanct in this way; and more significantly because Marshall was, despite his best intentions and fine sensitivity, unable to achieve the clear definition he desired, however much he succeeded in identifying the basis of a practical policy. The reasons for this are obvious enough in his description, as he outlines the complicated motives behind the various relationships which developed between the European and the Indian nations. Self-interest was the paramount consideration; and whatever the particular situation, each sovereign authority was anxious above all else to preserve its freedom to exercise its rights and thereby to confirm its sovereignty. This, it was felt, would provide a sufficient basis for the maintaining of peaceable, or at the very least orderly, relations with its indigenous inhabitants.

Much later, in the early part of the twentieth century, the Canadian government would assert its sovereignty in the Arctic along much the same basic lines, and for many of the same basic reasons, though the criteria of civilization and of orderly relations had changed somewhat: instead of the cul-

tivation of the land, which was impossible in any case, the
government sought to ensure that the vast domain would fit
into a more contemporary pattern of civil orthodoxy, and
provided a police force and social assistance checks.[11] It is
worth noting that many of the most recent and dramatic
exercises of the sort have involved the aboriginal people of
the north and have exposed the kinds of apparently intractable situations which are typical in the long history of native
affairs. Although it is no longer widely held, as it was in
Shakespeare's day, that from the New World come natives
"whose heads do fall beneath their shoulders," a host of
other irrational prejudices and ethnocentric expectations
cooperate to ossify relations between native and non-native.
From the New World Bantustans of the Arctic,[12] to the
suburban idiocies of the newly integrated welfare communities of the north such as Frobisher Bay, a wide range of
conditions reflects the equally wide range of sins of omis-
sion and of commission that is the sorry result of over three
hundred years of development in North America. The subtle seductions of adversary and negotiated "settlements" of
disputes, defined by such inventions as wars and dictated
treaties (both of which have appeals to native as well as
non-native traditions and sensibilities), are as apparent in
the recent legal and confrontation strategies emerging in the
North of Canada as they are in the neat solutions of the
Alaska Native Claims Settlement Act. There is no necessary reason to scorn those "solutions," but one should be
careful to recognize precisely which problem it is that they
resolve.

The context within which Imperial policy operated during
the years leading up to the union of the rebellious American
colonies provides a convenient model and must at some
time be understood because the exercise of sovereign prerogatives of various kinds figures first and very largely in
the scheme; and the basis of future practice was laid at that
time. And the chief architect of this policy, Sir William
Johnson, was conveniently explicit in defining the situation.

Johnson had been active in dealing with the Indians since 1744, when he was appointed an Indian agent (one of thirty in New York); and in 1746 he had appeared at a meeting held in Albany between Governor George Clinton and the Six Nations and the River Indians. (The Tuscaroras had joined the five nations [Onondaga, Cayuga, Mohawk, Oneida, Seneca] of the confederate League in 1715 as a lesser partner. Their influence, both civil and military, was immense and their allegiance earnestly sought.)[13] Johnson represented the colony of New York as a commissioner for stores and provisions; and, always anxious (as Cadwaller Colden said of him) to comply with the humors of the Indians in his dress and conversation with them, he appeared dressed and painted as a Mohawk warrior. His mission was to recruit warriors to fight the French in King George's War, which was then in progress; and he was so obviously adept that he took over the management of Indian affairs from the group of locally elected Albany commissioners who had since the days of Robert Livingstone (appointed town clerk of Albany and secretary of Indian affairs in 1675) been primarily responsible for some of the most blatantly fraudulent acquisitions of land in the history of colonial days. Their actions, and obvious contempt for the rights of the Indians, as well as their disregard for the prerogative which the Crown claimed over all matters concerning the acquiring of Indian land, were an example of the kind of conflict between local jurisdictions and the central authority which led to the growth of revolutionary sentiments and to the later conflict between the Congress of the United States and the individual states themselves about jurisdiction over Indian lands.

The maintenance of peace, and the furthering of orderly settlement and trade, were of paramount concern to the central authority; so also were they to the local interests, but the sense of appropriate means to those desirable ends differed, in some cases drastically. In times of war and threat of Indian aggression, mutual interest prevailed. For example, during the years (1744–1748) of King George's War, the powerful Dutch (Albany) faction of the New York Assembly, though in fairly vocal opposition to Clinton and Johnson, cooperated with them. In 1748, however, they refused to grant a peacetime allowance (which was required for the very necessary purchase of presents for the Indians) to Johnson and he was forced to resign, leaving authority over Indian affairs to the Albany merchants. By 1753, however, the Albany commissioners had sufficiently offended the Indians of the Six Nations that Kendrick, one of the nine Mohawk sachems—there were fifty altogether in the council of the League—declared to Clinton that the "covenant chain of friendship" was broken and Indian-English accord at an end. The British Lords of Trade became mildly apoplectic (as they tended to become about once in each decade during the mid-eighteenth century) and ordered the new Governor (Sir Danvers Osborne) to attempt to regain the allegiance of the Six Nations.

The result was the Albany Conference of 1754, which was called "to investigate and, if possible, to satisfy the Indians' complaints about fraudulent purchases and grants," as well as their concern over the gross neglect by the Albany commissioners of their general welfare.[14] The Conference has been widely celebrated by some writers on early colonial history, partly because it was there that Benjamin Franklin first espoused the idea of a strong federal control over Indian affairs which he and James Wilson were to support so energetically during the American constitutional discussions later in the century. Of course, this concept was part of a more general plan, which was also drawn up at Albany by Franklin, for a confederation of the American colonies; and it is generally held that the model of the great Iroquois (Six Nations) confederacy was a significant influence on both the Albany Plan and the later Articles of Confederation.[15] But so far as the Indians were concerned it was a rather empty business, presided over (after the sudden death of Osborne) by Lieutenant-Governor (later Chief Justice of New York) James De Lancey, who had earlier been identified by Clinton as the head of the Albany faction which was acting in opposition to the British home government and making "encroachments upon the rights and prerogatives of the Crown" by dealing themselves in Indian land. The anxiety of the Indians was simply expressed by a Mohawk spokesman:

> We told you a little while ago that we had an uneasiness on our minds, and we shall now tell you what it is; it is concerning our land.[16]

The response of the Albany Conference was to state, in well-intentioned platitudes, that all future purchases of land would be invalid unless made "by the Government where such Lands lye, and from the Indians in a Body in their public Councils"; and that complaints of past injustices or fraudulent purchases would be investigated. In addition, there was a provision that the lands acquired would have to be improved within a reasonable length of time, thereby tacitly advancing that eighteenth-century argument that would be put to relentless use in the nineteenth—that the Indians did not cultivate, and therefore did not either profitably use or reasonably need, the land which they occupied, and that the land should consequently be turned over to those who knew what land was for.

And what precisely was land for? For both the settler and the statesman of the eighteenth century, it was intimately associated with the importance of private property and was a fundamental *political,* as well as economic, element. By the conservative political tradition which was one of the most significant legacies of British thought to affect the development of North America, the importance of private property was that it ensured the individual with rights vis-à-vis the state and ensured the state of a commitment to its values and institutions. The political logic which sustained this position also insisted that such rights were consubstantial with certain duties, duties that flowed from membership in a civil society. In this vein, Samuel Taylor Coleridge wrote, addressing the subject of Sir Robert Peel's Bill (1818), that

> between the acknowledged truth that in all countries both governments and subjects have duties—duties both to themselves and to each other . . . between this truism and the Jacobinical doctrine of the universal inalienable right of all the inhabitants of every country to the exercise of their inherent sovereignty, there is no middle step, no middle meaning.

It is an extreme description, but by the time it was written the confusions surrounding the concepts of rights and duties, and their relationship both to natural and to civilized existence, were formidable, and nowhere more (or more dangerously) so than in the new states and old colonies of North America, and especially with respect to relations between its aboriginal and its European population, which each claimed a different kind of political sovereignty. Land and private property were at the center of this confusion, which was further complicated by (usually non-native) political conflicts varying from petty local disputes to the kind of major disagreements that led to the Revolutionary War. And attitudes towards the Indians were drastically, even if understandably, unstable at this time. On the one hand, George Washington (heavily influenced by General Philip Schuyler, who came from a long line of Albany settlers and military men, and who could therefore boast that he knew in his bones how to deal with Indians) remarked in 1783 that

> the gradual extension of our Settlements will as certainly cause the Savage as the Wolf to retire; both being beasts of prey tho' they differ in shape. In a word there is nothing to be obtained by an Indian War but the Soil they live on and this can be had by purchase at less expense.[17]

On the other hand, in a quite different frame of reference, Thomas Jefferson commented in his Second Inaugural Address of 1805 that the Indians were "endowed with the faculties and rights of men."[18]

In such a context, it was difficult to determine exactly what constituted the inherent sovereignty of the Indian nations and what were their rights and duties with respect to the government of which they were loath to call themselves subjects. Questions, and "middle meanings," of just the sort that Coleridge's remark raises were becoming rather awkwardly evident in this time; and the concept of tribal sovereignty with which the new Union operated both reinforced and contradicted the principles which the American states had accepted and were hoping to celebrate. In addition, what an English radical of the same generation as the English conservative Coleridge called "the [Government's] one great duty of protecting the property of individuals"[19] was not being effectively performed for the Indians; and both theoretically and practically this was a very serious, though hardly a simple, neglect. For one thing, it did have a distracting influence upon the native perception of rights and duties.

And yet in the final analysis eighteenth-century Indian policy was, in the main and in practice, a fairly singleminded business, informed by the need to maintain the peace and security with the Indians which was necessary for the proper establishing of social and economic structures and for an appropriate civil and religious ordering of affairs. Washington's comment indicates this in cynical terms; and Sir William Johnson's correspondence is filled with his continuous insistence upon this need, conveyed in wonderfully British tones.

Now as the Indians who possess these countries are by numbers considerable, by inclination warlike, and by disposition covetous (which last has been increased from the customs in which the French have bred them), I find on all hands that they will never be content without possessing the frontier, unless we settle limits with them, and make it worth their while, and without which should they make peace tomorrow they would break the same the first opportunity . . . I know that many mistakes arise here from erroneous accounts formerly made of Indians; they have been represented as calling themselves subjects, although the very word would have startled them, had it been ever pronounced by any interpreter. They desire to be considered as Allies and Friends, and such we may make them at a reasonable expense and thereby occupy our outposts, and carry on a trade in safety, until in a few years we shall become so formidable throughout the country as to be able to protect ourselves and abate of that charge; but until such measures be adopted, I am well convinced, there can be no reliance on a peace with them, and that as interest is the grand tie which will bind them to us, so their desire of plunder will induce them to commit hostilities whenever we neglect them.[20]

In 1755, Johnson was appointed superintendent for Indian affairs for a newly organized Northern department; a Southern department superintendent, Edmond Atkin, was appointed a year later and replaced in 1762 by the formidable John Stuart.[21] These superintendents had responsibility for all political relations between the British and the Indians, which mainly concerned land and the administration of suitable rewards, presents and guarantees of mutual interest. Certain clear principles guided the activities of Johnson, in particular, as he illustrates in a letter written in 1765 about the disputed Philipse patent;

I have laid it down as an invariable rule, from which I never did, nor ever shall deviate, that wherever a Title is set up by any Tribe of Indians of little consequence or importance to his Majestys Interest, and who may be considered as long domesticated, that such Claim unless apparently clear, had better remain unsupported than that Several old Titles of his Majestys Subjects should thereby become disturbed—and on the contrary, Wherever I found a Just complaint made by a People either by themselves or Connections capable of resenting and who I knew would resent a neglect, I Judged it my Duty to support the same, altho it should disturb the property of any Man whatsoever.[22]

Of course, it is obvious that these guiding principles were political in a very basic sense, for they were intended to reinforce the structures of civil responsibility and interest upon which British and now North American society were established. From Johnson's point of view, there were *only* political considerations, since these were taken to include the social, economic and legal prerogatives which were later atomized by the well-intentioned theorists of the late eighteenth and nineteenth centuries. The chief concern in Johnson's time was, quite simply, the maintaining of a stable polity; and to further this end the Lords of Trade attempted to establish coherent guidelines by which land and trade matters—the only matters which were really significant—should be conducted. In 1761, they were instrumental in having a Royal proclamation sent to the governors of New York, Nova Scotia, New Hampshire, Virginia, North Carolina, South Carolina and Georgia. In due course, and under urgent circumstances, these instructions were codified in the Proclamation of 1763, which formed the basis of the treaty-making practices of the sovereign authority at whose pleasure the native people found their circumstances ordered, and which clearly enunciated the principles of "interest" behind these ambivalent practices.

CHAPTER TEN

Property,
Rights and Liberty

For a long time, these principles of interest went unquestioned, for there were more than enough political questions to occupy the time and the energy of those who were in authority or wished to be. But by the 1850s, many of those in the United States who were involved in relations with the native people had serious misgivings about the basic elements of the treaty-making process, misgivings which had been growing since the 1820s, when the administration of Indian affairs had taken on something of a life of its own. Henry B. Whipple, for example, who was later such a powerful force in the furthering of a new "peace" policy after the Civil War, was strongly advocating the abolition of the policy of treating with the various Indian tribes as if they were semi-independent nations, and instead proposed that the country essentially make a virtue of necessity and accept the Indians as "wards" of the nation. This policy was also proposed by a number of influential writers around the middle of the nineteenth century, including G. W. Manypenny, a former United States Commissioner of Indian Affairs, in his book *Our Indian Wards* (1880). Basically, the tide was turning against the implications of separate status for the Indian tribes that the treaties sustained; and the advocates of "treating the Indian as an individual—like the white man"[1] were about to have their devastating innings. But there was another, even more compelling consideration.

The Senate Judiciary Committee had reported in 1870 that "an act of Congress which should assume to treat members of a tribe as subject to the municipal jurisdiction of the United States would be unconstitutional and void." This, to put it baldly, was rather startling; and in addition, the Senate (whose business it was to ratify the treaties) was felt by the House of Representatives (who had to vote appropriations if the provisions of and the compensations provided by the treaties were to be honored) to be getting rather out of hand; and appropriations were not always forthcoming. The consequence of all of this was an amendment to the Indian Appropriation Act, passed by Congress on March 3, 1871, which provided that "hereafter no Indian nation or tribe within the territory of the United States shall be acknowledged or recognized as an independent nation, tribe, or power with whom the United States may contract by treaty." The policy continued to be the establishing (if necessary, by conquest) or the maintaining of peaceable relations with the Indians and the furthering of their progress in the arts of civilization. The practices changed significantly, however, and the change concerned the attitude toward Indian land. For while Canada proceeded to develop its own version of the practice of establishing separate "homelands" for the native people which had been first proposed in an authoritative and explicit way by the Proclamation of 1763, the United States was abandoning this practice in favor of attempting to force the Indians to an understanding of the political and economic importance of private property by allotting their land in severalty rather than to the tribe as a whole. To understand this shift, however, we must first understand the basis of the separatist, basically "apartheid," practice which developed from the provisions of the Royal Proclamation.

Now the Proclamation of 1763 was not a treaty in any sense, but it did attempt to establish a coherent policy which would determine the future course of relations between native and non-native inhabitants of North America and which would further the advance of civilized life there. It was put together quickly, but had been stewing for some time. There were two major concerns: to establish *and maintain* peace with, and eventually to civilize, the Indians; and to provide for orderly settlement and the development of such trade in the new colonies as would benefit Britain. The main feature of this policy was to promote the idea of a boundary line between the lands of the Indians and those of the whites, a move which had been recommended for some years by Johnson, out of concern for wise settlement practice and the maintenance of peaceful relations; by his lieutenant, George Croghan, who urged the fixing of "a natural Boundary between them and us" for military reasons; and by his secretary, Peter Wraxall, out of a humane and practical concern for the Indians and their livelihood. In addition, it was recommended in several reports which the Lords of Trade had at hand, including one probably written by Lord Egremont, Secretary of State for the Southern Department, and entitled "Hints relating to the Division and Government of the Conquered and Newly Acquired Countries in America," which suggested that

> it might also be necessary to fix upon some Line for a Western Boundary to our ancient provinces, beyond which our People should not at present be permitted to settle, hence as their Numbers increased, they would emigrate to Nova Scotia, or to the provinces on the Southern Frontier, where they would be usefull to their Mother Country, instead of planting themselves in the Heart of America, out of the reach of Government, and where, from the difficulty of procuring European Commodities, they would be compelled to commence Manufacturs to the infinite prejudice of Britain.[2]

Here, in its crudest form, was the rationale for an economic, social and political structure which established the pattern for many of the most significant developments in the New World, a pattern which distinguished in power as well as place between the metropolis and the hinterland. This distinction has perhaps determined the course of social and economic development in Canada more completely than in the United States and has certainly been of immense influence in providing a peg for major economic historians such as Harold Innis and Donald Creighton.[3] Initially, of course, as in 1763, the relationship was between the Imperial power and the colony; but it is fairly easy to discover an imperialistic pattern in later developments after the British Imperial authority had vanished from the scene, especially with the provisions of the Indian Trade and Intercourse acts which were promulgated in the United States between 1790 and 1834; and with the strong central administration of both trade (through the virtually autonomous Hudson's Bay Company) and native affairs in Canada which led to the troubles in Manitoba during the several decades following Confederation.[4] In fact, there were specific attempts made by the Lords of Trade to centralize North American economic activity at the time of the Royal Proclamation and a plan for centralizing trade was drawn up in 1764. But when it was finally sent, in a desperate gesture, to the Governor Sir Guy Carleton in 1775, it was much too late—the American colonies were about to go their own way and impose their own central administration on their lands.

The administrative problem was quite apparent and it was defined as early as the mid-eighteenth century by the movement West. The intent of the Proclamation was to institute an effective land freeze in the colonies, encouraging what Johnson referred to as "the thick settlement of the frontier," and forcing expansion to take place northward into Quebec rather than westward, while at the same time defining "all the lands and territories lying to the westward of the sources of the rivers which fall into the sea from the West and North-West" as Indian Country. The actual laying out of the line followed the Proclamation by several years, since it needed at least nominal Indian consent. The principle was of a "natural line" determined by the ridge of the Appalachians and the Mississippi, and at the Treaty of Fort Stanwix in 1768 a northern line was established; the southern line was determined shortly after, but was modified a number of times during the following decade.

The Indians were being separated from the European settlers and were assigned homelands upon which they would be free to live according to traditional customs,[5] modified to take into account the fact that their new "home" often bore little relation to the environment which had shaped their culture and habits. They would live in such homelands, according to this scheme, until such time as the civil and religious values and properties of European civilization which were being established in the New World would have had time to effect and change their indigenous values by some sort of beneficent cultural contagion. It was rather naïvely supposed that this moment in time would correspond with pressure for settlement of their lands.

There were also military reasons for the creation of an Indian Country, for it provided a buffer zone between the British colonies of the Atlantic seaboard and French Louisiana. In what is now Canada, and particularly in the province of Quebec, the situation was not so simply ordered, for by the Articles of Capitulation following the fall of New France it had been provided that

> the Savage or Indian allies of his most Christian Majesty, shall be maintained in the lands they inhabit, if they choose to remain there; they shall not be molested on any pretence whatsoever, for having carried arms, and served his most Christian Majesty; they shall have, as well as the French, liberty of religion, and shall keep their missionaries.

Nonetheless, Governor James Murray was given supplementary instructions in 1763 that

> Whereas Our Province of Quebec is in part inhabited and possessed by several Nations and Tribes of Indians, with whom it is both necessary and expedient to cultivate and maintain a

strict Friendship and good Correspondence, so that they may
be induced by Degrees, not only to be good neighbours to our
Subjects, but likewise themselves to become good Subjects to
Us. You are therefore, as soon as you conveniently can, to
appoint a proper Person or Persons to assemble, and treat with
the said Indians, promising and assuring them of Protection and
Friendship on Our Part, and delivering them such Presents, as
shall be sent to you for that purpose.

From the differing conditions in the colonies arose differing practices; and the strict delineation of Indian land that
was possible in what were to become the united American
states was neither possible nor very desirable in the more
northerly areas. For one thing, the American colonies
wanted more control over their own affairs and land for
settlement. The Proclamation attempted to provide both, by
strictly establishing the boundaries and government for the
colonies and by recognizing the native rights to use of their
traditional hunting grounds only "beyond the bounds of the
respective Governments" (comprising the newly formed
provinces of Quebec, East and West Florida, and Gre-
nada). Another, and the crucial, point was that the Proclamation forbade, as Murray was firmly told,

on pain of Our Displeasure, all Our Subjects from making any
Purchase or Settlements whatever, or taking Possession of any
of the lands reserved to the Several Nations of Indians, with
whom We are connected, and who live under Our Protection
without Our special leave for that Purpose first obtained.[6]

This principle was intended to defend both Imperial
sovereignty and Indian usufructuary rights in land,[7] but its
force was considerably impaired by the sheer and insistent
pressure of local interests and frontier settlement. Eventually, the sword of Imperial righteousness was hammered not
into a plowshare but a pen, and the native people slowly lost
their birthright more by the sweep of a hand than by the
force of arms, though the latter continued to be a useful
persuader for many years.

The impact of the decision to set aside an Indian Country did not much affect the northerly areas in what is now Canada, because the land was in general either long settled and alienated from Indian interest, along the river or lake systems, or had been granted to the Hudson's Bay Company; and by the time settlement began to spread to the Northwest the neat lines of the eighteenth century had been smudged and blotted so many times that they were unrecognizable. In what would shortly become the American colonies, where much of the non-native population had congregated, the desire further to consolidate non-native settlements depended upon the assumption that when future needs should arise

> the Indians will ever retreat as our Settlements advance upon them and they will be as ready to sell, as we are to buy; That is the cheapest as well as the least distressing way of dealing with them.

Indeed, the economics of waiting would be argued often in the new nation during the years following the Treaty of Paris, as when Timothy Pickering (later the Secretary of War, with full responsibility for Indian affairs) argued in 1785 against acquiring more land at that time:

> The demand for what we now have would lessen in proportion to the additional acquisitions. The purchase will be as easy made at any future period as at this time. Indians having no ideas of wealth, and their numbers always lessening in the neighbourhood of our Settlements, their claims for compensation will likewise be diminished; and besides that, fewer will remain to be gratified, the game will be greatly reduced, and lands destitute of game will, by hunters, be lightly esteemed.[8]

The combination of this logic, with that of men like John Sevier, the first governor of the state of Tennessee, proved to be devastating so far as Indian rights in land were concerned, especially with the absence of the inefficient righteousness of the British Crown to impede progress.[9] Enunciating the typical opinion of the frontier settler, imbued with a strong sense of the rightness of the movement of which he was a part, Sevier remarked in 1798 that

> by the law of nations, it is agreed that no people shall be entitled to more land than they can cultivate. Of course no people will sit and starve for want of land to work, when a neighbouring nation has much more than they can make use of.[10]

This frontier in the United States, as Frederick Jackson Turner reasonably described it, was not a place, but a changing stage in a process that swept across the country. This has meant that there was a certain rather awesome continuity in the development of affairs between the Indians and the intruding settlers as this process continued its organic development. In Canada, on the other hand, settlement was discontinuous and a series of geographically discrete areas developed. The treaty-making policy, based on the promises of the Royal Proclamation, is the one single and consistent element which binds together much of the history of relations between native and non-native inhabitants of the two countries; but because of the nature of political and national developments it is the more purely administrative practices which defined changing patterns in Canada, and these patterns cannot be easily fitted to any organic model. By the time that the Revolutionary War was seen to be inevitable, this distinction was beginning to emerge and to display its central importance.

In 1775, having discovered that "the Pain of His Majesty's displeasure" was a very inadequate deterrent, the Imperial government sent some explicit instructions to the Governor of the colonies, Sir Guy Carleton, which provided for the strict maintaining of ordered trade and intercourse with the Indians, and which empowered the superintendent and his agents to "transact all affairs relative to the Indians." The Imperial authorities were anxious to diminish so far as possible the contact that the colonists might have and use with the Indians for the purpose of soliciting their support in the coming rebellion, and they were also wanting to take all measures to prevent offenses being given to the Indians, especially with regard to their lands, by anyone associated with the British. The early administration of Indian affairs in the British colonies was ostensibly under civil control but its primary concern was military, under the direction of the northern successor to the Indian Department which had been formed in 1755. But after the Revolutionary War certain limitations became obvious, for the Department lacked the necessary local authority and legislative capability to effect any change in the status or much change in the condition of the Indians under its jurisdiction.

As a consequence, most of the actions taken by the Indian Department under Imperial jurisdiction were narrowly protective and, to a certain extent, patronizingly generous, out of an interest in preserving alliances at almost any cost. Sir William Johnson had described the basis of this practice earlier in a letter to Lord Shelburne written in 1767.

We should employ men acquainted with their manners to put forth measures adapted to win upon their affections, to coincide with their genius and dispositions, to discover all their designs, to prevent frauds and injustice, to redress grievances, to remove their jealousies and apprehensions, whilst by annual or other stated congresses, as practised among themselves, we mutually repeat our engagements, refreshing the memories of those who have no other records to trust to—this would soon produce most salutary effects; their apprehensions removed, their attachment to us would acquire a solidity not to be shaken, whilst time, intercourse with us and instruction in religion and learning would create such a change in their manners and sentiments as the present generation might live to see; together with an end to the expense and attention which are as yet so indispensably necessary to attain these great purposes and to promote the safety, extend the settlements and increase the commerce of this country.[11]

It is a shabby fact that two hundred years later, with the "great purposes" long since attained and the safety, settlement and comerce of the country well ensured, the Canadian government, in its centennial year, was still mumbling about the "expense and attention" which the native people required; and two years later it put together a new policy to relinquish both which displayed about as much understanding of the native people and their situation as one might easily balance on the head of a pin.[12] Treaties were described, predictably enough, as "anomalies"; and the Prime Minister (Trudeau) joined the dancing angels (as well as Andrew Jackson) by suggesting that it was "inconceivable" that there should be treaties between sub-groups in a given society.

The years between 1783 and the treaty negotiated by John Jay in 1794, by which the British agreed to withdraw from their western interests, were troubled ones, and the military interests were understandably predominant. But by 1795 the Lieutenant-Governor of the Province of Upper Canada, John Graves Simcoe, was having great difficulty dealing with the legislative restrictions respecting Indian affairs in his province and flooded the Governor-General, Lord Dorchester, with correspondence overflowing with the political pieties and practical difficulties of the time. His concerns are exemplified by this letter of March 9, 1795:

> The members of the Legislature, therefore, as well as the People of the Province will not see with secret satisfaction and confidence the lives and properties of themselves and of their families at this momentous period, dependent on the discretionary conduct of the Indian Department. The legislature also can alone prevent improper Encroachments being made upon the lands of the Indians. It can alone regulate the Traders and prevent their Vices from being materially injurious to the Welfare of the Province; and it will in all probability exert its authority, as seems most just, to effect these popular objects. The legislature alone, can give due efficiency to those general principles of Policy which his Majesty shall think proper to adopt in

respect to the Indians, and which the Lieutenant Governor or Person administering the Government of Upper Canada, the Confidential Servant of the Crown in the Province, can alone carry into execution with safety, Vigilance, and promptitude.[13]

Simcoe, who had a genuine concern for native affairs, had some success in his endeavors, for the next year the Indian Department was placed under his management, but military priorities continued to prevail. In 1816, in fact, the Secretary of State for the Colonies ordered that not only the priorities but the superintendence of the Indian Department were to be specifically military; and military ranks and uniforms were to be part of Indian administration for the next fifteen years. In 1830, however, the Department was divided into two, representing Upper and Lower Canada (or what are now, roughly speaking, the provinces of Ontario and Quebec) and placed under a civil administration, with the pay for officers no longer coming from the military treasury for the use of Army Extraordinaries, but from the Imperial grant for the Indian department, whence monies for presents had flowed. The argument in favor of the change to a civil administration was simple: under military authority and personnel, the policy of progressive "civilization" of the Indians, which had been an important part of the Royal Proclamation, had not been furthered. Instead, the need to "appease" the Indians and thereby maintain their allegiance, which had been recognized by John Pownall (secretary to the Lords of Trade) in his "Sketch of a Report Concerning the Cessions in Africa and America at the Peace of 1763," and had been implicitly recognized throughout the Proclamation, had become the explicit, and the sole, practice during the succeeding years in both the American and the British colonies. The "protection from vices which were not his own, and instruction in peaceful occupations, foreign to his natural bent [which] were to be substituted for necessary generosity," as D. C. Scott described the policy,[14] had not been effected at all, so that in

1830 an exasperated Sir George Murray could comment in a letter to Sir James Kempt that

> it appears to mc that the course which had hitherto been taken in dealing with these people, has had reference to the advantages which might be derived from their friendship in time of war, rather than to any settled purpose of gradually reclaiming them from a state of barbarism, and of introducing amongst them the industrious and peaceful habits of civilized life.[15]

Pressure to shift direction and to work towards the eventual "civilizing" of the Indian came from various philanthropic organizations, such as the Aborigine Protection Society, which was founded in 1836 in London by politicians and public figures who had been instrumental in forming a select Committee of the British House of Commons in that year to report on the conditions of colonial natives;[16] and from an unlikely source—a report submitted by Inspector General Darling, Superintendent of Indian Affairs, in 1828, in which he "offered a remark" which proved to be distressingly accurate throughout North America, suggesting what

> may perhaps be worthy of consideration, as applicable to all Indian tribes having lands assigned to them for their support, viz. that if by vigilant superintendence and effectual legal protection they are not maintained in the possession of their lands, one of these results must follow, as the consequence of the rapid progress made in the clearing and settling of the forest through which they have been accustomed to hunt.
>
> 1st. They must be entirely maintained and supported by Government.
> 2nd. Or they will starve in the streets of the country towns and villages, if they do not crowd the gaols of the larger towns and cities.
> 3rd. Or they will turn their back with indignation on their father, in whose promises of protection they have with confidence for so many years relied and will

throw themselves, with vengeance in their hearts, into the arms of the Americans, who are ever ready to receive them, and who are now endeavouring to induce the tribes in Upper Canada, with whom they have the readiest intercourse, to accept the lands on the Mississippi.[17]

Accordingly, Darling recommended that the Indian Department should be strengthened to allow the exercise of more "vigour, vigilance and activity" in the prosecution of the end of civilizing the Indian and bringing him into the non-native community. Civil and religious, and anti-American, interests were combined, and the home government was requested by Sir James Kempt in the following year to send out

active and zealous missionaries for the Indians . . . and Wesleyan Missionaries from England to counteract the antipathy to the Established Church, and other objectionable principles which the Methodist Missionaries from the United States are supposed to instil into the minds of their Indian converts.[18]

Affairs in Canada during these years were not very entertaining, yet in many ways they provide an instructive contrast to the equally unstable situation and the equally erratic course of development in the United States. Basically, the new Union was more concerned to deal with the existing situation than to tackle new problems, of which they already had more than enough. After the Treaty of Paris in 1783, and in the first flush of revolutionary righteousness, the American authorities dealt with the Indians who had remained or turned loyal to the British as conquered peoples; and the treaties at Fort Stanwix (1784), Fort McIntosh (1784-1785) and at the mouth of the Great Miami on the Ohio River (1786) were rather wretched affairs, in which the federal commissions took obvious pleasure in reminding the Indians at every opportunity that you are mistaken in supposing that having been excluded from the United States and the Kingdom of Great Britain, you are become a free and independent nation, and may make what terms you please. It is not so. You are a subdued people; you have been overcome in war which you entered into with us, not only without provocation, but in violation of most sacred obligations.[19]

Of course, there were compelling reasons for seeking to expedite the transfer of Indian land as quickly, and with as little cost, as possible. The American government needed to have land to give to its soldiers, to accomodate the increase in population, and to provide collateral for the mounting public debt. Asserting the right of conquest, however, proved to be somewhat tactless, for it encouraged a militant defense by the Indians of their rights. So the Americans changed their policy, on the strenuous advice of Secretary of War Knox,[20] to establish (by the treaties of 1789 signed with the Six Nations and the Northwest Indians at Fort Harmon) the principle of purchase of land; and the lands previously ceded at Forts Stanwix and McIntosh were paid for. It was a principle which was consistent with British colonial practice and therefore taken by Knox to be in tune with the traditional modes and customs of the Indians. For it was becoming obvious that the British manner of establishing relations and dealing with the Indians was, for better or worse, the norm; and the Americans tacitly acknowledged this in their famous Northwest Ordinance of 1787, which emphasized that

> the utmost good faith shall always be observed towards the Indians; their lands and property shall never be taken from them without their consent; and in their property, rights, and liberty they never shall be invaded or disturbed, unless in just and lawful wars authorized by Congress; but laws founded in justice and humanity shall, from time to time, be made, for preventing wrongs being done to them, and for preserving peace and friendship with them.

In the same year, at the Constitutional Convention, there was something of a dispute over the powers to be given to Congress to deal with the Indians; and the final phrasing, that "the Congress shall have Power to . . . regulate Commerce with foreign Nations, and among the several States, and with the Indian Tribes . . . ," was one of those ambiguous concessions that provided the basis for future difficulties regarding state and federal rights, as well as the status of the Indian tribes themselves.

It was true that at the very time that the Americans were effectively enshrining British colonial principles with respect to Indian affairs into their constitution, they were in the midst of a dispute (which was eventually settled by the negotiation of John Jay in 1794) with the British over the control of the Indians, as well as of trade, in the Northwest. But this was not so much a dispute over policy as over a contentious practice. The British were refusing to withdraw from the Northwest frontier posts; and when they finally agreed to do so in 1794, they insisted that the Indians be allowed free passage, with peltries and personal possessions, across the border. The status of this privilege continues to be the subject of dispute at the present time and provides a focus for renewed Indian claims, especially among the Six Nations, to a sort of independent sovereignty.[21]

American attitudes were curiously ambivalent with respect to specific features of British Indian policy, but they tended to fashion the British as despicable dealers. More than anyone else, Francis Parkman[22] contributed to establishing this bias as historically orthodox; and he wrote of the British "scorn and neglect" of the Indian, from whom they were divided by "a thorny and impracticable barrier." This was contrasted by Parkman with the attitude of the French, who, being blessed with a "plastic and pliant temper," "embraced and cherished" the Indian. Aside from the rather important fact that there is little justification for this view, it is more to the point that, whatever the Americans might explicitly affirm, they implicitly adopted the British respect for what the Northwest Ordinance referred to as the "property, rights and liberty" of the Indians and Indian land. But it is here that we enter the snake pit.

Indian land, quite simply, was what was defined as such by the sovereign or federal authority. The consent of the Indians for the cession of lands was never very difficult to achieve, since it was the policy of the colonial, and later the American and Canadian, authorities to deal with the Indians in Balkanized tribal groups. In the early years of the Union these groups were endowed, in a kind of legal fiction, with the status of nations. Leaders or chiefs willing to be persuaded of the inevitable were usually forthcoming, and all of the attempts by the Indians to form large confederacies or alliances were discouraged by one means or another; tribal differences were played upon and traditional antipathies usefully exploited. This aspect of the story is an involved one, which has naturally received most attention by the Indians who have felt unfairly dispossessed.[23] In the extreme, "just and lawful wars" were entered into. In 1793, for example, Thomas Jefferson showed this ace, noting that

> our negotiations with the Northwest Indians have completely failed, so that war must settle our difference. We expected nothing else, and had gone into negotiations only to prove to all our citizens that peace was unattainable on terms which any one of them would admit.[24]

The Indian "banditti," as Knox called those who did not come to quick terms, were to be taught a lesson.

Most important is the fact that the very ordinance which might have appeared to secure for the Indians a certain protection of their rights to the use and occupancy of their land also affirmed the determination of the American authorities eventually to settle the area from the Ohio to the Mississippi rivers, an area which had been placed under

federal control on the understanding with the thirteen founding colonies that the land would be settled and formed into
states in due course. Indian land would then be what was
west of the Mississippi, a separate Indian Country consistent with the principle laid down as early as the Royal Proclamation of 1763. Of course, the Proclamation itself had no
legal binding on the new republic, but the principles which it
endorsed were in effect codified by the constitutional
documents which emerged.

An analogy with the African Homelands policy of South
Africa might be useful here, not because the manner of
effecting the end, or even the end itself, are similar, but
because the broad framework is surprisingly congruent.
Under the Bantu Administration Act, the Minister of Bantu
Development may, whenever he deems it expedient in the
public interest, order any tribe, or portion thereof, or any
Bantu community, to move from one place to another
within the Republic. The Minister must consult with the
tribe or community and the Bantu government concerned in
order to procure their consent: if it is not forthcoming, Parliament would have the final say. Until 1973, it was provided in the Act that if a tribe refuses or neglects to withdraw, no removal order shall be of any force or effect until a
resolution approving of the withdrawal has been adopted by
both Houses of Parliament. The Act was amended, however, to insert "unless or" before "until," so that if Parliament has approved a broad plan for consolidation, specific
removal orders will have no appeal to Parliament.[25]

It is no exaggeration to say that a broad consolidation
policy for the Indians was presented in the Royal Proclamation and received tacit approval in the enactments of the
early congresses of the United States and in the statements
of its early Presidents and cabinet members. President
Jackson's removal program was perfectly consistent with
United States policy, despite the cries of those who see
Jackson as a diabolical force in Indian history, for it involved a modified (or "modernized") employment of the
theory of environmentalism that was fast becoming canoni-

cal in Indian affairs, and which was used to argue not only
that all things are molded by their environment, but that this
process can be programmed by a judicious attention to the
functions of evolutionary change.[26] The shift from a
mechanistic process of incorporation of the native population into the non-native, to a teleological commitment to the
eventual product of that process, and the consequent sense
of freedom to order or design the causes which might produce such an effect, was both easy and ultimately inescapable.

For there was no question but that the gradual extension
of settlement would require, and would therefore cause to
be effected, the retirement of Indian use and occupancy of
the land; and that this extension was co-existent (though
few but the foolish would argue that it was co-extensive)
with the spread of civilized habits and an acceptance of the
virtues of industry and thrift. The American policy was only
tactically one of apartheid or separation of the native group
from the white settler. The strategy was for eventual assimilation, through instruction in the proper use of land and in
the methods of non-native economic enterprise. Even the
missionary groups recognized the priority which must be
assigned to the encouraging of the proper civil impulses, so
that the religious ones might germinate. Isolation from the
evils, and controlled instruction in the benefits, of civilization appeared to be the obvious solution.

It was increasingly recognized that the civilizing of the
Indian could not be done quickly or easily—indeed, there
was some argument as to whether it could be done at all.
But most had great faith in man's infinite capacity and
would have agreed in theory (if not always in practice) with
Washington's Secretary of War, Henry Knox, whose attitudes and pronouncements provided much of the basis for
the later policy of Jefferson and his administration.

> To deny that under a course of favourable circumstances, it
> could not be accomplished, is to suppose the human character
> under the influence of such stubborn habits as to be incapable of

melioration or change—a supposition entirely contradicted by the progress of society, from the barbarous ages to its present degree of perfection.[27]

But it was in practice that the thing was to be done, if at all, and there was much confusion as to the best method of teaching the alphabet of civilized truths.

The Northwest Ordinance, with its promise of "utmost good faith" in the protection of the "property, rights and liberty" of the Indians, was a hopelessly inadequate instrument to safeguard native interests in the face of all this confusion, for it was the simple truth that the Indians were not recognized as having any property, rights or liberty except insofar as the property was private, the rights corresponded with duties, and the liberty fitted into some structure of civil responsibilities. It was not that the Ordinance was in itself a piece of treachery, but that the assumptions upon which it was effectively based all but obliterated whatever guarantees it might have claimed to provide. Habits of industry and thrift, which were roughly defined as those habits which distinguished the non-native from the native, were the pre-requisites for the possession of rights and the liberty to enjoy them; and there was little difference in the application of this equation on either side of the border. In both countries there was an obsessive concern to promulgate what were accepted as the cardinal virtues of civilized existence, and very little inclination to respect any rights and liberties which might be imagined to exist outside the axiomatic system by which the energies and priorities of the two nations were sustained. In general, the feeling was that the Indians were "pampered wards" and must be encouraged or forced to exercise their own initiative if they were to enjoy the bountiful blessings of civilization, and to receive the rights and be trusted with the duties upon which civilization was based—if, in other words, they were to be part of the only game that was going. Outside of the structures of civilization—which in practical terms meant outside the res-

ervations, since nomadic life was by definition uncivilized—the Indians were not vested with any (other
than , for a time, hunting) rights. The Canadian government
was undoubtedly more efficient at dealing with the *wrongs*
which were done to and by the Indians, largely owing to
their establishing a police rather than a military presence in
the West. In both countries, however, Indian *rights* were
construed in the most limited terms, because the over-
whelming pressure was to consider rights as those privileges
which the non-native enjoyed, and in the enjoyment of
which the native had therefore to be instructed, even as he
had ironically to be instructed in the "laws of nature" according to which his life was to be ordered. Some of this
instruction was rather dramatically unsuccessful and led to
the wars and rebellions which colored the western plains red
in the latter half of the nineteenth century. Much of it, however, was "accomplished" by *fiat*—specifically, by legislative enactments and bureaucractic definitions which paved
the way along which the inexorable engines of progress
could parade.

CHAPTER ELEVEN

A
Conscious
Design

"If I knew for a certainty that a man was coming to my house with a conscious design of doing me good," remarked Henry David Thoreau with malign superiority, "I should run for my life." For ultimately, as one writer has observed, "the white man's sympathy was more deadly than his animosity. Philanthropy had in mind, the disappearance of an entire race."[1] By the time that Thoreau was writing, however, the Indians had few places left to which they could run and within a very few years would be almost entirely at the mercy of those who knew what was best for them. It was a terrible mercy, which fell like gentle rain from the billowy Indian reform movement which counted among its supporters many of the most powerful Indian administrators in the United States in the years following the Civil War, and which culminated in the three-day Mohonk Conferences organized by Albert H. Smiley in 1883.[2]

The tradition of patronizing philanthropy was already a long one and had as its early spokesman Thomas L. McKenney, the energetic and humane superintendent of Indian trade from 1816 to 1822 and (under Secretary of War John C. Calhoun) first head of the Bureau of Indian Affairs from

1824 to 1832. "Our Indians," wrote McKenney in 1821, "Stand pretty much in the relation to the Government as our children do to us. They are equally dependent, and need, not infrequently, the exercise of parental authority to detach them from those ways which might involve both their peace and their lives."[3] This was the thesis that informed the entire "wardship" theory which had been popularized by G. W. Manypenny and which was so generally accepted in the latter part of the century.

But parents must themselves be disciplined; and it was the abiding concern of such men as Secretary of Interior Carl Schurz to further the civil-service reform that was so necessary if the Indians were to be well served by the government. Yet even this was only an aspect of the problem, for Schurz and so many of his contemporaries represented a devastating liberal attitude which already had the status of holy writ in the temple of progressive concern.

> We must not expect them . . . to evolve out of their own consciousness what is best for their salvation. We must in a great measure do the necessary thinking for them, and then in the most humane way possible induce them to accept our conclusions.[4]

It was a pernicious and contagious response, with both civil and religious application, and it was questioned by very few. One of the doubters was Theodore Bland, a founder (in 1885) of the National Indian Defence Association and editor of *The Council Fire,* a monthly publication which ran for ten years beginning in 1878. Bland argued that the Indians should be allowed to make up their own cultural mind; most of his opponents simply countered that since what was accepted as the environmental and social basis of the native culture had been almost destroyed, or had at least had its independence shattered, the choice had been made for them. And no one, not even Bland, really entertained the possibility that the native culture was inseparable from its religious, as well as its civil processes, so that the idea that there was a choice left for a culture which had already experienced a civil transformation of immense proportions was an absurd fiction, just the sort of thing that sentimentality or perversity encourages.

The stubborn survival of native cultures is problematic, but also admits as many explanations as there are cultures; and it is in any case a difficult matter to discuss coherently in a book which is attempting to cover the entire range of relationships which have existed between native and non-native groups and individuals. Yet there is one point which must be made and it is that the supposed pre-eminent importance of land in the native pattern of existence, while undoubtedly indispensable when hunting was the means of subsistence, may be exaggerated. It may well be that land, to which I along with so many other writers on this subject have attached central significance, is not nearly as central, or even as significant, as has been suggested, and that its unique and traditional use by native groups was more a sufficient and sustaining effect than a necessary and controlling cause of their cultural distinctiveness. For it is true that native cultures have not only survived, but in marvellously Faulknerian ways prevailed, in situations which are so discontinuous with their traditional association with the land as almost to defy any logic, whether anthropological, sociological or psychological, that we have at present to structure our thinking. It is perhaps worth contemplating the limitations of our disciplines and methodologies and the inappropriateness of some of the definitions and distinctions which we bring to bear on the matter. For the process that we are dealing with is one in which both native and non-native are intimately involved, as D'Arcy Thompson said of differing explanations of biological process, "like warp and woof, and in their union is rooted the very nature of totality."

The litany sung by Indian spokesmen is of a familiar enough design, from the speech by the Mingo Chief Logan, given in 1774 and ending "Who is there to mourn for

Logan?—Not one" to the famous surrender speech of the Nez Percé Chief Joseph in 1879 with its poignant conclusion, "From where the sun now stands, I will fight no more forever."[5] Whether one lamented over the past glories, or the past innocence, of the Indians, there was agreement that a change had come upon them, and writers groped to find suitable ways of expressing this transition. Some, like the writer for the *Cheyenne Daily Leader* in 1870, foresaw the imminent extermination of the Indian:

> The same inscrutable Arbiter that decreed the downfall of Rome, has pronounced the doom of extinction upon the redmen of America. The attempt to defer this result by mawking sentimentalism in favor of savages is unworthy a great people.[6]

Others were more romantically picturesque, especially if they were purporting to present "the Indian side of the trouble—something usually omitted by writers upon the subject of Indian difficulties with the whites":

> There have been able and brave Indians, but gradually their power and influence has waned from the east to the west. In the language of Ossian, 'The chiefs of other days are departed. They have gone without their fame. The people are like the waves of the ocean: like the leaves of woody marven, they pass away in the rustling blast and other leaves lift their green heads on high.'[7]

These green heads rising above the leaves bore the flowers of civilization, according to this scheme. The days of an Edenic past, when

> Free as the day when nature first made man,
> Ere the base laws of servitude began,
> When wild in woods the noble savage ran . . .[8]

these days were gone forever; and although the idea of *once* noble savages was immensely appealing, and used as an argument both for humanitarian treatment of them now, and (more cynically) for a "continued primitivism" which would keep them as useful functionaries in the fur trade, it did not succeed in what Hoxie N. Fairchild has called its "classic function" of exhibiting virtues which raise doubts as to the value of civilization.[9] Or at least, these doubts were not very strong, since the main effect of the fiction of a pure and noble savagery was to provide the debased version, the wretchedly poor, wandering mendicant, as a model of what the white man would become if he did not progress. The Edenic myth was a shaping force in American history perhaps, but the shape it gave to it was almost comically baroque.

For while this myth provided the curiously imaginative "composition of place" which was necessary for the various quasi-mystical revelations which entertained the nineteenth century, it was more significant for what it concealed than what it exposed. And what it concealed was not a pattern of benevolence but a riot of licence, not civil charity and order but an apparent chaos of interdependence and contradiction, which explanations of an organic or natural process of evolutionary development only partly described and could never be trusted to prescribe. Of course, there were those who sought to reconcile the ambivalent tendencies of this novel imaginative structure of innocent (because) natural idleness, in which ironically a sense not of idleness but of energy prevailed. The disturbing conflicts which beset the sensitive or sentimental observer who was schooled in the pieties of the enlightenment were easily fitted into this scheme; and if one happened as well to be an enthusiast, such as Benjamin Franklin, one was quickly caught up in a tense and often quiet dramatic play of opposing forces. The compelling attractions of the "unshackled life" in which man's "innate capacities of soul [are] imaged"[10] were perceived not only within but by means of a pattern of understanding in which balance, order and expectation were cleverly confused, yet for which they provided the informing conditions. Everywhere, in all experiences and enterprises, the tensions between energy and design become obvious; and nowhere is this more obvious or more grotesque than in the picture which emerges of the advance of "civilization" across the American frontier. That this picture differed in Canada is owing not so much to the fact that the non-native population was any less nervous about the uncertain energies which native life and traditions embodied, and which found an answering voice within their own imaginative traditions (though the American non-native literary heritage was much more fitted to reinforce this nervousness),[11] nor that there was any less greed or stupidity, but that the mannerist contortions of the American frontier history were sustained by the stricter sense of national and individual purpose and design within which the energies had to be contained. These designs were mainly civil, though the religious ones have received most attention; and they were, ironically enough, the product of an attempt to avoid the hazards of authoritarian restriction. But they became, ironically, more limiting and rigid than that which they sought to control; and the catatonic mannerist[12] poses which were struck in the face, for example, of cultural pluralism, or differing economies, or alternate value systems, or conflicts between non-native civil and religious and military orderings, would have been comical had the consequences not been so serious.

The general policy, in both Canada and the United States, was one of enforced change for the native people, a change which would be discontinuous with native values and beliefs but continuous with the civil and religious progress which was earnestly felt to be indispensable for eventual native assimilation to the social and economic standards of non-native society, of education in habits of industry and thrift and individual responsibility. But the relationship between means and ends which was perceived in the two countries was very different, as we have seen, and reflected the quite distinct political values which prevailed and of which the non-native citizens of both countries became acutely aware in the latter part of the nineteenth century at a time of acute national self-consciousness.

The Canadian government had, in enacting the legislation which we have previously discussed, thrown a very large spanner into the machinery of native progress towards assimilation, at the very time that the Americans were earnestly pursuing their policies of integration or extermination and were engaged in a grotesque reinterpretation of the function of majority and minority elements in their society. Yet the Canadians had their own role to play in this particular drama, for they had effectively excluded the half-breeds or Métis from the special status accorded to Indians, and had thereby put them in an especially invidious position in the society of which they were an inevitable part.

Initially, the presence of the Métis was most conspicuous in Manitoba, where they constituted a unique and readily identifiable segment of the population. They were the descendants of alliances (sometimes invalid, usually common law, occasionally orthodox marriages) between the Indians (generally women) and the early explorers, traders and settlers. Many of the earliest of these latter were of French descent; and the Métis in Manitoba had to a great extent been brought within the fold of the Catholic church, which tended to have a monopoly on the ministering to the spiritual needs of the French Canadian population. This was important insofar as the conflicts which developed after Manitoba joined the Confederation were in part related to religious distrust between Catholic and Protestant, inflamed by Fenian and Orange agitation.

But the Métis people of Manitoba had gained wide fame and respect for their own unique qualities and way of life, though many tended to see their sterling attributes in the light of particular racial as well as cultural prejudices or preoccupations. For example, Alexander Ramsay, the superintendent of Indian Affairs in Minnesota at the time of the transfer of the United States Indian Department from military to civil authority, wrote in the course of an extensive report on the tribes of the West (submitted from St. Paul, in 1849) a glowing tribute to the half-breeds of Red River, "the Métis of the North."

> They are large, strong, courageous, and inured to hardships, possessing much native intelligence, and only need to be emancipated from the monopolizing rule of the Hudson's Bay Company to attain the best degree of social and intellectual refinement . . . a superior race who, partaking largely of the Anglo-Saxon blood, are marked by many of its energetic and better characteristics.[13]

Ramsay's criteria were basically those of the fur trade; and while his words are certainly enthusiastic, they exhibit no sense of the attachment to land which would prove the partial salvation of many of the Indian tribes of the plains, and the absence of which would have devastating consequences for the Métis. The significance of the Hudson's Bay Company at the time Ramsay wrote was immense. Ever since the forming of the union of American states, the sometime presence and the constant activity of the British traders, and in particular the Hudson's Bay Company after it merged with the Northwest Company, frustrated the economic, and to some extent the social, aspirations of Americans. The evil consequences of frontier activity, including the encouraging of native debauchery—the word originally meant a seduction from an allegiance—were often blamed on the traders of the Hudson's Bay Company; and men like Alexander Ramsay did not hesitate to condemn in a manner that brings to some sort of focus the peculiar situation in the area from St. Paul to Winnipeg in the mid-nineteenth century.

> It is inexplicable to me that the British Government, which parades its morality and stretches its pretensions of benevolence all over the world, should countenance its agents of the Hudson's Bay Company in poisoning the Indian race for the purpose of trade, tempting even our Indians to resort to their

factories and exchange their furs for ardent spirits, and sending also their agents within our territory to induce the Indian to sell his wild rice and winter's food for their cursed fire-water . . . If the British Government much longer permits this species of demoralizing trade, so destructive to the Indian race, national hypocrisy will cease to be without a synonym.

By 1850, the border was just becoming a feature of the prairie landscape. Within twenty years, the new nation of Canada would have come into existence, the Hudson's Bay Company would have sold their vast land holdings in the Northwest to the Canadian government, and the former frontier hinterland of the Red River lands would have developed its own metropolitan structures with which to exercise Imperial control over the new frontiers to the West. The crucial importance of land, especially land in proximity to the traditional (river) and the new and coming (railway) transportation routes, was becoming obvious. There was a Métis rebellion in Manitoba in 1869, which was in part a response to a desperate concern on the part of the half-breed population over their land rights. In the rush to put things in order, the Canadian parliament created the distinctions between Indian groups, according both to the racial characteristics and to the mode of existence, that we have examined. The choice which was given to the half-breeds was awkward: if they "took treaty," they opted for a sedentary existence. If, on the other hand, they "took scrip," accepting payment in compensation for their surrender of their interest, they opted for private rather than inalienable reserved property. Since most of them immediately traded their scrip for money or liquor, this choice effectively meant a continued nomadic life until their fortune finally ran out with the spread of settlement, the demise of the great buffalo herds, the absence of any demand for their skills as guides and hunters, the epidemic economic prerogatives based on the possession of private property, and the assumption that all land was potentially marketable under this scheme save that which had been or would be reserved for Indians. The half-breeds, squatters on what they considered to be their own land, understood but little of the new dispensation. Those still in Manitoba who had not elected to take treaty had given up their rights in land; and by 1876 the government had assumed that they were outside the terms of special federal attention by defining Indian and half-breed status in the new Indian Act to exclude them, though the option was still open to those in the Northwest who had not yet taken scrip to take treaty instead.[14]

It was clear to the half-breeds in the West, if not to the authorities in the East, that the progress of civilization was not just a non-native, but more specifically an Upper Canadian imposition. The Rebellion of 1885, precipitated by the actions of the gifted Métis leader Louis Riel, was the climax of a long period of discontent and an extreme embarrassment for a government that was trying very hard to create an illusion of a peaceful if resolute (and very expensive) expansion of the nation westward to the Pacific. After the event, there was little enough sympathy with the Métis, at least in Ottawa, for in the East they had never been graced with the kind of heroic mantle that frontier spokesmen such as Ramsay had cast upon them. But there was considerable agitation about the state of Indian affairs in the Northwest; and after Riel was safely hanged (on November 15, 1885), the government of Canada was called upon to explain the fact that several "status" Indian tribes had joined in the rebellion. The British North America Act by which the Dominion came into existence had placed "Indians, and lands reserved for Indians," under federal control. The Métis had been consistently ignored and their urgent appeals that their special interests be respected went unheeded in Ottawa. This, quite simply, was used to explain the disaffection towards the Métis not only by the government but by its opponents. As Edward Blake remarked in the House of Commons, reading from a letter written by one of the jurors in the Riel trial,

had the Government done its duty and redressed the grievances of the half-breeds of Saskatchewan . . . there would
never have been a second Riel Rebellion.[15]

But this exposed a more serious matter. Perhaps the
Métis revolt could be explained away, but that left the Indians, such as the bands which were led by Poundmaker
and Big Bear, in support of Riel. These groups were quite
clearly a part of the federal system of native supervision;
they had signed treaties, and there was a separate department to look after them. Somehow, things had obviously
gone very wrong; the specter of such Indian wars as had
spectacularly defined American expansion was a terrifying
one, especially for a government that was seriously short of
funds.

It quickly became apparent in the debates in the House of
Commons during 1886 that the government's practice had
been rather less than benign, for it had attempted to force
the Indians onto their reserves (which had been secured to
them by treaty) by a "policy of starvation," out of frustration and impatience at their stubborn reluctance to embrace
a new social and economic order, and with an earnest conviction that only on the reservation could they be properly
instructed in the appropriate civil and religious ambitions.
In the words of the Canadian Agent-General of Indian Affairs, speaking in 1880,

> it was a dangerous thing to commence the system of feeding the
> Indians. So long as they know they can rely, or believe they can
> rely, on any source whatever for their food they make no effort
> to support themselves. We have to guard against this, and the
> only way to guard against it is by being rigid, even stingy in the
> distribution of food, and require absolute proof of starvation
> before distributing it.[16]

This, of course, was reported in the debates (on April 15,
1886) by an opponent of the government, and a staunch
advocate of improved Indian administration and of Indian

self-sufficiency, Mr. M. C. Cameron of West Huron. But the supporters of the government, in the absence of Sir John A. Macdonald, were scarcely comforting to those who were concerned about the Indians' welfare, or (more usually) about the possibility of an Indian uprising. Sir Hector Langevin immediately rose to remark that

> we do not propose to expend large sums of money to give [the Indians] food from the first day of the year to the last. We must give them enough to keep them alive; but the Indians must, under the regulations that have been sanctioned by Parliament, go to their reservations and cultivate their land. They must provide partially for their wants. And therefore, if, by accident, an Indian should starve, it is not the fault of the Government nor the wish of the Government.

Others who jumped to the defense of the government spoke in similar terms and talked of "giving the Indian sufficient food to keep him exactly in a state in which he is driven from sheer necessity to exert himself." "I think," commented one Mr. O'Brien,

> that in dealing with Indians hereafter, the great trouble will be to feed them just exactly in that proportion which will stimulate them to work, and, at the same time, will be sufficient to keep them from suffering from want of food. I may have expressed myself clumsily, but I think the honourable gentlemen understand the difficulty, and that it is in endeavouring to hit that happy medium that the Indian officials have failed and have not supplied them as far as they ought.

It is worth noting that there was a pamphlet published later in the year, after the long and very specific attack in the House on April 15, 1886, by Mr. M. C. Cameron on the government's Indian policy in the Northwest, by the Department of Indian Affairs. It was entitled, predictably, *The Facts Respecting Indian Administration in the North-West* and had as its motto (inscribed on the title page and obvi-

ously directed at Cameron) a wonderful passage from the
writings of Dugald Stewart:

> Every breach of veracity indicates some latent vice or some
> criminal intention which the individual is ashamed to own.[17]

Yet despite its energetic defense of government policy
(which consisted of the "correction" or "refutation" of
thirty-four "misstatements," an "explanation" of twenty-
six "inaccuracies," and several general comments), the
tract does not counter, or indeed even attempt to counter,
the charge that the government was attempting to force the
Indians onto reserves by a policy that was both inhumane
and (more importantly, in the minds of some, given the
recent uprising and the reports of Indian troubles in the
United States) that was foolish and impolitic, since it drove
the Indians to desperate acts.

It was not that the Canadian government did not, in the
main, honor the provisions of the treaties which had recently been signed. Although there certainly were inexcus-
able failings in this regard, little that was of great consequence could be laid at the door of the government here except possibly that the provisions themselves were such as
only the most thrifty and penurious of commissioners could
have drawn up. It was rather that the government was
keeping too much to the letter, which was specific and certain, and ignoring the spirit of the agreement, which was
that the government would help the Indian through a difficult and very uncertain process of change. The ambivalence of government policy is perhaps most strikingly apparent in a general remark by D. C. Scott, at that time
the senior civil administrator of Indian Affairs in Canada,
in 1914. Scott was a most sensitive and imaginative man, a
poet of distinction, and an administrator of long experience. His writings on Indian Affairs in Canada are among
the most important, for they are marked by a clarity and
an honesty which is distressingly unusual in this area. But
commenting on the treaties, Scott is oddly ambiguous:

As may be surmised from the record of past Indian administration, the government was always anxious to fulfil the obligations which were laid upon it by these treaties. In every point, and adhering closely to the letter of the compact, the government has discharged to the present every promise which was made to the Indians. It has discharged them in a spirit of generosity, rather with reference to the policy of advancement which was long ago inaugurated in Upper Canada than in a niggardly spirit as if the treaty stipulations were to be weighed with exactitude.[18]

How a close adherence to the letter of the compact can be effected with a spirit of generosity is puzzling, and it certainly baffled the Indians of the plains, who were in desperate straits by the 1880s. Comments such as that of Sir John A. Macdonald, who was both Prime Minister and Minister of the Interior (and therefore had responsibility for Indian affairs), to a question in the House of Commons in 1885 about the poor quality of food which was given to destitute Indians beyond strict treaty allowance, is illuminating.

The honourable gentleman says there is a fraud on the Indians because the food is imperfect. It cannot be considered a fraud on the Indians because they have no right to that food. They are simply living on the benevolence and charity of the Canadian Parliament, and, as the old adage says, beggars should not be choosers . . . Even in Ontario, the honourable gentleman has seen and heard of contractors sending in inferior articles, which were afterwards condemned. Up there, they are sent to a distant post, they cannot be condemned, they have to be used. I do not think there has been any unwholesome food given, although it has not, perhaps, come up to the standard.[19]

As always in the consideration of Indian affairs, a number of issues converge here: the nature of the treaties and of native administrative priorities and legislative provisions in both Canada and the United States; the attempts to "civilize" the Indian and to accomplish his eventual assimilation into non-native social and political structures; the decline of the traditional means of sustenance (in particular, the buffalo); and the spread of non-native habits (with liquor playing a major role) and disease.

The background was either grim or resolute, depending on one's perspective. In the foreground (since the Indians especially did not really understand either the administrative priorities or the legislative provisions) were the treaties, those monuments of sovereign grace and compulsion, to the premises and assumptions of which too little attention is generally given. For they were, without any exaggeration, the codification of all that was involved in the relations between native and non-native on this continent. Their importance was immense; and an understanding of the reasons, conditions and consequences which sustained the process of which they were the most visible product is absolutely essential to an understanding of white attitudes toward native Americans and of all that followed from those attitudes.

In Canada, the treaties were rather specific instruments and, at least in the government's understanding, did not establish or allow for much independent status on the part of the Indian tribes, although some tribes were clearly unaware of the significance of the treaties and of the cession of lands to the government upon which they were based. There are many indications of this, the most recent being the evidence gathered in 1973 by Mr. Justice Morrow of the Supreme Court of the Northwest Territories in Canada from Indians who were present at, and in one case signed, Treaty No. 11, which was effected in 1921, and was the last treaty entered into by the Canadian government. Another indication, less certain but more picturesque, is to be found in the "winter count" of the Blackfoot leader Bad Head (or Father of Many Children, as he was also known).[20] The winter count was a method of reckoning time by which an outstanding event (usually one affecting the whole tribe but, failing that, a local or personal incident) is recorded to mark each year, the "recording" generally being in the memory of the individual keeping the count, or on a tanned skin or a stick. Bad Head signed the Blackfoot treaty with the American government in 1855, an event which had little effect, but which is recorded in the winter count for the year as "When we were first paid/soldiers." The treaty with the Canadian government which was signed in 1877, and which had a profound effect on the tribe, was *not* recorded, even though Bad Head was an old and influential leader of the tribe at the time; he would probably have been head chief but for his age, and he would certainly have had a part in the discussions which preceded the signing. Yet the entry for 1877 reads "When we had a bad spring," a reference which, however true, was not intended to indicate the treaty.

The year before the 1877 treaty is memorably recorded by Bad Head: "When there were plenty of buffalo." The entry for 1879 tells another story: "When first/no more buffalo"; and by 1880, both stories had ended: "When we all moved camp." When Queen Victoria's son-in-law, the Marquis of Lorne, came west as Governor-General in the following year, the Indians took the opportunity to set their case before him. One of them, Yellow Quilt, was particularly plain spoken:

> I was glad to hear you were coming, I think my women and children will live now. Let us see the kindness you will show us here. I live by the ground here. Our forefathers could see Buffalo and game all round. We used to live at that time. I am asking you and what is it that I ask. I do not understand the Treaty. Now I see what has been done to us. Our property has been taken from us. I cannot live by what I was then told. You do not see horses because I have eaten them. We have also eaten our dogs. That is what your work has done for me. I shall not be able to live by the good words that are told me. You see me naked as I am . . . We think that because this excellency has the power he can do what we ask. The reason is we cannot live by the first Treaty: we shall die off. Provisions are the only thing that will enable us to live long. They cannot hold to the Treaty that was made before.[21]

The general reply, given by the Marquis of Lorne, could easily pass for a present-day reaction against welfare and social-assistance programs.

I have been very glad to hear many of the Chiefs . . . I have
heard very eloquent speeches, I am quite sure that men who
speak so well can work as well as their red brethren in the East,
hands were not given by Manitou to fill pipes only but also to
work. I am sure that red men to the East when they work do
well and do not starve and I have heard that the men who talk
most and ask most do not work.

By the end of the Civil War, the policy in the United
States, which had long been latent, was finally made perfectly explicit: away from separate status and towards assimilation. The reconstruction of the Indian, as well as of
the South, was to be undertaken in earnest. The tensions
were still present, of course, but they were transformed into
evangelical obsession. To this end, the "peace policy" of
President Grant was instituted and its main element was an
expansion of educational facilities provided mainly through
the offices of various religious denominations.[22] It was an
unusual alliance of church and state, or churches and states,
particularly in a country which officially frowned upon such
marriages, however convenient; yet the new power of militant reformism was felt to be the only match, short of the
military, to the crude but surprisingly effective cultural inertia displayed by the Indian tribes. There was also a very
practical side, recognized by a number of zealous educators
such as Captain Richard H. Pratt, a Presbyterian who
started a school at Carlisle, Pennsylvania, in 1879, and who
argued that the educating of the children—and especially
the children of the chiefs and headmen—of defeated Indian
nations (Pratt suggested the Nez Percé as one example)
would "civilize" the children as well as ensure the good
behavior of their elders at home in the West. By 1880, two-
thirds of the children at the Carlisle school were of this sort,
hostages to the fortunes of American civilization.[23]
    In addition, the Americans officially abolished the prac-
tice of dealing with the Indian tribes as semi-autonomous
nations; and they also tried to break up Indian lands and

tribal governing structures in an attempt to force the Indians out of their traditional social, economic and political orders and into ones which fitted more neatly into the non-native patterns. To the Americans, the cause of "Indianness" was tribal allegiance and the effect was limited entitlement to reserve lands. In Canada, on the other hand, the cause was Indian land entitlement and the effect was tribal membership. In the United States, the authorities employed an inverted logic and attempted to act upon what they perceived as the effect, and thereby to subvert the cause. A specific instance of this practice in the United States was the Dawes Act, but in fact the practice had long been developing; and one of its most articulate advocates, George Washington Manypenny, had been allotting lands in severalty as early as 1854, in his role as Commissioner of Indian Affairs.[24] (The Interior Department had taken over control of Indian Affairs from the War Department in 1849; and the 1850's saw the new civil administrators anxiously enunciating the need for new policies, and instituting, often without Congressional authority, new practices, in an effort to discredit the previous military administration.) But the way for the Dawes Land Allotment Act was paved not by such practices, but by another piece of legislation enacted by Congress in 1885, by which seven major crimes were cited as being under the jurisdiction of federal law, whether committed by Indians on or off reserves.[25] Its effect was to replace tribal authority, which had up until that time been credited on reserves, with specifically non-native American codes of conduct. The legislation was challenged, and upheld (in *U.S. v. Kagama* [1886]) and the way was cleared for the legislating of other matters, such as allotment of land, on reserves.

A Court of Indian Offenses was another instrument of progress in this regard, for often its function was to enforce the anti-tribal rulings of the Indian agent. Thus the imposition of non-native patterns of civil order was accelerated, but without a corresponding acceleration of changes in the social patterns of the native group. The allotment scheme, which was intended to break down tribal groups into familial and individual elements, succeeded only in impoverishing the entire group. This, in a sense, was fortunate, because the tribal entity was in general maintained. And the failure of a bad policy, as well as of a good, can be instructive. Once again, a change which was intended to affect an entire group had been attempted by interfering with and influencing individual rather than group patterns of behavior. The old argument that the native individual was defined by his physical and cultural environment was applied to the situation to conclude that a change in the individual's attitude might be effected simply by changing aspects of that environment. The idea of autochthonous cultural development, as old as Joseph de Acosta, was still being abused; and the possibility of allowing native patterns of order and institution to adapt to a new, largely non-native, environment in a process of organic change was not simply unacceptable, it was never entertained. The reason for this was clear: native order was not civil order; and while it was assumed that a continuous process of development would bring the individual native to that higher stage which was enjoyed by the non-native culture, it was never accepted that the native group structures and institutions—in other words, the native cultures—were similarly capable of continuous development. Between native and non-native culture there was a discontinuity which was partly the product of that mannerist, dialectical tension between the seductions of primitivism and the compulsions of progressivism that I discussed earlier; and partly the product of sheer, satisfying ignorance. To change the native, one must replace his cultural institutions.[26] It was as simple as that. As long as the native tribes in the United States had an however arbitrary independent status, the issue of cultural distinctions did not need to be joined. When this fiction was rudely shattered, there was no escaping the matter.

Years later, there would be strong revival of the demand

for a separate status for native tribes. In 1971, Hank Adams, an Assiniboin Sioux who became director of the Survival of American Indians Association (a group formed to fight for treaty-guaranteed fishing rights for several Washington Indian tribes), chaired a committee which drew up a fifteen-point program for a new national Indian policy

> to remove human needs and aspirations of Indian tribes and Indian people from the workings of the general American political system and . . . reinstate a system of bilateral relationships between Indian tribes and the Federal Government.[27]

This program became the basis for the twenty demands presented by the Trail of Broken Treaties in their march to Washington (and takeover of the Bureau of Indian Affairs) in December 1972 in which a reinstitution of a treaty-making relationship between the United States and the "Indian Tribes and Nations" was called for. The original power of Congress (Article I, Section 8 of the Constitution 1787) "to regulate Commerce with foreign Nations, and among the several states, with the Indian tribes" would thereby be re-established and the independent status of the Indian reaffirmed.[28]

CHAPTER TWELVE

Dance Us
Back the
Tribal Morn

Medicine man, relent, restore—
Lie to us—dance us back the tribal morn!

—Hart Crane, from
"The Dance"*

Of the things that have mattered in Indian affairs, money
has certainly been among the most important. In fact, when
one has been through all of the less material instruments of
change (with the possible exception of land), it sometimes
seems as though Andrew Undershaft's religion has prevailed and all we are left with is George Bernard Shaw's
ironic consolation that, after all,

> The universal regard for money *is* the one hopeful fact in our
> civilization, the one sound spot in our social conscience.
> Money is the most important thing in the world. It represents
> health, strength, honour, generosity and beauty as conspicuously
> and undeniably as the want of it represents illness, weakness,
> meanness and ugliness . . . It is only when it is cheapened to

---

The Collected Poems and Selected Letters and Prose of Hart Crane, ed. Waldo
Frank. New York: Liveright, 1933, p. 21.

worthlessness for some and made impossibly dear to others, that it becomes a curse. In short, it is a curse only in such foolish conditions that life itself is a curse. For the two things are inseparable: money is the counter that enables life to be distributed socially: it *is* life as truly as sovereigns and bank notes are money. The first duty of every citizen is to insist on having money on reasonable terms . . .[1]

Deciding on these "reasonable terms" has been a long process, and life for the Indians has, at least insofar as their relationship with the whites is concerned, depended on little else. And their relationship with the white has, in so many ways, defined their life—indeed, has been their life.

From the earliest days, the spending of money on Indians became gradually separated from the notion of providing compensation for the loss of lands and livelihood and became an issue in itself. For Indians and their affairs have been, and continue to be, an expensive undertaking, or else so intimately related to land settlement, resource extraction and other enterprises that they have constituted a component of very real significance in the basic social and economic development of North America. Initially, land was wanted and presents were given; and although such presents appear to us grotesquely out of line with the concessions that were given by the Indians, they were still a considerable expenditure for a hard-pressed new Union, and a considerable nuisance for an Imperial government which was not at all sure why it should be bothered. Or, more exactly, it was fairly sure why, since the humane treatment of colonial natives was part of a package of early nineteenth-century liberal enthusiasms that included prison reform and the abolition of slavery, but not at all sure how or whether the mere distribution of goods and monies was the most suitable method of helping the native people to help themselves.

This question of presents was not a minor one, especially in the years which followed the War of 1812. Both the American and the British governments wished, if possible, to cut back this substantial expense, while the Indians and many of their non-native friends urged that it be continued as a vested right.[2] The practice had been established by the French and indeed was one of the reasons why the French had such apparently congenial relations with the native people. "Meeting the savage half way," for which Parkman praised the French in his book on *The Conspiracy of Pontiac,* was generally assured of success if one happened to take the precaution of meeting him there with a present in one hand and a bottle of whiskey or a gun in the other. As L. O. Saum remarks,

> the French, it is commonly assumed, often defeated their English rivals in their race into the interior because they more readily captured the esteem of the natives. Quite possibly, they captured the esteem of the natives because, at critical junctures, they won the race into the interior . . .[3]

and because they gave generously to the Indians those presents which they knew would please them and assure them of their loyalty and esteem.

In both Canada and the United States, one of the most demanding of tasks which the Superintendent-General or the Commissioner of Indian Affairs had to undertake was to convince Congress or the Imperial (and later the Canadian) government that this large apportionment for gifts was in the best interests of the Union or the Crown. Basically,

> the presents furnished the Indians and every member of his family with a complete suit of clothing. His food consisted of the game which he killed with the gun and ammunition supplied to him by the Government; of the fish which abound in the lakes and rivers, caught with the net and hooks supplied from the same source.[4]

Earlier issues, according to one source,

> consisted of ornaments such as arm-bands, brooches, ear-bobs, gorgets; of articles such as kettles, clasp-knives, looking-

glasses and thimbles; in addition to the more useful merchandise, clothes now unknown, molton, ratleen and caddies; blankets and Irish linen; shoes and ivory box combs; tobacco, ball & gun flints.[5]

Yet no matter how doubtful the merit of continuing such practices, discontinuing them was in some respects a still more dubious option. The cut-backs which were introduced at various times, particularly in the United States, were cause for grave concern. Lewis Cass, for example, who was a man experienced in these matters, remarked in 1814 that

> our trading factories, and our economy in presents have rendered us contemptible to the [Indian]. The Government should never Come into contact with them, but in cases where its Dignity, its strength or its liberality will inspire them with respect or fear.[6]

In Canada in 1830, a year when the Imperial Treasury was not inclined to be generous, the Indian budget was fixed at £20,000, of which over three-quarters (£15,850) was appropriated for presents and the remainder for the pay and pensions of the officers.[7] This was an especially unfortunate year for the administration to be short of funds and to be spending most of those which were available on presents which did not apparently serve a civilizing function. The government was just about to embark upon a program modelled on the experiment performed by the Wesleyan Methodists under the leadership of Peter Jones and his brother with the Mississaga Indians, whereby a very successful Indian community—which is to say, with non-native civil and religious structures—had been established on the Credit River near what is now Toronto. The more ambitious government plan was described by the Governor, Sir James Kempt, as one

> 1. To collect the Indians in considerable numbers, and settle them in villages with a due portion of land for their cultivation and support.

2. To make such provision for their religious improvement, education, and instruction in husbandry as circumstances may from time to time require.
3. To afford them such assistance in building their houses; rations; and in procuring such seed and agricultural implements as may be necessary, committing when practicable a portion of their presents for the latter.[8]

But while the plans were approved in principle, in practice they became impossible to put fully into effect, for there was no money.

It is here that the chief defect of the system of distributing presents is most apparent, for its inflexibility worked against the prosecution of new and possibly imaginitive experiments. Indeed, while the high cost was always criticized by those who urged that the giving of presents be abolished, their main objection, more clearly related to the obvious failure of the entire Indian policy, was that this particular practice

> encouraged their natural indolence and improvidence; kept them a distinct people; fostered their natural pride and consequent aversion to labour; and created an undue feeling of dependence upon the crown. The formalities or festivities which accompanied the distribution tended also to degrade the nations and to keep alive their old customs. The chief superintendent was usually accompanied by a party of visitors, and on these occasions the pride and superstition of the Indians was fostered in direct opposition to the policy of the government.[9]

The practice was, in Canada, effectively abolished by the early 1850s on the strong advice of a commission which reported in 1844-1845. It reappeared as an aspect of treaty provisions, although the gifts of powder, shot and twine to those Indians who wished to hunt were to be supplemented by agricultural implements, seed and cattle to those who would till the soil. It must be added that to call the money and commodities which were given as promised under treaty "gifts" or "presents" is a slight misnomer, since they were in fact given, whether explicitly or not, in exchange for a surrender of land rights. One could, no doubt, go further and claim that since the government had, and the Indians recognized that they had, the power (or "right") to extinguish title without any compensation at all, provided it was done as a specific act and openly (and therefore subject to the censure of those who elected the government, which of course did not in general include the native people), whatever the Indians received came by grace. However, few took this step, largely because the tradition of (often token) compensation was so firmly established.

In the United States, treaties had been for some time the basis of gifts and payments, but since there was in general no coherent program of instruction in the attainments of civilization, many of the presents had the appearance of being little more than baubles given to entertain the indolent savage. Also, there were substantial monies required for "persuasion", especially in the South, where the acquisition of land was often accomplished by greasing the palm of an influential chief. For instance, Doublehead, a chief of the Cherokees, was granted $1,000 by the President one day after the Cherokee cession of land between the Tennessee and Duck Rivers, on January 7, 1806,

> in consideration of his active influence in forwarding the views of Government, in the introduction of the arts of civilization among the Cherokee Nation Indians, and for his friendly disposition towards the United States, and for the purpose of enabling him to extend his useful example among the Red people.[10]

Over and above the obvious abuses of public money and public trust, there *was* cause for alarm. In the first place, the presents that were distributed were not an integral part of any scheme to improve the lot of the Indians or to provide them with a replacement, or the means to create a replacement, for the way of life and the traditions which they were slowly being forced to relinquish. The presents were, or at least became, a haphazard mixture of conscience money and cultural bribery, yet always retained some sense of their previous significance as the token of friendship and mutual self-interest between the two races. The natives needed much more, primarily of protection but also of assistance, but both of these cost money. Coordination of any sort was never the strong suit of the Indian Department, and the situation with respect to financial responsibility which Henry S. Schoolcraft castigated in 1828 might have been as easily applied to the programs and planning of the organization.

> The derangements in the fiscal affairs of the Indian department are in the extreme. One would think that appropriations had been handled with a pitchfork . . . there is a screw loose in the public machinery somewhere.[11]

When President Arthur remarked of Indian affairs in 1881 that

> it has been easier to resort to convenient make-shifts than to grapple with the great permanent problem, and accordingly the easier course has almost invariably been pursued,[12]

he was summarizing 100 years of the history of Indian administration, at the same time as Helen Hunt Jackson was summarizing the "century of dishonour" which that chaotic administration had superintended. In Canada, the same debate was in progress and the same conclusion being reached. Speaking in the House of Commons in 1885, M. C. Cameron noted that

> writers upon the Indian question, and especially writers such as the authoress of 'One hundred years of dishonour', speak of the Indian as easily managed, peacable, quiet, inoffensive, docile, so long as he is fairly and honestly treated; but as faithless, turbulent, and rebellious when he is injured, when he is de-

ceived, when he is wronged, when he is defrauded. In order to retain the confidence of the Indian, in order to educate, to elevate, to civilise and to christianise the Indians, it was of the first consequence that men of character, men of honesty, men of truthfulness, men of high moral standing, should have been selected to preside over and administer Indian affairs in the North-West Territories. I regret to say that, in so far as I have been able to gather the facts, such men have not been selected . . . I say, Sir, that the conduct of the officials of the North-West Territories, more than any thing else, created dissatis-faction and discontent among the Indians; I say that the mis-conduct and the mismanagement of the Administration in connection with the Indian affairs in the North-West Territo-ries, as much as anything else, produced uneasiness, dissat-isfaction and discontent among the Indians, which ultimately broke out into open rebellion.[13]

What he went on to say, though rather incoherently, was that such men of sterling character, could they be found—as they certainly could by a Liberal Government—would be quite clear as to what it was that they were doing and why they were there—would, in short, be in no doubt as to what they were presiding over and administering.

But the men who were there were in doubt, and little wonder, for the same piece of legislation which attempted to define their function, the Indian Act, was also serving to contradict the ultimate purpose of all that was being done in Indian affairs. That purpose was to assimilate the Indian; the Act separated them. Opposing the passage of some amendments to the Act in 1880, William Paterson, the member for the riding of Brant (which contained the most acculturated of the Indian tribes, the Mohawks), argued that

the whole Indian law discourages the assimilation of the whites and the Indians, and the solution of the Indian problem can only be found in wiping out the distinction which exists between the races, in giving the red man all the liberties and rights enjoyed by the white man, and entailing upon him all the responsibilities which attach to those rights & privileges. For those reasons I am opposed to the discussion of this subject at the present time. The Indian question is the question of the country. It means, as we know from the Estimates brought down yearly, the expenditure of millions for the maintenance of the Indians—it means one of the most pressing and vital questions of the hour, and I warn the honourable the First Minister, that legislation in the direction proposed, old-time legislation, simply means that it will entail upon the people, year after year, and for all time to come, the voting annually of hundreds of thousands of dollars to keep the Indians in the low, degraded state in which they are at present. What I advocate is this: That we should have an Indian policy, which will not only tend to relieve us from these heavy burdens, but will give to the Indians more rights than they now possess, and wipe out the race distinctions that now exist. The policy adopted by this Government, whether mistaken or not, has had in view the object that the Indian should not have a wrong done him. We have endeavoured to show ourselves superior to our neighbours in the management of those men.[14]

Paterson spent much of his career hammering away at the ambiguities in and the inefficiencies of the Indian department, and at the burden upon the national treasury as well as the national conscience which the Indian represented. Six years later he was reminding the government once again of their responsibilities, emphasizing that

the people will demand that the money given the Government to be expended in relieving the necessities of these people shall not be used in upholding a horde of officials who are not properly discharging their duties; they will demand that two or three prices shall not be paid for provisions or implements of agriculture; and that the cost of travelling shall not be paid up to an exorbitant sum; and they will require that the whole cost of the machinery will not involve such a charge on the country as to cause the continued existence of a feeling, which has already pervaded to some extent the minds of the people, that the Indian problem is becoming a grave and serious one, and threatens to load us down with a burden too heavy for us to bear. Out of the vast expenditure charged on Indian account, only half a million dollars have gone to supplies for destitute Indians, and that has gone in prices paid for articles such as I have described . . . If the money were properly expended, if some better system were established, if the Government's agents dealt with the Indians honestly, the money spent by the Government and properly put to use would have prevented any such tales of destitution and misery as those we have heard.[15]

One obvious step was to abolish all but the most acutely needed charitable aid, while insisting that such aid as was furnished have a productive multiplier effect; and this was attempted. Writing to one of his agents at Shubenacadie in 1880, L. Vankoughnet, the Deputy Superintendent-General of Indian Affairs, advised that

you should by every means in your power endeavour to persuade the Indians within your district to pursue industrial employment by cultivating the soil, etc. for a living; and no encouragement should be given by you to idleness by gratuitous aid being furnished to able-bodied Indians.[16]

But the line between encouraging idleness and allowing starvation and utter destitution was a fine one. The governments of both countries, sensitive as they were to the liberal enthusiasms of the uninformed and to the dangers of fomenting Indian rebellion, as well as to their international reputations for ordering a humane and just society, tended to err on the side of what was felt to be "generosity," though it was never hard to get some red-neck support for a program of "natural attrition."

Much money was spent, at least by normal administrative standards, but there was and continues to be what one might charitably call a central ambivalence in the character of native administration. It is, sadly and stupidly enough, far from a new tale; in the 1820s Schoolcraft was complaining bitterly that

now the subject [Indian affairs] drags along as an incubus on Congress. Legislation for them is only taken up on a pinch. It is a mere expedient to get along with the subject; it is taken up unwillingly, and dropped in a hurry. Nobody knows really what to do, and those who have more information are deemed to be a little moonstruck.[17]

It would be foolish, of course, to think that the answer is simply to follow the counsel of experts, at least regarding matters of policy, for the scope of the question goes far beyond the purview of simple experience. And since thought is invariably more demanding and more difficult than action, there has been much action but very little thought—indeed, one is tempted to see some of the action as an excuse for thought, and even as a euphemism for theory, whereby "getting things done" becomes a theoretical stance and the means replace the ends.

Nowhere is this confusion more apparent than in one of the thorniest of all problems which have arisen in Indian affairs, that of local government and control (which, along with status and land, effectively defines the subject). The Americans, as we have seen, permitted extensive local autonomy in the initial instance, going as far as to treat the Indian tribes as having quasi-national status. There was some opposition to this strategy from the beginning, but the impulse of the revolutionary independence which had been attained worked powerfully to define individuals and groups as either with or against, either inside or outside. Since the Indian tribes were clearly outside if not always as clearly against the principles and practices upon which the Union was established, it was much easier to treat them as distinct entities, about to be introduced to but not yet enjoying the pleasures and rewards of civilization. The early treaties which were signed with the Indians of the Five Civilized Tribes, under the Continental Congress, forbade whites from settling on Indian lands under threat that "such person shall forfeit the protection of the United States and the [particular tribe] may punish him, or not, as they please"; and this provision was included in the first treaties (in 1790

[Creek] and 1791 [Cherokee]) made after the Constitution. Although fines and imprisonment were specified shortly thereafter (in 1793, under one of the numerous revisions of the Trade and Intercourse Act), the force of the law against encroachment on and alienation of Indian land and property was never effective in the territories under the control of the United States, for the jurisdiction of local judicial authorities, and their influence by local (non-native) political pressure was so strong that the Indians were very much encouraged to think of themselves as beyond the pale of conventional enforcement.

The most celebrated instance which underlined the anomalous character of native civil responsibility came in Georgia, during the 1820s and 1830s. But although the supremacy over state rights of such native jurisdiction as had been guaranteed by treaty was upheld in the courts, Andrew Jackson is reported to have remarked that "[Chief Justice] John Marshall has made his decision; now let him enforce it." He could not, of course, and Jackson's point was proven.

While the idea that the Indian tribes were indeed *sui juris,* or "subject, within themselves, to no law but the law of their own making," was still in a certain though limited sense intact, there were clear indications that this was rather a matter of convenience than a matter of principle. Even so, the principle was to die very hard, along with a number of Indians and whites, as the interpretation of "convenience," and most importantly, whose convenience should predominate, became critical. Even by the end of the century, and even in Canada, where the fiction of the "semi-independence" of Indian tribes had never really been entertained, there was still a basic core of rights which the Indians were denied and duties from which they were exempt. Perhaps the focus of all of these is to be found in the matter of taxation, from which Indians have traditionally been free. Now there are few political instruments of such power and visibility. The dumping of crates of tea into Boston harbor is only one example of the focus unpopular taxation can provide for social and political resentment and the basis it can establish for remarkable solidarity, but it is no exaggeration to see its importance for the Indian people in equally dramatic terms.

The Indian people of both Canada and the United States naturally identify the exemption which they generally enjoy from land and property, as well as from some income and sales, taxes with their special status, and with their sense of having paid their debt to the non-native community through their original surrender of an interest in the land. In addition, their staunch and passionate defense of their rights in this matter is closely related to their unsettling reluctance to involve themselves in and to take advantage of the normal political processes, and the normal pattern of rights and duties, which are available to the population at large. Partly, this is out of a fear of being obliterated by a process which is of awesome cultural, social and economic influence; and partly, it is out of a recognition that this process is in many respects foreign to their indigenous civil and religious values. There is at present a strong sense of this eminently understandable cultural paranoia and an insistence upon the retention of an administrative structure which, however antediluvian, has somehow worked to preserve something of their distinctive identity. The following is taken from a recent announcement by the American Indian Civil Liberties Trust:

> Among the successes to which its subsidies have contributed are the defeat in a statewide referendum of the extension of state jurisdiction by South Dakota over Indian Reservations, the rejection by the U.S. Supreme Court of the state imposition of sales taxes on the Navaho and Popago Reservations . . . and the slowing down of the movement of Government for the termination of federal supervision over Indians.[18]

Indeed, there was more than just a sense of this attitude in the response of frantic betrayal that greeted the Canadian government's 1969 White Paper on Indian Policy, which advocated a gradual relinquishment of federal responsibility for Indians, and a gradual increase in native control of their own resources in line with non-native patterns of private ownership and individual responsibility.

"The vast majority of Indians," suggested one writer,

> still prefer cultural separateness because they have never known anything else, and those who do know something of the white man's world and are willing to undertake the limited experiment of sifting out of their culture those aspects which they can combine with aspects of the alien culture in such a way as to get on working terms with modern life . . . want to remain distinctive . . . But they are ready for functional integration, particularly in any economic sense.[19]

The issue, however, is not so simply handled and it is furthermore basically an issue not so much of economics as of civil jurisdiction and political authority.

At its extreme, the disengagement of the native people from non-native civil structures was clearly a non-native device and varied in effect from the disallowing of native testimony in courts of law to the denial of the franchise. In other instances, however, an even more severe disengagement has resulted from the best of non-native intentions and in particular from the establishing, supporting and central funding of native organizations which are in many cases not of indigenous origin, and which do not conform to any pattern of constituent responsibility and answerability that would be acceptable or even recognizable in the North American non-native *or traditional native* community. The most dramatic examples of this are to be found in the tribal government councils which were uniformly imposed upon the Indians in the United States as a consequence of the Wheeler-Howard Act of 1934. These councils have been given increased power and greatly increased funding in recent years as a result of the enthusiasm of the Nixon administration for native self-determination. The provincial, territorial and national native associations which were dramatically encouraged, and in many cases created, in response to the Canadian government's Indian policy of 1969 are of a somewhat similar character and reflect an eager government rather more than they do a responsive native population, though the latter is certainly developing.

The relationships which exist between the Department or the Bureau of Indian Affairs on the one hand, and the tribal governments and native associations on the other, vary from cooperation and constructive tension to coercion and antagonism. Both the Bureau in the United States, and the Department in Canada, are clientele government organizations. They attempt to provide a wide range of services to their clients, from those of a trustee administrator to those of a technical consultant and financial advisor. In addition, they attempt to make up for the fact that most of the native people function outside the normal economic processes which operate in North America. The conditions, limits and general terms of reference for these services are provided by the British North America Act and the Indian Act in Canada, by the various Acts and statutory regulations enacted in the United States from time to time, by administrative traditions of fairly long standing in both countries, and by responses to needs identified and (ideally) agreed upon by both the government departments and the native people.

Because of this structure, and the administrative context which has been developed to give direction and purpose to it, some fairly clear trends emerge. Most important of these is the implication that the Bureau or the Department is derelict in its duties if it does not respond positively to native requests. Furthermore, it is even more culpably negligent if it fails to defend the concerns and positions of its clients in inter-departmental negotiations, putting forward the native position in the most effective way possible. The failure of the Bureau and the Department to do the latter is one of the sorest spots in native affairs. While in many cases the reason is quite obviously negligence, or worse, in some instances the difficulty of defining that elusive "native position" is acute, and the failure to do so rather more understandable. It is here that the tribal governments and provincial and national associations become such useful yet ambivalent instruments; for while in specific areas the Indian Act, or tribal agreements and programs, cover the matter, in many and often the most contentious areas these are not nearly adequate.

This puts the Bureau and the Department in a most awkward position, in that they must decide what will be the consultative structure and must operate as one of the parties to that consultation. Admittedly, the situation has had a much longer time—since 1934, in fact—to develop in the United States, while Canada has moved in this direction only since 1969; but the troubles at Wounded Knee, South Dakota, in the spring of 1973 have brought the matter to a focus which involves both countries. The political structures which function as consultative and decision-making processes for the non-native segment of North American society do not operate with special reference to the native people, though there is increased evidence that a number of other minority and even majority groups also feel themselves ill served by the existing structures. Nonetheless, the native people are uniquely disorganized to deal politically in any manner to which the federal, much less the state or provincial, structure is capable of responding sensitively. The Department and the Bureau therefore possess, in some measure by default, an enormous degree of latitude in their dealings with the native people. They identify, fund and deal with groups which are either of their own choosing or the result of a crystallizing of opposition to their own unilateral actions, and which develop their own, often startlingly inappropriate, justifications for acting or reacting as they do.

The difficulty is that good, and constructive, intentions are not sufficient in a situation such as this, both because it is organizations (the government department and the native council and associations) and not individuals which are parties to the compact, and because the possibilities for understanding and cooperative action are limited by often quite divergent organizational aims or values or beliefs. The situation is further complicated by the fact that each side operates from what we might call political premises, but their sense of polity or civil organization is generally different.

Finally, both government and native organizations are sustained to a surprising degree by the often bizarre relationships which develop between them. Often it appears that much of the energy generated by this relationship goes into supporting the reliance of both sides upon it, rather than into moving in new directions independent of that reliance. Although this is not generally admitted, it is clear that both the government and the tribal councils and native associations depend for much of their present organizational validity, as well as for much of their strategy, upon the existence of the other, and upon the dependent interests that are created between them. It is therefore perhaps understandable that often more effort is spent in maintaining what are assumed to be desirable, but may well be intractable, relationships, than in developing new strategies for improving the lot of the native people. One indication of the stalemate which is so quickly reached in such a situation is the tendency for the Bureau and the Department of Indian Affairs to act as a focus for the political, as well as the economic and social, activities of the native people: the buildings of the bureaucrats are fairly routinely occupied or otherwise besieged, but the tactic is about as effective as trying to trap water in a sieve.

It is currently orthodox to speak of encouraging the native people to achieve a fair social, economic and political equality with the rest of the American and Canadian population. But social and economic matters are not of the same order as—indeed, are simply an aspect of—political matters; and they cannot all be thrown together on the rather classical scales of justice that this way of talking implies. Political, more than economic, and far more than social or cultural, functions can *only* be exercised in any way that gives the word any sense in a context which includes the non-native population. The only alternative is for the Bureau or the Department to function as the non-native element. If they do so, however, they cannot also hope to function as apolitical and disinterested advisors. (I do not mean to suggest that a native "homelands" or apartheid policy is not *possible;* simply that it is not now, and has really never been, a central element in North American political thought and action.)

There is a danger that, once again, the native people may be done a grave disservice out of the best of intentions. In political matters, and to a lesser extent in economic matters, the native circumstances are inextricably interwoven with the total Canadian and American political and economic situation, which creates the body politic within which the native people must eventually work out their own priorities. Political as well as economic links must be established with the majority society, possibly through control of land resources, possibly even through some kind of new federal structure, though this is most unlikely, given that neither country is at present exactly a model of federal harmony and cooperation; and it is unlikely that present federal structures could maintain their sometimes precarious integrity in the face of such pressures. Some form of political bond is necessary, however, not in order to obliterate native traditions and values, but on the contrary to allow them to develop in accordance with the possibilities which the native people perceive, and with the energies which will be part of an organic process of natural development realized in light of that perception. The alternative is the frustrating dependence on non-native decisions and the debilitating vulnerability to non-native prerogatives which has too long been the story. The native people must have the opportunity to allow their sense of community and identity to develop and function in something other than a hot-house climate. From the root-cellar to the hot-house may betoken commendable progress in native affairs, but one should keep in mind the open air, which may well be something other than the cold blast of winter.[20] The incompatibilities and irreconcilable conflicts between the values and beliefs of native and non-native society may never disappear and perhaps must not be allowed to; native culture depends upon them to a very great extent since its sources of purely indigenous inspiration and sustenance have largely disappeared. But they must not be preserved under the glass of a bureaucratic family compact.

There is still the vexing question of responsibility. In earlier days, when the extension of franchise was being argued, this issue appeared in its crudest form. But even there, when discussed with the most intemperate (and often untimely) logic, the complications of the matter were readily apparent. For example, the Franchise Bill was introduced into the Canadian House of Commons in 1885, but on a most inauspicious date, March 19. It was the feast of St. Joseph, the patron saint of the Métis, and the very day upon which Louis Riel announced his second provisional government at Batoche, the final brave and desperate attempt to assert a kind of native sovereignty in Canada. Naturally, there was some consternation:

> Mr. Mills: What we are anxious to know is, whether the honourable gentleman proposes to give other than enfranchised Indians votes.
>
> Sir John A. Macdonald: Yes.
>
> Mills: Indians residing on a reservation?
>
> Macdonald: Yes, if they have the necessary property qualification.[21]
>
> Mills: An Indian who cannot make a contract for himself, who can neither buy nor sell anything without the consent of the Superintendent-General—an Indian who is not enfranchised?

Macdonald: Whether he is enfranchised or not.

Mills: This will include Indians in Manitoba and British Columbia?

Macdonald: Yes.

Mills: Poundmaker and Big Bear?

Macdonald: Yes.

Mills: So that they can go from a scalping party to the polls.[22]

The anxiousness was apparent not only among the whites. Many of the Indians were suspicious that the extension of the franchise would signal the end of their special status—as, indeed, it eventually would, if the logic which was applied (against the limited Franchise Bill) by William Paterson were to become the logic of the government.

> If [the Prime Minister's] desire is to benefit the Indians, let him give greater facilities for them to attain the full status of their rights and liberties, to emancipate them from the guardianship of the Government of the day, to make them free agents, with the right to manage their own affairs.[23]

Naturally the Indians did not wish to be emancipated from the guardianship of the government just yet. They realized full well that the right to manage their own affairs could quickly become a shoddy euphemism for the right to be robbed and cheated out of, or themselves out of inexperience mismanage, what were left of their resources, their livelihood and their traditions. Once again, their specific concern was the possibility of losing treaty privileges and in particular their exemption from taxation.

> Many of the Indians on the Grand River Reservation have been told, that in case they receive the right to vote, their *Treaty Rights* with the Government would be in danger—that afterwards they would not be able to compel the Government to observe and carry out the treaties. They have also been told

that the granting of the Franchise to them, was a scheme of the Government with the object of imposing a direct *taxation* upon them.

These two subjects are being used successfully in many cases to induce the Indian to either vote against your government or not to vote at all.[24]

Now the paying of taxes, however annoying, is a fairly basic non-native political function, and acts as a financial and political control, involving the taxpayer in the actions to which he is contributor in a direct psychological, if usually an indirect administrative, way. It is a process which informs the social, economic and political structures of the non-native community. If the native people are to benefit from these structures, it is in their interest eventually to involve themselves in some way in the processes by which these structures are sustained and influenced. "Some way," however, will not be a simple way, for the native exemption from taxation is closely bound up with the sense of "property" that the native people maintain, which does not include the function of property as a political instrument in the manner upon which non-native local political structures often rely. This is an ambiguous advantage. On the one hand, the native people have a real interest in the land which has been reserved for them under government trusteeship, and the present structure maintains their interest. But on the other hand, they often wish to have what is effectively a political advantage flow from that interest and to be involved in the wide range of decisions which might affect it. The desire is both entirely understandable and commendable, yet how such advantage and influence might be exercised is not at all obvious, nor has much energy or imagination been expended, by either native or non-native individuals or groups, to develop new civil and political structures. Unfortunately, since the present form of native land tenure does not admit of its use as an economic asset in some of the usual ways—for instance, it cannot be alienated and consequently cannot be used to raise capital—many of the much-vaunted political successes of local groups in non-native society, which are often solidly based on property rights or privileges which have been threatened, provide few lessons that are useful, even though they often form something of a model for community animation in native areas.

It would be refreshing to be able to conclude with a flourish of startling answers to the numbing questions, and breathtaking solutions to the quixotic problems, which have defined the relationships between the native and the non-native people of Canada and the United States during the past centuries, and which are still very much present. Yet I am utterly unable to do so. In the company of many others, I should like to see the native people assume much more control of matters which concern them, while retaining those indigenous patterns of responsibility and decision which have served them well in the past, and might be modified to current needs and future possibilities. The native people of Canada and the United States suffer, in too many cases, from awful poverty, debilitating apathy, and humiliating prejudice. But they are with us still, which is no mean, indeed is in some respects a glorious, feat. The relationship of which they are a part is itself a part of the story of their survival, as it is of the times and the ways in which they have prevailed, and as it must be of the manner in which they will continue to live beside or among us.

Nonetheless, this relationship must be more fully a part of the pattern of self-interest which compels our social, economic and political structures and activities.[25] Otherwise, the same sad story will be told over again, by those who will come after us. There is every reason for the native people to distrust the benevolence of the white man, as the Oriental fable tells.

Once upon a time a monkey and a fish were caught up in a great flood. The monkey, agile and experienced, had the good fortune to scramble up a tree to safety. As he looked down into the raging waters, he saw a fish struggling against the swift current.

...anitarian desire to help his less fortunate fel-
...down and scooped the fish from the water. To
...urprise, the fish was not very grateful for this

...Marie Guyard, Mère de l'Incarnation, arrived
in Que... and founded (with Madame de la Petrie) the
Ursuline Convent, of which Madame Guyard became
Superior. "When we arrived in this country," she remarked,

> the Indians were so numerous that it seemed as if they were
> going to grow into a vast population: but after they were bap-
> tized God called them to Himself either by disease or by the
> hands of the Iroquois. It was perhaps his wise design to permit
> their death lest their hearts should turn to wickedness.[27]

Several hundred years later, General William T. Sherman
would suggest that "the only good Indian is a dead Indian."
There is little enough difference between these two responses, but the general perception of what it is to be a
"good" Indian has fortunately been somewhat more generous, though it has often changed with the passing of years
and of fashions, and has been different from native and
non-native perspectives. Still, the dilemma is harsh. "Work
or starve" is one crude expression of it: the "starvation"
may be physical or cultural, of course; and "work" has
meant something different to each generation. Cultivate the
land; 'become an individual—like the white man'; develop
habits of industry and thrift; seek wage employment . . .
The basic issue remains constant, and yet is always changing with the changing attitudes toward self-interest and
mutual interest that each age expresses. The native people
must somehow be free to act out of their own self-interest,
and yet become a part of our mutual interest so that their
interest is shared by us, and ours by them.

NOTES

Chapter 1. Our Dance Is Turned Into Mourning

1. Quoted by Jean-Jacques Rousseau in "A Discourse on the Origin of Inequality," *The Social Contract and Discourses,* trans. G. D. H. Cole (New York: Dutton, 1950), p. 242.

2. There is a good account of this topic under the general heading "Metaphysics" and the chapter headings "Environmentalism," "Origins," "Deficiency," "Noble Savage" in Bernard W. Sheehan's *Seeds of Extinction: Jeffersonian Philanthropy and the American Indian* (Chapel Hill: University of North Carolina Press, 1973), pp. 15-116. For a more general discussion of the background to these arguments, see Lee Eldridge Huddleston, *Origins of the American Indians: European Concepts, 1492-1729* (Austin: University of Texas Press, 1967).

3. It should be noted that many believed the civilizing of the Indian to be possible only if he were isolated from the pernicious influence of the white man, and therefore advocated the paradoxical policy of removal, that a garden might be planted in the wilderness, or a flower in the desert, rather than in the rather messy backyard of a European tenement. One of the most energetic advocates of such a program was the Baptist missionary Isaac McCoy. For an account of the issue, see Robert F. Berkhofer, Jr., *Salvation and the Savage: An Analysis of Protestant Missions and American Indian Response, 1787-1862* (Lexington: University of Kentucky Press, 1965),

pp. 100-106; or, more specifically, George A. Schultz, *An Indian Canaan: Isaac McCoy and the Vision of an Indian State* (Norman: University of Oklahoma Press, 1972). McCoy's arguments and information were frequently used by those who argued in favor of the Cherokee Removal Bill in 1830.

4. Colonel Nelson A. Miles, "The Indian Problem," *North American Review,* CXXVIII (1879), p. 309.

5. See Randolph C. Downes, "A Crusade for Indian Reform, 1922-1934," *The Mississippi Valley Historical Review*, XXIII (1945), p. 343. Quoted in Michael T. Smith, "The Wheeler-Howard Act of 1934: The Indian New Deal," *Journal of the West,* X (1971), p. 521.

6. Vattel was the author of *The Law of Nations; or Principles of the Law of Nature, Applied to the Conduct and Affairs of Nations and Sovereigns* (1760; pub. in Northampton, Mass., in 1820), from which the following phrase is taken. He was widely quoted and extremely influential; for the pattern into which his arguments nicely fitted, see Wilcomb E. Washburn, "The Moral and Legal Justification for Dispossessing the Indians," *Seventeenth Century America: Essays in Colonial History,* ed. J. M. Smith (Chapel Hill: University of North Carolina Press, 1959), pp. 15-32; and *Red Man's Land/White Man's Land: A Study of the Past and Present Status of the American Indian* (New York: Charles Scribner's Sons, 1971). On the use of Vattel's arguments in the Removal debates, see Albert K. Weinberg, *Manifest Destiny: A Study of Nationalist Expansionism in American History* (Baltimore: Johns Hopkins Press, 1935), pp. 77-99.

7. *Indian Atrocities: Narratives of the Perils and Sufferings of Dr. Knight and John Slover Among the Indians.* The first part is quoted in *Great Documents in American Indian History,* ed. Wayne Moquin with Charles Van Doren (New York: Praeger, 1973), p. 109; the second, included in *This Country Was Ours: A Documentary History of the American Indian,* ed. Virgil J. Vogel (New York: Harper and Row, 1972), p. 105.

8. Lamentations 5:2-4, 13-16. Used as the motto of a *History of the Indians of Connecticut from the Earliest Known Period to A.D. 1850* (Albany, 1871), by John W. deForest.

9. Cadwaller Colden to the Lords of Trade, September 20, 1764, referred to in Georgiana C. Nammack, *Fraud, Politics, and the*

*Dispossession of the Indians: The Iroquois Land Frontier in
the Colonial Period* (Norman: University of Oklahoma Press,
1969), pp. 96-97; Reginald Horsman, *Expansion and American
Indian Policy, 1783-1812* (East Lansing: Michigan State University Press, 1966), pp. 42-43; Report of United States Commissioner of Indian Affairs George W. Manypenny, November 22, 1856, and included in *The American Indian and the
United States: A Documentary History*, ed. Wilcomb E. Washburn (New York: Random House, 1973), Vol. I, p. 62.

Chapter 2. To Lyve More Vertuously

1. Published as "A new interlude and a mery of the nature of the
iiij elements, declarynge many proper poyntes of phylosophy
naturall, and of dyvers straunge landys, and of dyvers straunge
effectes and causis," between 1510 and 1520. Reproduced in
the Tudor Facsimile Texts series, ed. John S. Farmer, Vol.
85 (London, 1908); and as "The Interlude of the Four Elements," ed. J. O. Holliwell, in *Early English Poetry, Ballads,
and Popular Literature of the Middle Ages*, Vol. 22 (London,
1848).

2. Isaiah 28:9.

3. The speakers here are, respectively, Thomas Pickering
(quoted in Sheehan, p. 36); H. H. Brackenridge (quoted in
Vogel, p. 105); and Andrew Jackson (quoted in D'Arcy
McNickle, *Native American Tribalism: Indian Survivals and
Renewals* [New York: Oxford University Press, 1973], p. 56.)

4. This comment was made in the course of an article in the
North American Review, XXX (1830), pp. 62-121, in which
Cass expressed his support of President Jackson's removal
policy. Cass was an active force in Indian affairs in the United
States, as Governor of Michigan Territory from 1813 to 1831,
and then as Secretary of War under President Jackson from
1831 to 1836—in many ways, he is a latter-day American
counterpart to Sir William Johnson (see Chapters Nine and
Ten). His initial concern was to maintain peace and security
and he formulated his policy accordingly.
    "However we may despise [the Indians], it is the part of
    true wisdom to consult their prejudices, to draw physical
    strength from their intellectual weakness, and to attach
    them to us through the medium of their affections and
    interest, or to compel them to join us by a display of our
    strength. The only question is, by which of these
    methods, by presents and gentle treatment or by force and

fear we may expect with the most economy to attain our object.''

When he turned to benevolent considerations, he was sincere and honest, but his principles were incorrigibly established, and incorrigibly liberal.

"We must think for them. We must frequently promote their interest against their inclination, and no plan for the improvement of their condition will ever be practicable or efficacious, to the promotion of which their consent must in the first instance be obtained.''

He was very much a part of, and in many ways the most eloquent spokesman of his times.

"What ignorance, or folly, or morbid jealousy of our national progress does it not argue, to expect that our civilized border would become stationary, and some of the fairest portions of the globe be abandoned to hopeless sterility. That a few naked wandering barbarians should stay the march of cultivation and improvement, and hold in a state of perpetual unproductiveness, immense regions formed by Providence to support millions of human beings?''

(F. P. Prucha, *Lewis Cass and American Indian Policy* [Detroit: Wayne State University Press, 1967], pp. 2, 8-9, 12-13.)

5. See Huddleston, pp. 38-40.

6. For a discussion of some of these, see Sheehan, pp. 45-65; also Roy Harvey Pearce, *The Savages of America: A Study of the Indian and the Idea of Civilization* (Baltimore: Johns Hopkins Press, 1965), pp. 61-62, esp. n. 14. Rev. Dr. Elias Boudinot's *A Star in the West* (Trenton, 1816) is perhaps the most famous of these; and Barbara Simon's *The Ten Lost Tribes of Israel Historically Identified with the Aborigines of the Western Hemisphere* (London, 1836) is one of the last in a fairly dismal series.

7. Quoted in L. O. Saum, *The Fur Trader and the Indian* (Seattle: University of Washington Press, 1965), p. 29.

8. The majority opinion in this case was expressed by Chief Justice John Marshall, who decided that the court had no jurisdiction. "If it be true that the Cherokee nation have rights," he reflected, "this is not the tribunal in which those rights are to be asserted." Marshall took the opportunity, however, to discuss the larger question and to develop his concept of "domestic dependent" Indian nations.

"Though the Indians are acknowledged to have an unquestionable, and, therefore, unquestioned right to the lands they occupy, until that right shall be extinguished by a voluntary cession to our government; yet it may well be doubted whether those tribes which reside within the acknowledged boundaries of the United States can, with strict accuracy, be denominated foreign nations. They may, more correctly, perhaps, be denominated domestic dependent nations. They occupy a territory to which we assert a title independent of their will, which must take effect in point of possession when their right of possession ceases. Meanwhile they are in a state of pupilage. Their relation to the United States resembles that of a ward to his guardian. They look to our government for protection; rely upon its kindness and its power; appeal to it for relief to their wants; and address the president as their great father.''

Johnson's contribution to the decision was more specific, for he held that Indian treaties were little more than contracts; and thereby he forestalled the argument that the judicial power of the United States extended to all cases which involved treaties.

A year later, the allegation that the laws of the state of Georgia were invalid in Cherokee Territory was sustained (in *Samuel Worcester et al. v. The State of Georgia*), in an inspiring (but politically ineffective) decision by Marshall. A discussion of this, and of the arguments which surrounded the removal debates of the 1830s, will be taken up in later chapters.

9. Washburn, Vol. IV, pp. 2564-2565. A memorable dissenting opinion in this case was given by Mr. Justice Smith Thompson; see Washburn, Vol. IV, pp. 2580-2602.

10. From his Annual Reports for 1830 and 1831 (Washburn, Vol. I, pp. 18, 23).

11. In a letter from businessman E. S. Mety of the Wm. E. Storer Co. at St. Louis to President Hayes, February 19, 1878.

12. Quoted in Henry E. Fritz, *The Movement for Indian Assimilation, 1860-1890* (Philadelphia: University of Pennsylvania Press, 1963), p. 111.

13. From his Report of November 25, 1838 (Washburn, Vol. I, pp. 37-38).

14. *Journals of Samuel Hearne and Philip Turnor,* ed. J. B. Tyrell (Toronto: Champlain Society, 1934), p. 458; *The Explorations*

of Pierre Esprit Radisson, ed. Arthur T. Adams (Minneapolis: Ross and Haines, 1961), p. 144. Quoted in Saum, pp. 33, 38.

15. H. A. Innis, *Peter Pond: Fur Trader and Adventurer* (Toronto: Irwin and Gordon, 1930), p. 57.

16. *The North American Indian,* Vol. X, p. 4. Curtis spent over 25 years developing a photographic and ethnographic record of the Indians and Eskimos of the western part of Canada and the United States, and his work appeared as a 20-volume set between 1907 and 1930. It was, in his words, "a series of volumes picturing and describing the Indians" and "represent[ed] the result of a personal study of a people who are rapidly losing the traces of the aboriginal character and who are destined ultimately to become assimilated with the 'superior race.'"

17. G. E. Ellis, "The Red Indian of America in Contact with the French and the English," *Narrative and Critical History of America,* ed. Justin Winson (Cambridge, Mass., 1889), p. 283.

18. Edwin Thompson Denig, *Five Indian Tribes of the Upper Missouri: Sioux, Arickaras, Assiniboines, Crees, Crows,* ed. J. C. Ewers (Norman: University of Oklahoma Press, 1961), p. 61. Quoted in Saum, p. 231.

19. Report of United States Commissioner of Indian Affairs Elbert Herring, November 19, 1831 (Washburn, Vol. I, p. 21).

20. E. R. Curtius, *Essays on European Literature,* trans. Michael Kowal (Princeton: Princeton University Press, 1973), pp. 472-473.

21. Elbert Herring, in his Report of November 22, 1832 (Washburn, Vol. I, p. 26).

22. Modern "single-purpose" projects, such as hydro-electric dams or oil pipelines, continue in this tradition of defining native habits and expectations in the way that is most suitable to their purposes. It is not an unusual device, for it is simply one tactic in the ubiquitous strategy of posing a question—an "Indian question," say—for which one knows, or at least knows that there is, an answer.

23. As the Commissioner of Indian Affairs Samuel S. Hamilton remarked (in his Report of November 26, 1830), "the act to regulate trade and intercourse with the Indian tribes, and to preserve peace on the frontiers, passed in 1802, is the principal one which governs all our relations with the Indian tribes" (Washburn, Vol. I, p. 16).

Chapter 3.   Them and Us

1. See Fritz, pp. 43-44, 74-108, 206-208; and R. W. Mardock, *The Reformers and the American Indian* (Columbia, Mo.: University of Missouri Press, 1971), pp. 57-59, 129-131.

2. *The Administration of Indian Affairs in Canada* (Washington, 1915).

3. From *Recollections of the Last Ten Years* (Boston, 1826). Quoted in Sheehan, p. 163.

4. Duncan Campbell Scott, Deputy Superintendent-General of Indian Affairs at the time of Abbott's study, from which this quotation is taken.

5. In 1860, control of Indian affairs was transferred by the Imperial government to the Crown Lands department of the Provinces of Canada. (See D. C. Scott, "Indian Affairs, 1840-1867," *Canada and Its Provinces,* ed. Adam Shortt and Arthur G. Doughty, Vol. 5 (Toronto: Publisher's Association of Canada, 1913-1914), pp. 357-358. This article and its companion pieces covering the years 1763-1841 (Vol. 4) and 1867-1912 (Vol. 7) constitute the best account of Indian affairs in Canada during the Imperial years and the early years of the Dominion; they also provide a useful context for an understanding of American policy and practice. In addition, see J. E. Hodgetts, *Pioneer Public Service: An Administrative History of the United Canadas, 1841-1867* (Toronto: University of Toronto Press, 1955), pp. 211-219, 223-224. The entire Chapter XIII, "Indian Affairs: The White Man's Albatross," pp. 205-225, is invaluable as a source for the history of Indian administration.)

   This transfer was appropriate enough, since the Indian lands were the most important Indian asset to be administered. The government had already acted, in 1850, to protect the Indian lands, and it is here that one of the ambivalent features of Canadian Indian affairs begins to emerge. Two Acts were passed in that year, "An Act for the better protection of the Lands and Property of the Indians in Lower Canada" and "An Act for the protection of the Indians in Upper Canada from imposition, and the property occupied or enjoyed by them from trespass or injury." Prior to this legislation, there had been little enabling authority to protect Indian lands from trespass or imposition, even though it had been a matter of policy to do so. These Acts attempted to fill that gap, but in doing so they did one thing which has, more than any other single element, influenced the course and practice of Indian administration in Canada; for they provided the first legal definition of Indian status, of who is an Indian, and therefore of who is to be instructed in and exposed to the force of the laws and the ways of natural progress towards civilization and of civilized tenure of land.

Initially, the definition in the act for Lower Canada included
"—all persons of Indian blood, reputed to belong to the particular Body or Tribe of Indians interested in such lands, and their descendants.

—all persons intermarried with any such Indians and residing amongst them, and the descendants of all such persons.

—all persons residing among such Indians, whose parents on either side were or are Indians of such Body or Tribe, or entitled to be considered as such; and

—all persons adopted in infancy by any such Indians, and residing in the Village or upon the lands of such Tribe or Body of Indians and their descendants."

This was amended a year later to exclude non-Indian males intermarried with Indians, but the significant feature of the definition is the requirement that Indian status is contingent upon membership in a band or tribe. The Upper Canada act was more general and included sweeping provisions to protect Indian lands, forbidding conveyance without permission of the Crown, exempting such lands from taxes, and providing that no debt could be collected from any Indian unless such was possessed of private property to the value of £25 or more. (This provision was later modified to become a critical qualification for the exercise of the franchise.)

6. The case was the *Attorney-General of Canada v. Jeannette Lavell* (1973). All of the native associations appeared as intervenors to oppose the application of the Bill of Rights to the Indian Act; and the arguments which prevailed to support this view asserted the principal legislative authority of Parliament. The Indian Act is in fact at present undergoing an extensive revision, in cooperation with the native people. For a recent discussion of the matter of equal rights, see John Whyte, "The Lavell Case and Equality in Canada," *Queen's Quarterly,* LXXXI (1974), pp. 28-42.

7. Report by the Special Commissioners appointed on September 8, 1856, to investigate Indian affairs in Canada. In particu-

lar, they were instructed to inquire into and to report upon
      —the best means of securing the future progress and
      civilization of the Indian Tribes in Canada;
      —the best mode of so managing the Indian property as to
      secure its full benefit to the Indians, without im-
      peding the settlement of the country.
Essentially their task was to facilitate the transfer of the Indian
Department from Imperial to home rule. Unlike the Royal
Commission appointed by Sir Charles Bagot in 1842, which
reported in 1844, the 1856 Commissioners did not accept the
Imperial government's view that the Indian Department was
an "expiring" one.

8. Washburn, Vol. IV, p. 2515.

9. Flora Warren Seymour's arguments were presented in "Trying It on the Indians," *New Outlook*, CLXIII (May, 1934);
   Kirkland's were repeated in the Hearings before the House
   Committee on the proposed bill (1934). Quoted in Smith, pp.
   527-528.

10. Quoted in D. S. Otis, "History of the Allotment Policy,"
    *Hearings Before the House Committee on Indian Affairs on
    the Indian Reorganization Act of 1934*, 73rd Congress, 2nd
    Session.

11. See Kirke Kickingbird and Karen Ducheneaux, *One Hundred
    Million Acres* (New York: Macmillan, 1973), esp. Chapters 1
    and 2. This book is clearly intended as a successor, one
    hundred years after, to Helen Hunt Jackson's *A Century of
    Dishonour* (1881). It contains useful and often startling infor-
    mation.
        Both of these books were introduced by earnest apologists
    for native rights—Henry B. Whipple in 1880 and Vine Deloria
    Jr. in 1973; each introduction embodies the orthodoxies of its
    time and the commitments of its author, and together they
    provide an instructive contrast.

12. Riggs was a missionary to the Santee Sioux, who had in 1878-
    1879 drafted a bill designed "to get the homestead wedge in
    to all Nebraska [and eventually all Dakota Territory] Re-
    serves," as a means of preventing the further removal of the
    Indians there. In March, 1879, the A.B.C.F.M. recommended
    the bill to Senator Dawes; and it eventually provided the basis
    for the allotment, citizenship and inalienability clauses of the
    Dawes Act. Though an instrument of the allotment scheme
    which eventually was so destructive of native cultural solidar-

ity, Riggs was opposed to the fashionable enthusiasm for obliterating native languages as a necessary adjunct to an education in the civilized arts. (See Fritz, pp. 207-209; and Roy W. Meyer, *History of the Santee Sioux: United States Indian Policy on Trial* [Lincoln: University of Nebraska Press, 1967], p. 277.) The A.B.C.F.M. had, along with the Catholics, been rather left out when authority was granted in 1869 to various of the religious organizations to appoint agents to particular agencies; and they were somewhat churlishly impatient to further President Grant's inaugural promise to support any course which might lead the Indian to "civilization and ultimate citizenship." In general, they supported the concept that Indians should be civilized first and Christianized in due course. (See Robert F. Berkhofer, Jr., *Salvation and the Savage*, pp. 5-6, n. 10.)

13. For comments on Painter's role, and on the general situation which led to the passing of the bill, see Fritz, pp. 198-213.

14. Quoted in Vogel, pp. 193-194.

15. In his Report of September 30, 1905 (Washburn, Vol. II, pp. 738, 740).

16. A. G. Price, *White Settlers and Native Peoples: An Historical Study of Racial Contacts between English-speaking Whites and Aboriginal People in the United States, Canada, Australia, and New Zealand* (Melbourne: Georgian House, 1949), pp. 41-42.

17. Report of United States Commissioner of Indian Affairs Cato Sells, October 2, 1916 (Washburn, Vol. II, p. 849). The quotation is from a letter sent by Sells to all Indian Service employees and to other interested parties on January 10, 1916.

18. From a later Report by Sells, September 30, 1920 (Washburn, Vol. II, p. 904).

Chapter 4.   Social Credit

1. One of the most effective instruments in this regard was the United States Homestead Act of 1862. It was not simply that it provided an incentive to white settlement, but it also provided a model for the encouraging of individual habits of industry and thrift, and therefore a logical model to apply to the native people, who were not exactly paradigms of virtue

in that respect. The General Allotment Act was the product of such logic.

It should be noted that there is still a substantial amount of land to which the native title has not been extinguished. This is particularly true in Canada, and although there is a dispute about the nature and extent of this issue in British Columbia and northern Quebec, there is no question at all in the Yukon and the Northwest Territories. Treaties (8 and 11) were signed with some of the Indians in this area, but reserves were never parcelled out; and the Eskimos have never been engaged in land-cession formalities with the sovereign (federal) government. The next few years will see this matter brought to the forefront, particularly as development proceeds in the North and as the Yukon and Northwest Territories move towards some kind of provincial status.

2. The attitude of those whites who were signing the treaties was straightforward:

> "Let us have Christianity and civilization to leaven the mass of heathenism and paganism among the Indian tribes; let us have a wise and paternal Government faithfully carrying out the provisions of our treaties, and doing its utmost to help and elevate the Indian population, who have been cast upon our care, and we will have peace, progress, and concord among them in the North-West; and instead of the Indian melting away, as one of them in older Canada tersely put it, 'as snow before the sun', we will see our Indian population, loyal subjects of the Crown, happy, prosperous and self-sustaining, and Canada will be enabled to feel, that in a truly patriotic spirit, our country has done its duty by the red men of the North-West, and thereby to herself."
>
> (Alexander Morris, *The Treaties of Canada with the Indians of Manitoba and the North-West Territories* [Toronto, 1880], pp. 296-297).

3. This model is, of course, that of C. H. Douglas, the architect of the useful political philosophy of Social Credit. (See his *Economic Democracy* [London, 1920].)

For an imaginative discussion of this topic, and of the interest which it generated in the early years of this century, see Hugh Kenner, *The Pound Era* (Berkeley: University of California Press, 1971), pp. 301-317.

4. Scott, "Indian Affairs, 1840-1867," notes an occasion in 1829 at the Island at St. Joseph when the tribes had gathered to

receive their presents and the *government* distributed "milk" (a euphemism for liquor) to the Indians.

Colonel Mackey, who was the government officer in charge, responded to the Indian request for "a little of your milk to do away with the parching of our throats" as follows:
"Children,
   I will do all in my power to supply your different demands for guns, kettles [etc.]; and although your Great Father does not wish to give you anything that is unjurious to you—still, because you so earnestly desire it, I will give to those who ask for it a few drops [gallons] of milk."
Scott notes that "this was one of the last occasions on which intoxicants were issued to Indians by a government officer" (pp. 334-335).

5. From an article on the "Influence of Missions on the Temporal Condition of the Heathen," *Baptist Missionary Magazine,* XXIX (1849), pp. 101-105.

6. A statement of purpose made by the Board of Managers of the United Foreign Missionary Society, May 5, 1823. Quoted in Berkhofer, pp. 9, 10-11. For the Protestant missionaries, the diffusion of Christianity meant the diffusion of the Gospel, and the earliest missionary societies included this ambition in their titles: the Society for Propagation of the Gospel among the Indians and Others in North America, and the Society of the United Brethren for Propagating the Gospel among the Heathen, both founded in 1787.

7. Saum, p. 68.

8. In a letter written in the spring of 1817. Quoted in F. P. Prucha, *American Indian Policy in the Formative Years: The Indian Trade and Intercourse Acts 1790-1834* (Lincoln: University of Nebraska Press, 1962), p. 79, in a chapter (V) full of illuminating examples of the kinds of compromises which were made to further trading interests.

9. Canada, House of Commons, *Debates,* March 31, 1879, p. 844. The speaker was Mr. S. J. Dawson.

10. The speaker was the Prime Minister, Sir John A. Macdonald, Canada, House of Commons, *Debates,* May 5, 1880, p. 1991.

11. It should also be noted that the extension of the franchise was part of a Conservative strategy to provide federal, rather than various provincial, regulations governing the exercise of the franchise.

12. Canada, House of Commons, *Debates,* February 26, 1884, p. 542.

13. Canada, House of Commons, *Debates,* May 4, 1885, pp. 1575-1576.

14. E. R. Curtius, p. 132.

15. See W. T. Hagan, *Indian Police and Judges: Experiments in Acculturation and Control* (New Haven: Yale University Press, 1966). As part of the encouraging of the process of acculturation, it was, for example, specified in the Dawes Act of 1887 that preference for police appointments should go to those who had received allotments. Furthermore, "the policeman was supposed to give up his long braids, cease painting his face, trade moccasins for boots, and eschew any other outward manifestation of the blanket Indian" (p. 70).

   "The police force is a perpetual educator," commented United States Commissioner of Indian Affairs Hiram Price in his Report of October 24, 1881 (Washburn, Vol. I, p. 307). "It is a power entirely independent of the chiefs. It weakens, and will finally destroy, the power of tribes and bands. It fosters a spirit of personal responsibility."

16. *North American Review,* CXVI (1873), p. 357.

17. Fritz, p. 163.

18. Report of United States Commissioner of Indian Affairs Francis A. Walker, November 1, 1872 (Washburn, Vol. I, p. 186).

19. Included in the report was an extensive account of Indian affairs in the West during the latter part of the nineteenth century.

Chapter 5.   Indian Giving

1. For a brief discussion of this see Diamond Jenness, *Eskimo Administration,* Vol. II *(Canada),* p. 67, and Vol. IV *(Greenland)* p. 19. (The volumes cover Alaska, Canada, Labrador and Greenland but not the Soviet Arctic, and conclude with a volume of *Analysis and Reflections:* Technical Papers 10, 14, 16, 19 and 21 of the Arctic Institute of North America, published in Montreal from 1962-1968.) See also Sheehan, pp. 216-217; Price, pp. 37-38; and Elémire Zolla, *The Writer and the Shaman: A Morphology of the American Indian,* trans. Raymond Rosenthal (New York: Harcourt Brace Jovanovich, 1973), pp. 243-244.

For a fuller account of one of the most spectacular of such messianic revivals, see James Mooney, *The Ghost Dance Religion and the Sioux Outbreak of 1890* (Washington, 1896). A more modern account of a similar phenomenon is given by H. G. Barnett in *Indian Shakers: A Messianic Cult of the Pacific Northwest* (Carbondale: Southern Illinois University Press, 1957).

2. The central figure in much of this controversy was the enigmatic Edgar Dewdney. He was elected as a Conservative member to the British Columbia legislature when the province joined Confederation and to the Canadian House of Commons in 1872. He was appointed Indian Commissioner for the Northwest Territories in 1879 and lieutenant governor in 1881. In 1888, he returned to the federal House of Commons and became Minister of the Interior and Superintendent General of Indian Affairs. His relations with the Indians were generally good; with the friends of the Indians (especially Grit friends), bad; with the enemies of the Indians, once again good.

3. See S. W. Horrall, "Sir John A. Macdonald and the Mounted Police Force for the Northwest Territories," *The Canadian Historical Review*, LIII (1972), pp. 179-200.

4. For a very perceptive recent account of this complicated matter, see Hugh Brody, *Indians on Skid Row* (Ottawa: Department of Indian Affairs and Northern Development, 1971).

5. There is adequate testimony of this, most of it in the mass of "reminiscences" which have characterized western Canadian casual history. Professional historians, who like to scorn such reminiscences, become much more tractable if one refers to them as "papers" or (better still) "documents."

6. In a letter written on January 9, 1870. Quoted in James Ernest Nix, *Mission Among the Buffalo: The Labours of the Reverends George H. and John C. McDougall in the Canadian Northwest, 1860-1876* (Toronto: Ryerson Press, 1960). Needless to say, the Catholics were themselves not all that impressed by the Protestant missions. Archbishop F. N. Blanchet, of Oregon, infuriated by the parcelling out of western agencies to Protestant groups under Grant's "peace policy," wrote to United States Commissioner of Indian Affairs Ely S. Parker on July 8, 1871:

   "How can the government expect that a true civilization may be given to our Indians by Sects, not christian but

infidel? No we are not of those who think . . . all . . .
denominations are equally good, though teaching doctrines diametrically opposed to each other. Woe to the
Indians to whom those contradictory doctrines are taught
by dissenting sects."
(Quoted in Fritz, p. 89.)

7. Canada, House of Commons, *Debates*, April 15, 1886, p. 721.

8. This was originally published in the *Mail* newspaper on January 13, 1886. Quoted by Cameron in the same debate.

9. Originally appeared in the rival newspaper the *Globe* on
March 20, 1886. Quoted in *The Facts Respecting Indian
Administration in the North-West* (Ottawa, 1886), p. 14.

10. Canada, House of Commons, *Debates,* April 15, 1886, pp.
783-784.

11. *Indian Administration in the North-West, p.* 15. He had written earlier, on February 22, 1884, that "of course they know
that your policy with the Indians has always turned for the
best, both for the Government and the Indians."

12. Quoted in Desmond Morton, *The Last War Drum: The
North-West Campaign of 1885* (Toronto: Hakkert, 1972), pp.
164-165.

13. In an article entitled "A Great Chieftain," written after Crowfoot's death, and printed in the *Macleod Gazette,* May 22 and
29, 1890. Quoted in Hugh A. Dempsey, *Crowfoot: Chief of
the Blackfeet* (Edmonton: Hurtig, 1972), p. 166.

14. The Report was dated November 1, 1872 (Washburn, Vol. I,
pp. 183-184, 190).

15. Dempsey, *Crowfoot,* pp. 89, 145-147.

16. In particular, in the Debates of April 15, 1886, though he was
so widely disliked by some parties in Ottawa that he was often
mentioned as doing what ought not to be done, and usually in
the wrong way.

17. Both the Sioux Commission and the earlier Peace Commission
operated under all but impossible conditions. The latter effected treaties which were then not ratified by Congress. The
former, under the chairmanship of G. W. Manypenny, was
subverted by the administration's desire to remove the Sioux
out of Dakota, by the antagonism of the military, and by the
inattention of the press. The Sioux Commission issued its
report on December 16, 1876 (see Fritz, pp. 180-187); but it

was another incident, the removal of the Ponca tribe, which captured the attention of the eastern public and reinforced the reform cause.

18. This practice was legion; for example, curious arrangements with the powerful I. G. Baker Company of Montana were often brought to public attention in Canada; and the list of similar abuses in the United States would be a story in itself. There is a brief discussion of such "Indian rings" in Fritz, pp. 27-29, 144; and in Hagan, esp. Chapter 2, *passim*.

19. Quoted in Nammack, pp. 101-102.

20. Writing to the President in 1862, Bishop Whipple noted that
    "The Indian agents who are placed in trust of the honor and faith of the government are generally selected without any reference to their fitness for the place. The congressional delegation desire to reward John Doe for party work, and John Doe desires the place, because there is a tradition on the border that an Indian agent with fifteen hundred dollars a year can retire upon an ample fortune in four years."

    (Quoted in Lawrence F. Schmeckebier, *The Office of Indian Affairs: Its History, Activities and Organization,* [Baltimore: Johns Hopkins Press, 1927], p. 47.)

    The Indian Peace Commission which reported to President Andrew Johnson on January 7, 1868,
    "insisted that the present Indian service is corrupt, and [a] change should be made to get rid of the dishonest. That there are many bad men connected with the service cannot be denied. The records are abundant to show that agents have pocketed the funds appropriated by the government and driven the Indians to starvation. It cannot be doubted that Indian wars have originated from this cause."

    (Washburn, Vol. I, pp. 159-160.)

21. See, for example, the Report of United States Commissioner of Indian Affairs N. G. Taylor, November 23, 1868 (Washburn, Vol. I, pp. 164-175.) Basically the (intelligent) objection, very powerfully stated by Taylor, was that "the nature and objects of the War Department, as indicated by its very name, WAR, are essentially military, while the nature of our relations with the Indians ought to be, and the objects aimed at in their conduct are, essentially civil" (p. 170).

22. Quoted by General G. A. Custer in *My Life on the Plains; or, Personal Experiences with Indians* (Norman: University of Oklahoma Press, 1962), pp. 178-179.

23. See Fritz, pp. 220-221; and Schmeckebier, pp. 83-85.

24. In 1966, Professor James Coleman of Johns Hopkins University carried out a massive survey of 4,000 schools and 600,000 students, under the mandate of the American Civil Rights Act (1964). His findings were somewhat ambivalent, but the general tenor was "that schooling had little effect in raising the achievement or reducing the disparate standard of black children relative to white. . . . What Coleman was saying was that public schools—or the process of education itself—were not the social equalizers American society imagined them to be" (Daniel Bell, "On Meritocracy and Equality," *Public Interest*, 29 [1972], pp. 44-46).

    This thesis was carried further by Christopher Jencks, in his book *Inequality*, where it was argued that the aim of social policy must be equality of result—by sharing and redistributive policies and in effect changing the rules of the game to reduce the capacity of some for a competitive advantage—rather than equality of opportunity.

25. Reported in the House of Commons, *Debates*, April 15, 1886, p. 719.

26. *Indian Administration in the North-West*, p. 7.

27. Saum, p. 104. This was a very common theme and used especially to argue for policies of removal and separation. "It is a melancholy truth," a Royal Commission appointed to investigate the management of Indian affairs in Canada (after the Union of Upper and Lower Canada in 1841) was told,

    "that the example and encouragement of vicious white neighbours have been among the chief causes of the deterioration of the Indian character. In his native state the Indian is simple-minded, generous, proud and energetic, his craftiness is exhibited chiefly in the chase and in war . . . In his half civilized state, he is indolent to excess, intemperate, suspicious, cunning, covetous, and addicted to lying and fraud."

    Sir Francis Bond Head, Lieutenant Governor of Upper Canada during these years, was a staunch advocate of "removing and fortifying the Indians as much as possible from all communication with the whites." His tenure of office, however, was taken up by other, more urgent, matters.

28. *The Writings of 'Colonel William Byrd of Westover in Virginia Esqr'*, ed. J. S. Bassett (New York, 1901), pp. 102-103.

29. Ewers, ed. Denig's *Five Indian Tribes,* pp. 70-71. Quoted in Saum, p. 147.

30. *Forty Years a Fur Trader on the Upper Missouri,* ed. M. M. Quaife (Chicago, 1933), p. 351.

31. *Ibid.*, pp. 359-360.

Chapter 6.   Constructing the Unreconstructed

1. For a good account of his proposals, and the assumptions upon which they were based, see Richard N. Ellis, *General Pope and U.S. Indian Policy* (Albuquerque: University of New Mexico Press, 1970).

2. The spokesman is one Rev. James Coleman, giving evidence before a Royal Commission in 1847.

3. Prucha, *American Indian Policy,* p. 146.

4. See Fritz, pp. 53-54; Meyer, Chapter 10, pp. 198-219.

5. For example, the building of the Union Pacific and the Kansas Pacific across the plains during the 1860's and 1870's, and the building of the Canadian Pacific during the following decade. The relationship of the railroads to the native situation has never been well studied. It is a complex matter, for it changed the attitudes of the whites, as well as of the Indians. The airplane has had a somewhat similar effect, albeit different in degree, in the North.

6. Jenness, *Eskimo Administration,* Vol. II (Canada), p. 9.

7. See Jenness, Vol. II, pp. 17-34.

8. Jenness, Vol. II, pp. 40-41. There is a good study of the constitutional questions involved by Kenneth Lysyk, "The Unique Constitutional Position of the Canadian Indian," *The Canadian Bar Review,* XLV (1967), pp. 513-553.

9. This was finally resolved in the summer of 1973 when the Canadian government committed itself to such a recognition, and to the funding of Indian and Eskimo (Inuit) associations to undertake research to establish traditional land use and occupancy and to proceed towards negotiations to extinguish native title after the manner of the treaties which were signed between 1871 and 1921 with the Indians of the Northwest.

10. Jenness, Vol. II, p. 74, and pp. 99-110 *passim*. Also Peter J. Usher, *The Bankslanders: Economy and Ecology of a Frontier Trapping Community* (Ottawa: Department of Indian Affairs and Northern Development, 1971), Vols. I and II.

11. The chief difficulty with native reserve land has been that, since it is inalienable, it cannot be used to raise capital, nor can it form any tax base by which the native people could become involved (or entangled) in non-native political, economic and social activities.

12. See Smith, "The Wheeler-Howard Act," pp. 522ff.

13. Downes, "Crusade for Indian Reform," p. 342.

14. There are many accounts of Roosevelt's "New Day for Indians," but one of the best and most sympathetic is in Price, pp. 41-58.

15. From *Every Zenith: A Memoir and Some Essays on Life and Thought* (Denver, 1963), p. 203. At the beginning of his book on *The Indians of the Americas* (New York: Norton, 1947) Collier made a remark which is memorable:
    "They had what the world has lost. They have it now. What the world has lost, the world must have again, lest it die. . . . It is the ancient, lost reverence and passion for human personality, joined with the ancient, lost reverence for the earth and its web of life."

16. In Hearings before the House Committee (1934). Quoted in Smith, p. 528.

17. William H. Kelly, "Indian Adjustment and the History of Indian Affairs," *Arizona Law Review*, 10 (1968), p. 567, n. 31.

18. The cruel story of this "orgy of exploration" which resulted in the destruction of a wonderfully adapted civilization, and the theft of a way of life, is told in Angie Debo's classic *And Still the Waters Run: The Betrayal of the Five Civilized Tribes* (Princeton: Princeton University Press, 1972; first published in 1940).

19. In the Report of United States Commissioner of Indian Affairs John R. Nichols, June 30, 1949 (Washburn, Vol. II, p. 975).

20. Included in the Report of Acting United States Commissioner of Indian Affairs W. B. Greenwood, June 30, 1953 (Washburn, Vol. II, p. 989).

Chapter 7. An Anomaly Upon the Face of the Earth

1. See Washburn, Vol. IV, p. 2752. In combination with the earlier Tillamooks case (1950), the opinions expressed have substantially influenced subsequent legal and political decisions in both Canada and the United States. One of the obvious spectres raised by these actions was that accumulated interest would outweigh the (claimed) principal if compensation were allowed. (For once, the figurative and the factual were aligned.) The basis of the decision, that aboriginal title is not a property right, reinforced the paradoxical nature of the Indian claim, since few native spokesmen would claim otherwise.

2. Stewart French, *Alaska Native Claims Settlement Act,* published by the Arctic Institute of North America (Washington, 1972), p. 12.

3. This comment is included in an excellent study by C. D. Rowley, entitled *The Destruction of Aboriginal Society: Aboriginal Policy and Practice* (Canberra: Australian National University Press, 1970). It is the first volume in an excellent series on *Aborigines in Australian Society,* of which Mr. Rowley is general director.

4. Price, pp. 196-197.

5. Dempsey, pp. 11-12.

6. *New North West* (Deer Lodge, Montana), October 29, 1869. Quoted in Dempsey, pp. 59-60.

7. See Jenness, Vol. II, Chapter 14 (Eskimo Health [1950-60]), pp. 139-149.

8. The booklet was written and prepared by Dr. J. S. Willis of the Northern Health Service.

9. *Eskimo Mortality and Housing*, pp. 61, 70.

10. D. K. Thomas and C. T. Thompson, *Eskimo Housing as Planned Culture Change* (Ottawa: Department of Indian Affairs and Northern Development, 1972), p. 9.

11. This provision was revised in more general terms in 1895 and, by including the prohibition of "wounding or mutilation," effectively embraced the Sun Dance of the Plains tribes.

12. Quoted in S. H. Blake's *Memorandum on Indian Work.*

Chapter 8. The Indian Question `

1. See Huddleston, *passim*. Much in the following paragraphs is taken directly or indirectly from this useful book.

Chapter 9. Alas for Caliban

1. "Le Sueur, The Explorer of the Minnesota River," *Minnesota Historical Collections*, I (1850-1856), p. 273. Quoted in Meyer, p. 11.

2. A full account of several of such "transactions," and specifically of the Delaware purchase, is given in Nammack, pp. 22-38. In addition, her book contains valuable information about the early Imperial and colonial land policy leading to the Albany Conference of 1754, to which I am indebted in the following pages. See also Allen W. Trelease, *Indian Affairs in Colonial New York: The Seventeenth Century* (Ithaca: Cornell University Press, 1960).

3. Edited by Charles Howard McIlwaine, as Vol. 21 of *Harvard Historical Studies* (Cambridge, Mass., 1915). Other sources of interest are the *Bibliography of the English Colonial Treaties with the American Indians, Including a Synopsis of Each Treaty*, ed. Henry F. DuPuy (New York, 1917); and, particularly with reference to the Six Nations and early Imperial policy, *Documents Relative to the Colonial History of the State of New York*, 15 Vols., ed. E. B. O'Callaghan (Albany, 1853-1887).

4. Mr. Justice Judson, in reasons given for the decision of the Supreme Court of Canada in *Frank Calder et al. v. Attorney-General of British Columbia* (1973). This is the most recent case in Canadian jurisprudence in which the issue of aboriginal rights has been contended. In particular, the dissenting reasons given by Mr. Justice Hall provide a reasonably full survey of the matter, as it affected British Imperial, as well as American and Canadian responses. The literature on this subject is gathering some momentum, especially in Canada where the issue is still very much alive. The most significant publication is *Native Rights in Canada*, 2nd edition, ed. Peter A. Cumming and Neil H. Mickenberg (Toronto: Indian-Eskimo Association of Canada, 1972).

5. Scott, "Indian Affairs, 1763-1841," p. 699.

6. The captivity narrative is a unique genre in American letters and has received generous attention by Pearce in *The Savages of America*, pp. 58, 198-199; and in "The Significances of the Captivity Narrative," *American Literature*, XIX (1947), pp. 1-20); by Leslie Fiedler in *The Return of the Vanishing American* (New York: Stein and Day, 1968); and most recently by Zolla, in *The Writer and the Shaman*, esp. Chapter III entitled "Missionaries, Demonologists, and Puritan Captives" (pp. 41-60).

Some of these narratives are marvellously related, in more than one sense: for example, *The Redeemed Captive Returning to Zion*, or A Faithful History of Remarkable Occurences in the Captivity and Deliverance of Mr. John Williams, Minister of the Gospel in Deerfield; Who, in the Desolation which befel that Plantation, by an Incursion of French and Indians, was by them carried away (in 1704), with his Family and his Neighbourhood, into Canada (pub. in 1706-1707). Williams' daughter had her own story told: *A Unredeemed Captive*, Being the Story of Eunice Williams, who, at the age of 7 years, was carried away from Deerfield by the Indians . . . and who lived among them in Canada as one of them the rest of her live (pub. in 1897). Eunice married an Indian and they had a son Thomas, who in turn received attention in a *Life of Te-Ho-Ra-Gwa-Ne-Gen (Two suns together)*, Alias Thomas William, A Chief of the Caughnawaga Tribe of Indians in Canada, by the Rev. Eleazer Williams, Reputed son of Thomas Williams, and by many believed to be Louis XVII, son of the last reigning monarch of France previous to the Revolution of 1789 (pub. in Albany in 1859)!

7. Preamble to Treaty No. 3 between Her Majesty the Queen and the Saulteaux Tribe of the Ojibbeway Indians at the Northwest Angle on the Lake of the Woods (1873).

8. There was a fairly extensive contemporary literature about the removal policy, which was naturally focussed on the Removal Bill of 1830. *Speeches on The Passage of the Bill, for the Removal of the Indians, Delivered in the Congress of the United States, April and May, 1830,* ed. Jeremiah Evarts (Boston, 1830), presented the arguments that were delivered against the action; and Evarts, who wrote under the name William Penn, also presented some *Essays on the Present Crisis in the Condition of the American Indians. First Published in the National Intelligences* (Boston, 1829).

Typical of a number of tracts published on the issue is

Heman Humphrey's *Indian Rights and Our Duties* (Amherst, 1830), with its righteous motto from Ezekiel:
> The people of the land have used oppression, and exercised robbery, and have vexed the poor and needy. . . .

9. From the majority opinion in the case of *Johnson and Graham's Lessee v. M'Intosh* (1823). The court rejected as invalid certain land titles granted to individuals by Indian tribes prior to the American revolution. The principle enunciated here has been generally, if rather crudely, respected in Canada and the United States; except, curiously enough, in the case of the Indians of California and British Columbia. "Lifted by those eternal swells, you needs must own the seductive god, bowing your head to Pan," writes Melville of the Pacific (in *Moby Dick*, Chapter 3). The authorities were otherwise seduced on its shores, and the Indians still watch fretfully from the no longer shadowy shadows.

10. Schmeckebier, p. 3.

11. For a full discussion of this, see Jenness, Vol. II *(Canada)*, pp. 7-98. A recent, and very fine, *History of the Original Peoples of Northern Canada* by Keith J. Crowe (Montreal: McGill-Queen's University Press, 1974) deals with this in perceptive detail.

12. The phrase is used by Diamond Jenness, Vol. V *(Analysis and Reflections)*, p. 4-5. Jenness was extremely upset over the way "in which European immigrants [were] discreetly confining the aboriginal Eskimos and segregating them from the rest of the continent"; and since at the time he was writing there appeared to be little chance of a stable economic base in the North, he counselled a policy of removal to the south and progressive assimilation. Despite his conclusions, the series is a remarkably acute one, exactly what one would expect of one of the most sensitive of modern anthropologists.

13. The question of the establishment and effect of such alliances, particularly with the powerful Iroquois, is among the most deliciously uncertain in the history of early Indian, French, British and American affairs, and it has produced some of the most famous historical writings on the continent, in particular those of Francis Parkman and Lewis H. Morgan.

14. Nammack, p. 42.

15. The influence of Iroquoian social models on Marxist theory was also significant; and Friedrich Engels was much indebted

to L. H. Morgan's description of the Iroquois (see Zolla, pp. 162-163).

16. Quoted in Prucha, *American Indian Policy,* p. 10.

17. In a letter to James Duane (September 7, 1783), quoted in Horsman, p. 9.

18. *A Compilation of the Messages and Papers of the Presidents,* ed. James D. Richardson (Washington, 1896-1899), Vol. I, p. 380. Quoted in Horsman, pp. 108-109.

19. From *The Brighton Guardian* of 1832, in the course of a long diatribe against taxes. Included in *The English Radical Tradition, 1763-1914,* ed. S. Maccoby (London: Adam and Charles Black, 1966), pp. 118-119.

20. Quoted in Scott, "Indian Affairs, 1763-1841," p. 699.

21. See John R. Alden, "The Albany Congress and the Creation of the Indian Superintendencies," *Mississippi Valley Historical Review,* XXVII (1940), pp. 193-210; *The Appalachian Indian Frontier: The Edmond Atkin Report and Plan of 1755,* ed. W. R. Jacobs (Lincoln: University of Nebraska Press, 1967); John R. Alden, *John Stuart and the Southern Colonial Frontier: A Study of Indian Relations, War, Trade, and Land Problems in the Southern Wilderness, 1754-1775* (Ann Arbor: University of Michigan Press, 1944); Arthur Pound, *Johnson of the Mohawks: A Biography of Sir William Johnson, Irish Immigrant, Mohawk War Chief, American Soldier, Empire Builder* (New York: Macmillan, 1930); Oliver M. Dickerson, *American Colonial Government, 1696-1765: A Study of the British Board of Trade in its Relation to the American Colonies, Political, Industrial, Administrative* (New York: Russell and Russell, 1962).

22. Quoted in Nammack, p. 77. The letter was written to Roger Morris, one of the contesting heirs of Adolph Philipse. Philipse had during the 1690's acquired a tract of land on the east side of the Hudson River from Jan Sebering and Lambert Dorlandt, who had themselves obtained a licence to purchase land from the Wappinger Indians and had paid them money, but had not obtained letters patent for the land. Title was placed in dispute in 1762 and the issue decided against the Indians by the New York Council in 1765; this decision was confirmed in 1767.

Chapter 10.   Property, Rights and Liberty

1. The phrase is from the First Annual Message (of 1901) of President Theodore Roosevelt. Quoted in Vogel, pp. 193-194.

2. Quoted in Prucha, *American Indian Policy,* p. 16. See also R. A. Humphreys, "Lord Shelburne and the Proclamation of 1763," *English Historical Review,* XLIX (1934), pp. 241-264. The Proclamation itself is included in *Documents Relating to the Constitutional History of Canada,* 1759-1791, ed. Adam Shortt and Arthur E. Doughty (Ottawa, 1907), pp. 119-123; and in a slightly abbreviated form in Washburn, Vol. 3, pp. 2135-2139.

3. For a useful discussion of this, with special and illuminating reference to the prairie-parkland region of Canada and the bordering United States, see B. Kaye and D. W. Moodie, "Geographical Perspectives on the Canadian Plains," *A Region of the Mind,* ed. Richard Allen (Regina: University of Saskatchewan Press, 1973), pp. 17-46. Two other essays in the same volume—"Historiography of the Fur Trade" by L. G. Thomas (pp. 73-86), and "Historiography of the Canadian Plains After 1870" by T. D. Regehr (pp. 87-102)—give a good perspective on the assumptions and terms of reference of the historians of the period.

   There is a perceptive discussion of the general relations between "metropolis and hinterland" as they have influenced the interpretations of historians and policy-makers alike in a very controversial third volume of Peter J. Usher's study of *The Bankslanders,* esp. pp. 17-21.

4. An account of this would be an account of the Northwest until the 1890's; something of this sort is supplied by G. W. G. Stanley in *The Birth of Western Canada: A History of the Riel Rebellions,* rev. ed. (Toronto: University of Toronto Press, 1961) and *Louis Riel* (Toronto: Ryerson, 1963); by A. S. Morton in *A History of the Canadian West to 1870-71* (London: Nelson, 1939) and by Marcel Giraud, *Le Métis Canadien* (Paris: Université de Paris, 1945).

5. A general history of this practice in several British colonies is provided in Price, *passim.* Both the advocates of assimilation and the proponents of a separate development or status for native groups have found it convenient to consider the establishing of native "homelands" as either a stage in, or the context for, the new indigenous Jerusalem that is envisaged.

6. Shortt, *Constitutional Documents,* Vol. I, Sessional Papers No. 18, pp. 199-200.

7. The success of the Proclamation of 1763 in this endeavor has been very mixed. As we have seen, it was referred to by United States Commissioner of Indian Affairs John R. Nichols in his Report of 1949 as having provided the basis of American Indian policy to that date, though the evidence is far from convincing. (Nichols argued for a "termination" of that policy, for he did not see a future role for the principles enunciated in the Proclamation.) It continues to be a major touchstone in the continuing struggle for native land rights in the North of Canada and in parts of British Columbia and Quebec.

8. In a letter to Rufus King, June 1, 1785. Quoted in Horsman, p. 100. The preceding quotation, in a similar spirit, is from an opinion given by George Washington on September 7, 1783, to a Congressional committee chaired by James Duane, which was meeting to formulate an Indian policy.

9. Even when this inefficiency was exercised, as it was with respect to Australia, for example, it was sometimes powerless to prevent the encroachments and exploitation that occurred. See Price, pp. 122-128.

10. In correspondence to James Orr, May 12, 1798. Quoted by Prucha, *American Indian Policy,* p. 38. Vattel's *Law of Nations* comes ringing clearly through here, as it does so often in this period.

11. Quoted in Scott, "Indian Affairs, 1763-1841," pp. 698-699.

12. This policy was formally presented as a White Paper, entitled "Indian Policy 1969," as part of the federal government's objective of achieving "a full and equal participation" of all its citizens "in cultural, social, economic and political life in Canada," and in particular a fuller integration of the native peoples into Canadian society. Basically, the government proposed a phased ending of special status for Indians registered under the Indian Act, and a relinquishment of federal trusteeship of Indian lands and interests by replacing the Indian Act with an Indian Lands Act that would transfer control of those lands to the Indians themselves. Corresponding to this, it was intended that the native people would be brought into the same sphere of influence as other Canadian citizens, through the transfer of responsibility for their welfare from federal to provincial and municipal jurisdictions.

The Indians in general reacted strongly against this proposed policy, arguing that they need and deserve a special and extraordinary status, some kind of Canadian "citizenship plus." Provincial authorities in Canada, like state authorities in the United States, have never displayed much inclination, nor have they always had sufficient means, to give special attention to the native people; and the possibility of being thrown to these and other waiting lions has never been attractive to the Indians and Eskimos.

There is little doubt that the policy was ill conceived: it ignored the practical realities of the situation, as well as the advice which should have been apparent both from the meetings which were held across the country with Indian groups during the preceding years, and from the government-sponsored *Survey of the Contemporary Indians of Canada, A Report on Economic, Political, Educational Needs and Policies,* ed. H. B. Hawthorn et al. (Ottawa: Department of Indian Affairs and Northern Development, 1966-1967), in which the concept of a "citizen plus" was given a full and sympathetic examination.

There were two positive effects of the policy statement, however. As a consequence of the government's expressed wish to deal only with Indian associations in discussing Indian policy, a number of such provincial, territorial and national associations were formed and federally funded and have provided a focus for native concern. In addition, a Commissioner on Indian Claims was appointed to facilitate the settling of outstanding treaty and other claims.

13. The political character of Indian affairs is an often neglected, but absolutely central, feature both of its history and of its present progress. See, for an aspect of this, Chapter Twelve below.

14. "Indian Affairs, 1763-1841," p. 695.

15. The 1830's were a time of unusual attention to reform of native administration in all of the British colonies, and of unusual satisfaction with existing principles and practices in the United States, once the removal debate was over.

16. In July, 1834, the (British) House of Commons unanimously passed an address stating that it was "deeply impressed with the duty of acting upon the principles of justice and humanity in the intercourse and relations of this country with the native inhabitants of its colonial settlement, of affording them protection in the enjoyment of their civil rights, and of imparting to

them that degree of civilization and that religion with which Providence has blessed this nation.''

"In 1836 and 1837 a select committee of the Commons under T. Fowell Buxton, who was the brother-in-law of Elizabeth Fry and the coadjutor of Wilberforce, the promoters of prison reform and the abolition of slavery, issued reports which painted a shocking picture of European injustice and urged reform in fervent language. The committee stressed that the incontrovertible right of the natives to their own soil, 'a plain and sacred right,' had not been realized. Europeans had entered native lands uninvited. They had acted as if they were lords of the soil. They had punished the natives as if they were aggressors on their own territories. They had treated them on their own property as if they were thieves and robbers, and had 'driven them back into the interior as if they were dogs or kangaroos.' ''

(Price, p. 122. See also Paul Hasluck, *Black Australians: A Survey of Native Policy in Western Australia 1829-1897,* 2nd edition [Melbourne: Melbourne University Press, 1970], pp. 45-56.)

17. In a letter to Lord Dalhousie, July 24, 1828 (in *Papers Relating to the Indian Department in Upper and Lower Canada,* 1837 [617], XLIV).

18. Reported in the "Report on the Affairs of the Indians in Canada," *Journals,* Legislative Assembly, Canada, 1844-1845. Appendix E.E.E., Section 1 ("History of Relations between the Government and the Indians"). Quoted in Hodgetts, p. 206.

19. From the Minutes of the Fort Stanwix Treaty Council, October 3-21, 1784. Quoted in Horsman, p. 19.

20. For a more detailed account of this change in policy, and of the interests which dictated it, see Horsman, pp. 32-52.

21. The major concern of Chief Justice Jay was to dislodge the Montreal-based traders and British garrison troops from that triangular section south of the Great Lakes to the confluence of the Mississippi and Ohio Rivers. Neither of the signatories wished to inhibit those Indians who were necessary adjuncts to the fur trade on both sides of the border; and Article III of the Treaty, while stipulating that *all* persons resident on either side of the border should be free to pass into the other territory, specifically exempted the Indian from payment of duty on any of their ordinary possessions. Whether the Jay Treaty

was terminated by the War of 1812 was a matter of dispute at the time; in any case, the provisions of Article III were revived by Article IX of the Treaty of Ghent (1815). International treaties, however, are not self-executing and require enabling legislation, which to date has not been passed by either country to the satisfaction of the Indians involved; and the clear implication of a case brought by Louis Francis of the St. Regis band before the Supreme Court of Canada in 1956 is that this provision has no current application in Canada.

The issue may appear somewhat trivial, but there is a more fundamental matter involved. The historical situation furnishes a notable instance in which the international boundary divides a single Indian nation; furthermore, the Iroquois, who were the principal beneficiaries of the Jay Treaty, constitute a particularly special case. The original home of the Iroquois was the Hudson Valley of what is now New York State, where they supported first the Dutch and then the British when the latter took over as the occupying power in 1674. As the Iroquois were more anti-French then pro-Dutch or pro-British, the French had sought to win at least some elements to their point of view by establishing groups converted to Catholicism from time to time at what was to become Caughnawaga. However, in 1760 the Caughnawaga people transferred their allegiance back to the British and led them to Montreal. (In the previous year French clerics had persuaded 100 Caughnawagans to form the settlement of St. Regis.) Most of the Six Nations Indians in New York supported the British during the Revolutionary War and many were brought to Canada after the cessation of hostilities. These formed the nuclei of the Iroquois settlements at Tyendinaga and Six Nations, Brantford.

None of the Iroquois was party to the sort of treaty entered into with the British or Canadian government by most other Indian groups; and the arrangements which were effected tended to reinforce their sense of supranational status. In addition, the form of land tenure under which certain of their lands are held is dissimilar to that which applies to other Indian lands. A recent court case which considered this matter in Canada upheld the right of hereditary rather than elected chiefs to exercise authority over these lands. Both the issue of the sovereign status of Indian nations, and the conflict between indigenous and essentially European political structures in the native communities, are so central as almost to define the "Indian problem" which has perplexed North America for the past several centuries.

22. Particularly in his book *The Conspiracy of Pontiac* (1851). For a brief discussion of this aspect, see Saum, pp. 69-88. Pearce considers Parkman's various historical fictions in *The Savages of America*, pp. 163-168. And Donald Davie, by no means the least perceptive of Parkman's readers, has written a splendid "Sequence for Francis Parkman" (1961) which concludes, enigmatically:

    The measure of concern
    Measures the truth, and in the *philosophe*
    A paradox of noble savages
    Has met no need more urgent than to scoff.
    (Collected Poems, 1950-1970, pp. 119-127)

23. Each native generation has produced its ritual objects of scorn, from the great Oglala chief Red Cloud, who signed the Fort Laramie Treaty in 1868 and became an agency Indian, one symbol of capitulation, to the Blood Indian leader Crowfoot, whose adopted son Poundmaker joined the Riel rebellion against the government in 1885, yet who as chief of the Blackfoot Nation held his people aloof from the conflict, and thereby became to many a symbol of self-interested compromise.

24. From a letter to Charles Pinckney, November 27, 1793. Quoted in Horsman, p. 98.

25. *A Survey of Race Relations in South Africa,* compiled by Muriel Horrell and Dudley Horner, for the South Africa Institute of Race Relations (Johannesburg, 1974), pp. 145-146.

26. For an extended analysis of this, see Sheehan, especially pp. 243-279.

27. From a report delivered on July 7, 1789. Quoted in Horsman, p. 58. This fascination with the 'stages' of development of human society, its institutions and its artifacts, found its way into the discussion of almost every human endeavor during the early years of the nineteenth century. For example, it informed T. L. Peacock's witty discussion of *The Four Ages of Poetry* (1820), and the much more serious response in *A Defence of Poetry* (1821) written by P. B. Shelby, wherein 'truths' such as that 'the savage is to ages what the child is to years' abound.

Chapter 11.   A Conscious Design

1. Sheehan, p. 278.

2. The Dawes Allotment Act had the strong support of the Lake

Mohonk Conference and its Reports. The Conference had been initiated by the Quaker brothers Albert and Alfred Smiley in 1883 in order to bring together annually various friends of the Indians and thereby to achieve a single focus for reform action. The Conference was fairly closely associated with the A.B.C.F.M.; Albert Smiley was a commissioner, and the Conference's first president was General Clinton Fisk, the Board Chairman (Mardock, p. 201).

By 1885, the Conference was an important gathering, attended by such influential public figures as Carl Schurz and Henry Dawes, and the *Proceedings of the Lake Mohonk Conference* (1886-1890) are significant. (The proceedings for previous years were published in the annual reports of the Board of Indian Commissioners.)

3. From a report delivered by McKenney to the Senate, December 27, 1871. Quoted in Sheehan, p. 153.

4. Quoted in Fritz, p. 204. Like so many who were interested in matters of public concern, Schurz took to the pages of the *North American Review* to express his opinions (in an article entitled "Present Aspects of the Indian Problem," *North American Review,* CXXXIII (1881), pp. 1-24. Lewis Cass, in particular, wrote a number of important articles which appeared there, including ones on the "Indians of North America" (XXII [1826], pp. 53-119), "Service of Indians in Civilized Warfare" (XXIV [1827], pp. 365-442), *"Schoolcraft's Travels"* (XXVI [1828], pp. 357-403), and "Aboriginal Structures" (LI [1840], pp. 396-433). The pieces were ostensibly review articles, but the books under review generally served as preacher's texts. The most significant review that Cass wrote was his article in support of the Removal of the Indians (XXX [1830], pp. 62-121), in which he effectively threw in his lot with Andrew Jackson, whose Secretary of War he became. The same year, the *Review* published an article by Jeremiah Evarts arguing the other side of the case.

5. There is a collection of such speeches, edited by W. C. Vanderwerth, and entitled *Indian Oratory: A Collection of Famous Speeches by Noted Indian Chieftains* (Norman: University of Oklahoma Press, 1971). Few books on Indians are without a selection of, or excerpts from, various speeches, statements, manifestos, books, or contemporary recreations (by eighteenth and nineteenth-century enthusiasts) of speeches by Indian leaders and spokesmen. A good bibliography, valuable for material published before 1972, is included in Virgil J. Vogel's *This Country Was Ours.* One cannot but

sympathize, however, with the exasperation displayed by Vine Deloria Jr. in a recent comment specifically on T. C. McLuhan's *Touch the Earth: A Self-Portrait of Indian Existence* (Toronto: New Press, 1971) (Deloria mistakes the title as *Touch the Wind,* a not entirely inadvertent slip, I suspect), but more generally on books of a certain sort.

> "A melodramatic scissors-and-paste job . . . in which the heartrendering [*sic*] surrender speeches were piled one on top of the other until the last century of life-and-death struggle for the American West became a convention of Indian poets standing on the hillside in the twilight reciting the wrongs of a mythical demon known as the government. . . . The concept of modern Indians [was] thus completely buried under a collection of trivia and nostalgia.
>
> (From the Foreword to *One Hundred Million Acres* by Kirke Kickingbird and Karen Ducheneaux, p. viii)

6. March 7, 1870. Quoted in Fritz, p. 172.

7. Daniel Buck, *Indian Outbreaks* (Mankato, Minn., 1904), p. 282.

8. John Dryden, *Almanzor and Almahide, or The Conquest of Granada,* Part I, Act I, l. 207-209. The speaker is Almanzor.

9. See Saum, pp. 91-113, especially p. 105. H. N. Fairchild's work, which is essential to a study of the idea, is *The Noble Savage: A Study in Romantic Naturalism* (New York: Columbia University Press, 1928). Also of interest are *Primitivism and Related Ideas in Antiquity* by A. O. Lovejoy and George Boas (Baltimore, Md., Johns Hopkins Press, 1935); and *The Quest for Paradise: Europe and the American Moral Imagination,* by C. L. Sanford (Urbana, Ill.: University of Illinois Press, 1961).

    The "idea of progress" also deserves some attention, for it was quite obviously an informing condition. Elémire Zolla deals with the notion in some detail, especially in Chapter I (pp. 5-27); and a classic on the subject is Arthur Ekirch's *The Idea of Progress in America, 1815-1860* (New York: P. Smith, 1951). See also Pearce, pp. 82-86, 151-160. Basic to the idea, as far as we are concerned here, was the assumed superiority of agrarian to hunter societies, reinforced by Vattel's "legal" arguments.

10. *The Excursion,* Book III, 933-935. Quoted (though the reference is wrong) in Zolla, p. 75.

11. What I have referred to as this "baroque" tradition has received limited attention by historians. Identifying aspects of "avant-garde" art with the baroque, Renato Poggioli recently suggested that "the primitive artist identifies vision and representation; the classical artist subordinates one to the other; the avant garde artist treats them as if they were in a state of opposition" (*The Theory of the Avant-Garde* [Cambridge, Mass: Harvard University Press, 1968]). It is this kind of opposition which characterizes a central aspect of American, and particularly American frontier, history. Irving Babbitt once called the baroque "romantic intellectualism." In the context of the tensions which the baroque also displays, this serves as a useful expression of the curious attitudes which informed the American expansion west. Baroque forms, noted Henri Focillon,

> "live with passionate intensity a life that is entirely their own; they proliferate like some vegetable monstrosity. They break apart even as they grow; they tend to invade space in every direction, to perforate it, to become as one with its possibilities."
> *(The Life of Forms in Art,* 2nd ed., trans. C. B. Hogan [New York: George Wittenborn, 1948], p. 13)

12. Mannerism is characterized by a curious kind of game, wherein opposites are juxtaposed "very delicately," or where one passes "from disorientation to hoped for reorientation with a subtlety evoked by the difficulty. Bacon's *New Atlantis* (for example), appearing to offer us a utopia, is actually concerned with the adjustment to one another of two incommensurable kinds of power" (See Roy Daniells, "The Mannerist Element in English Literature," *University of Toronto Quarterly,* XXXVI [1966], pp. 1-11). Usually, of course, the term is used to refer to an art form characterized by (though, some would argue, not by any means restricted to) a group of Italian painters working between about 1520 and 1600. Its peculiar quality, however, is the illusion it creates of a uniquely nervous sensibility, in which (it has been suggested by Frederick Hartt) disorientation from the source of political or social power is the critical issue, and from which one gains a new perception of the particular and the sometimes bizarre rather than of the universal or the ideal. It seems to me a term which is especially apt to describe white attitudes towards native Americans during the last century.

13. Quoted in the Report of the Chippewa Indian Commission (1892).

14. For a discussion of this in an historical perspective, see G. W. G. Stanley, *The Birth of Western Canada*; W. L. Morton, *Manitoba: A History* (Toronto: University of Toronto Press, 1957); Desmond Morton, *The Last War Drum,* especially Chapter I. Other aspects are more fully considered in Cumming and Mickenberg, pp. 6-9, 200-204 and 325-327, where an excerpt from the 1944 Report of the Honourable W. A. MacDonald on the Exclusion of Half-Breeds from Treaty Lists is included.

15. Canada, House of Commons, *Debates,* March 19, 1886, p. 255. Quoted in the Introduction by Desmond Morton to *The Queen v. Louis Riel* (Toronto: University of Toronto Press, 1974), p. xxx.

16. Canada, House of Commons, *Debates,* April 15, 1886, p. 724. The following remarks are taken from the same lively debate, pp. 730, 741-742.

17. This publication is undated, but presumably appeared later in the same year, 1886.

18. "Indian Affairs, 1867-1912," p. 600.

19. Quoted in the *Debates* of April 15, 1886, p. 738.

20. H. A. Dempsey, *A Blackfoot Winter Count* (Calgary, 1972).

21. From a Report of Meetings between Indians of the Northwest Territory and the Governor-General, November 16, 1881. The Marquis's reply, which follows, is from the same report.

22. This policy was in large part a consequence of the Peace Commission which was appointed in 1867, and directed

    "to ascertain the alleged reasons for [Indian] acts of hostility, and . . . to make and conclude with said bands or tribes such treaty stipulations, subject to the action of the Senate, as may remove all just causes of complaint on their part, and at the same time establish security for person and property along the lines of railroad now being constructed to the Pacific and other thorough fares of travel to the Western Territories, and such as will most likely ensure civilization for the Indians and peace and safety for the whites."

    There is a brief account of the work and the recommendations of the commission, and of the general policy which Grant instituted in 1869, in Schmeckebier, pp. 53-57. A more general and much fuller discussion is included in Fritz, *passim.* The differences between military and civilian attitudes to native affairs and the curious kind of control which was given to religious groups during this period make it a fascinating one for the study of non-native attitudes and responses to a particularly unsettled time on the western plains.

23. Fritz, pp. 164-166.

24. It must be realized that allotment in severalty, instead of to the tribe as a whole, was not only intended to break up the tribal group. It was also seen by many as the only way of securing for the native people permanent and irrevocable homes, since it was becoming obvious that forces beyond the control of the best-intentioned federal legislators or commissioners were working to render the reserves an inadequate guarantee and the treaties a poor excuse for a promise. And, of course, not all were well intentioned, which complicated the matter further.

25. An interesting example of an attempt to forestall the haphazard applications of non-native legal codes to native situations, and to allow traditional native procedures as much exercise as possible, is provided by the Canadian Judge Jack Sissons in *Judge of the Far North: The Memoirs of Jack Sissons* (Toronto: McClelland and Stewart, 1968).

26. For a slightly different approach to this question, see Kelly, *passim.*

27. See Alvin M. Josephy, Jr., "Wounded Knee and All That— What the Indians Want," *New York Times Magazine,* March 18, 1973, p. 74. This article provides a useful perspective on recent American Indian policy.

28. In a recent review of Elémire Zolla's book, entitled "The Indian and His Image" (*The Hudson Review,* XXVII [1974], pp. 101-105), Guy Davenport jumps in with both feet.

> "The Indians are probably more numerous now than at the time of Columbus' discovery. They are a vigorous people. After four hundred years of stubborn refusal to accept the gift of Europe which we have by now corrupted out of all resemblance to anything like a civilization, they should be brought to the council tables with all the old treaties in their hands. The idea that time cannot be reversed is mere Enlightenment dogma, Liberal twaddle. And the sovereignty of the State is a totalitarian idea useful only to collect taxes. Let the Indian Nations exist again within our borders."

Chapter 12. Dance Us Back the Tribal Morn

1. From the Preface to *Major Barbara.*

2. Experienced Indian department officers argued, in effect, that the presents were the only thing upon which the Indians could depend, and that to deny them this would be to condemn them to an early grave. In addition, it was pointed out that this "custom, long established" was an important factor in their attachment to the government. Various suggestions were made to commute the presents for money, but this was opposed because, as Lord Dalhousie remarked, "every man knows that money to Indians is instantly spent in spiritous liquors; and the system adopted in making useful presents as payment was intended expressly to avoid temptation."

3. Saum, p. 86.

4. Quoted in Scott, "Indian Affairs, 1840-1867," p. 341.

5. *Ibid.*, p. 341.

6. In a letter written on September 3, 1814 to John Armstrong. Quoted in Prucha, *American Indian Policy,* p. 89.

7. The predicament was similar on both sides of the border. Sheehan, p. 122, notes that "beginning in 1802, Congress authorized some fifteen thousand dollars annually for Indian affairs. Unfortunately, the elaborate system of Indian negotiations and presents absorbed these funds." Sheehan refers to G. D. Harmon, *Sixty Years of Indian Affairs: Political, Economic and Diplomatic, 1789-1850* (Chapel Hill: University of North Carolina Press, 1941), a useful book on the subject, with an especially valuable bibliography. See also A. W. Hoopes, *Indian Affairs and their Administration, with special reference to the Far West* (Philadelphia, 1932).

8. Quoted in Scott, "Indian Affairs, 1840-1867," p. 333.

9. *Ibid.*, p. 342.

10. Horsman, p. 128.

11. *Personal Memoirs of a Residence of Thirty Years with the Indian Tribes on the American Frontier* (Philadelphia, 1851), p. 319.

12. Quoted in Schmeckebier. As Lewis Cass so clearly perceived, there is no avoiding the political function of Indian affairs.

13. Canada, House of Commons, *Debates,* April 15, 1886, p. 719.

14. House of Commons, *Debates,* May 4, 1880, p. 1990.

15. House of Commons, *Debates,* April 15, 1886, p. 739.

16. In a letter of April 27, 1880.

17. Schoolcraft, pp. 318-319.

18. Part of the statement of purpose and interest, included in the Preface to *Uncommon Controversy: Fishing Rights of the Muckleshoot, Puyallup, and Nisqually Indians* (Seattle: University of Washington Press, 1970) p. xi.

19. From John Melling, "A Survey of the Present Situation of Indians in Canada," *Indian Truth,* 47 (1970), pp. 1-12. Quoted by McNickle (in *Native American Tribalism*), who comments that "the Indians wanted control of their lands, as they wanted control over other areas of their social and economic interests, but they were not prepared to abandon traditional values. . . . They saw no inconsistency in wanting control and at the same time maintaining the inalienability of the lands protected by treaty guarantees" (pp. 146-149). Some of the Indians did, in fact, see an inconsistency, though in general they were not attended to. (See, for example, William I. C. Wuttunee, *Ruffled Feathers: Indians in Canadian Society* [Calgary: Bell Books, 1971]).

20. In a speech before the Military Service Institution on December 10, 1885, Captain R. H. Pratt, superintendent of the Indian school at Carlisle, Pa., gave a chilling indication of precisely what the native people fear.

    "The policy of providing one teacher for from one hundred and fifty to two hundred Indians needs to be reversed to a policy that will provide from one hundred and fifty to two hundred teachers to each Indian. This will be the case when our two hundred and sixty thousand Indians are brought into contact with our fifty million people."

    This was quoted by Congressman Thomas Skinner of North Carolina in the House of Representatives, speaking (as the counterpart of Dawes in the Senate) in support of the General Allotment Bill in December, 1886.

21. As specified in Section 11e of the Act.

22. Canada, House of Commons, *Debates,* April 30, 1885, p. 1484. Repeated (by Mr. M. C. Cameron) in debate on May 4, 1885, p. 1580.

23. *Ibid.* See pp. 1571-1574.

24. Letter of Chief P. E. Jones to Sir John A. Macdonald, August 8, 1886.

25. In 1864, the Secretary of the Interior, E. H. Stanton, commented on the occasion of a visit of Bishop Whipple to Washington with a group of Indians:

> "What does Bishop Whipple want? If he has come here to tell us of the corruption of our Indian system, and the dishonesty of Indian agents, tell him that we know it. But the Government never reforms an evil until the people demand it. Tell him that when he reaches the heart of the American people, the Indians will be saved."
>
> (H. B. Whipple, *Lights and Shadows of a Long Episcopate* [New York, 1899], p. 144)

26. Included as the motto of *Patterns of Housekeeping in Two Eskimo Settlements* by Charles Thomas Thompson (Ottawa: Department of Indian Affairs and Northern Development, 1969), p. xi.

27. *Lettres Spirituelles*, ed. of 1681, p. 230.

INDEX